THE BUDDHA, THE BIKE, THE COUCH, AND THE CIRCLE: A FESTSCHRIFT FOR DR. ROBERT UNGER

Michael M. Dow, PsyD
Francis J. Kaklauskas, PsyD
Elizabeth Olson, PsyD

University
PROFESSORS PRESS

First Published in 2015, University Professors Press.

ISBN 13: 978-1-939686-11-4

University Professors Press
Colorado Springs, CO
www.universityprofessorspress.com

Cover art by Jean-Marc C. Wong
Cover photo by Amy Bianco Martin
Back cover photo courtesy of the Boulder Psychotherapist Guild
Cover Design by Laura Ross

"Buddhism and Psychoanalysis: Paths of Disappointment" was originally published in Kaklauskas, F., Hoffman, L., Nimmanheminda, S., & Jack, M. (2008). *Brilliant Sanity: Buddhism and psychotherapy* (pp. 347-353). Colorado Springs, CO: University of the Rockies Press. Reprinted with permission from the University of the Rockies Press.

"Sustaining Transference in the Treatment of Alcoholism" was originally published in *Modern Psychoanalysis*, *3*, 155-171, 1978. Reprinted with permission from *Modern Psychoanalysis* (Journal).

Dedications

To my wife, Amelie and my daughter, Natascha: the group that makes it all possible

Michael M. Dow

I dedicate this book to my husband, Francis, my companion in life, love and work, to my son, Levi, my heart and joy, and to my dear friends and family who walk with me on this path.

Elizabeth Olson

To my father, Adolf and son, Levi

Francis J. Kaklauskas

Table of Contents

Articles

The Birthday Kiss:
Artist's Note on the Cover

Jean-Marc C. Wong

In this oil painting entitled "The Birthday Kiss," Dr. Bob Unger holds court amongst familiar personal treasures not worthy of his home, and in the company of personal heroes physically dead, living, immortal and imagined. Brightly colored rocks—devoid of any magical power—fill a shallow bowl on the table beside him. The false promise of religion? Certainly for someone it's a metaphor for something. An old fashioned coin purse lies close to the table's edge as if questioning its own value. What the hell is money? And what's a rich man, but just a poor man with money? Alan Watts seems to float utterly content (not by any admitted oversight of the painter). Is he experiencing the heaven of the here-and-now? Just beside him, Bob Dylan appears miles away. Is he bored or deep in thought? It's all the same, for he clearly is resigned to suffer alone in a moment of existential angst, as if humming all the while, "It's alright Ma, I'm only bleeding." Here, are we observing the uncomfortable group silence which follows the annoying comment of an ungraceful participant, or the profound disquietude that comes with remembering? No matter. The show must go on, for time is money, and impatience is the convention. Dr. Bob's blue clock ticks above. The session's end draws ever closer. A lively dialogue ensues, or perhaps has been derailed by an egocentric rant. It seems to be all fun and games for the unflappable Dr. Bob, who manages the group with ease as he applies an oily horse salve to his thumb in a self-soothing maneuver. The greatest of leaders is not immune to the trivial! Bozo the Clown takes a disruptive stab at entertaining. But all attempts at spontaneity are welcome, for even the uninspired are healers. And besides, aren't we all Bozos on this bus? In a beautifully framed picture we observe a young and exuberant Marc Chagall engaging his fiancée Bella in a kiss. On the adjacent wall—as if part of an unexpected and dreadful dream—the couple seem to fall haphazardly through space in various unpredictable configurations of separation. Intimacy seems nearly out of reach, and evidently doesn't come without a struggle. Oh the terror of falling in love! The horror of falling apart! In the window a yellow taxi cab seems to wait patiently for its passenger, ever-prepared to whisk him off to a destination unknown. Might this taxi take Bob on a nostalgic joy ride of youthful days long since past? Or will the journey be more pivotal? What calamities lie ahead? And as it is his character to invite, must our leader go alone?

Acknowledgments

We would like to acknowledge the many people who helped us put this fun project together. Firstly, to all the contributors who put thought and vulnerability and energy into their entries and tolerated our various and sometimes endless email exchanges. We would like to especially thank Helena Unger who knew just the right way to support us with encouragement and practicality, and who was ever responsive with last minute late night emails. She was instrumental in helping us connect with many of the contributors in this collection. A big thanks to Amelie Bracher, Jeff Price, and Matthew Holloran who all helped tremendously with last minute copy-editing and formatting. We are indebted to *Modern Psychoanalysis* (Journal) and their managing editor Sam Dash for allowing us to reprint Bob Unger's 1978 article, "Sustaining Transference in the Treatment of Alcoholism," as well as to the University of the Rockies' Press and Executive Editor Christina Ganim for allowing us to reprint Bob's article "Paths of Disappointment: Buddhism and Psychoanalysis" from the 2008 book *Brilliant Sanity: Buddhist Approaches to Psychotherapy* (Kaklauskas, Hoffman, Nimmanheminda, & Jack). We also deeply appreciate Naropa University's Master of Arts in Contemplative Counseling and Psychotherapy program and Shawn Rubin and Louis Hoffman of University Professors Press for their passion and untiring assistance with this project.

Special Acknowledgment

For Helena

I want to acknowledge Helena Unger for her support in organizing this project, and also for her support in my life. Helena and Bob are community models for marriage, partnership, and individuality in relationship. When times have gotten difficult in my marriage, I think of Bob and Helena and it gives me a feeling of hope because I know that they have stayed together and worked through their difficulties. I know that they are really enjoying their lives together now, enjoying the fruition of their marriage, family, work, and personal interests.

When times were difficult financially for me, Bob would ask, "Are you getting close to the bread lines?" Shortly thereafter Helena would send me a referral. Helena sent me my first private practice client. She offered that I could come and meet with her and the little girl for the first session. I remember Helena joining with the little girl by agreeing with her and emphatically stating, "That is *so* stupid!" I was really surprised at the time and thought, "*Really*, you can say that, 'stupid', agreeing with a little girl who is angry?" It was very liberating for me to see and opened the door in my work with kids to freely say whatever would really match their emotional experience.

Helena brought my family a delicious meal when Levi was born, complete with cake and berries for dessert. She and I wrote an article together called "Mothering in the Moment" (she came up with the great title). We spent several hours together writing and taking care of Levi as we wrote the article for in her lovely flower gardens. She has been incredibly generous with her time and kindness over the years, from patiently escorting me (and many others over the years) through the Boulder Interdisciplinary Committee, introducing me to many of the members, to offering me professional clothing that she was clearing out of her closets (a wonderful treat as Helena is always very fashionable).

I love Helena's style, her bright spirit, her sharp mind and her kind heart. She is a strong independent woman who has the capacity to tolerate aggression very well herself. I remember hearing a story about Helena substituting for Bob in one of his classes at Naropa. When Bob came back to the group class the next week, legend has it that he said, "Who - Helena, that bitch?" It opened up the space for the group to have all of their feelings toward her, even though she was Bob's wife. He didn't feel that she needed to be protected, and she didn't.

Thank you Helena for all of your love and generosity! We could not have put this book together without your help. Thank you also for all the ways you have influenced the community. I appreciate you and the time we have shared together.

With love,
Elizabeth Olson

I would like to acknowledge Helena for her strategic problem solving, creativity, and enthusiasm that helped us move this project from a wonderful idea into an actuality. Like Bob, she was one of my group psychotherapy professors, and I also spent many years under her guidance in group supervision for Naropa groups. I learned a tremendous amount from her as she held the members of that group with tremendous presence, fearless acceptance and examination of all feelings, and a unique combination of clear boundaries yet boundless warmth and compassion. Beyond that, for me, Helena provided a powerful model of fearlessly and unabashedly being oneself. It has been an honor to work with her on this project.

Francis J. Kaklauskas

Never having become a Naropa group leader, I never had the pleasure of Helena's personal mentorship. However, in the course of this project, I have quickly come to appreciate Helena's unique charm. Elegance is the word that comes to mind when I try to describe the experience of interacting with Helena. She is elegant in both word and appearance, thought and deed. I have greatly appreciated her attention to detail, her efficiency, and warmth, her lightness and her wit, her deft ability to defer to our wishes, while also keeping the larger group in mind, and considering what is best for all. I only hope that this is but one of many future collaborations.

Michael M. Dow

Introduction

The old pond,
A frog jumps in:
Plop!

Basho (1686/1960)

This most famous of all Haiku reminds us of Bob. The stagnant old pond lies there still, unmoving, and suddenly, a sound – something new and unexpected, an awakening. Bob's words are like that. The "plop," the sound of the water, echoes in our psyche, making waves that ripple outwards concentrically across our lives. Our unconscious waters are transformed from sterile and asleep to alive with movement and sound.

And as editors, we quickly found out that we were not alone in this impression. As we first spoke to others about this project, everyone was so excited to share their stories and participate. Just when we thought we were finished, more entries would pour in. And they kept coming. Bob has held many roles in his life, all of which are represented here: father and son, client and therapist, husband, teacher, colleague, engineer, mechanic, artist, cyclist supreme, off-tune singer, and friend to name just a few. In all of these roles, Bob's essence has shone forth. Beyond all the many words and ideas, beyond the various hats and guises, have reliably been Bob's special sense of presence and playfulness, his aliveness and compassion, and his hope.

A Festschrift is a traditional celebration, originating in German academia, aimed at honoring an important teacher or scholar. It could literally be translated as "Feast Writing." Traditionally a festschrift consists of more academic articles, but in this case, since Bob's influence and legacy has primarily been through his teaching, supervision and psychotherapy, we have aimed at a more personal volume. But there are many lessons and offerings here that are intriguing and impactful regardless of whether one has had personal contact with Bob. Our hope is that readers from many backgrounds will indeed feast on the varied submissions, and find wisdom and enjoyment in the many courses offered here.

We should also mention that this Festschrift derives considerable inspiration from a previous Festschrift compiled for one of Bob's mentors, Dr. Hyman Spotnitz. (Sheftel, 1991). Like the Spotnitz Festschrift, this Festschrift aims, through personal reflections and anecdotes, to reach beyond the personal to something more enduring and far-reaching, to lessons about psychotherapy and life that are applicable to many.

Why a festschrift for Dr. Bob Unger? While not an academic, Bob has been prolific in his influence. The number of people whose lives he has not only touched, but transformed (as this volume is but small testament) is truly legion. For the past nearly 30 years Bob has been a Professor in the Master's Program in Contemplative Psychotherapy and Counseling (MACP) at Naropa University teaching his well known Evolution of Central Concepts in Western Psychology and Group Therapy classes (among others), and was one of the principle architects of the intensive group therapy training that forms the core of that program. To this day the MACP program remains one of the few Master's programs in the country where one can obtain thorough training in not only Buddhist approaches to psychotherapy (including but going considerably beyond training in mindfulness), but intensive group psychotherapy training. Such a Master's program, in good Buddhist fashion, aims, much as Bob himself does, to go beyond the self conceived as a separate, isolated, non-moving thing.

To give you a brief overview of Bob's other accomplishments, he has also been a fellow at the American Group Psychotherapy Association (AGPA) for the last 20 years, and has led countless 2 day group institutes, and a multitude of other panels and workshops at their annual conference. He is the founder of the local chapter of that organization, the Colorado Group Psychotherapy Society, which has also held yearly conferences on and off for the past 25 years which Bob has helped to lead. Here in Boulder, Bob has run some of the longest running and most sought after psychotherapy and consultation groups, and is well known as the therapist's therapist, and even the therapist to therapists of therapists! Somehow he has also found time to run regular process groups for staff at various local human service agencies such as the Boulder Shelter for the Homeless, the Boulder County Aids Project and the Denver Alternative to Family Violence program. In short, Bob's legacy in Boulder, in Colorado and beyond, is a flourishing culture of groups, of psychotherapists who are attentive to the unconscious and to humor, to systems and to hierarchy, and to their own awareness.

The title, *The Bicycle, The Buddha, The Circle and the Couch,* comes from some of Bob's major life interests, and also pays homage to his lineage by referencing Hyman Spotnitz's first book, *The Couch and the Circle: A Story of Group Psychotherapy* (1961). Like that collection of stories, this collection aims to be readable, enjoyable, and insightful.

This book is inevitably just a small sampling of some of the lives Bob Unger has touched throughout his life up to this point. In an effort to be inclusive, and in the spirit of Bob himself, we accepted most contributions and in almost any form—from the very brief, to longer pieces, from poetry to prose, from essay to personal reflection. And as you will see, the pieces contained here run the gamut. Most of the entries are by clinicians and students he has taught and trained, but there are also many colleagues, and co-conspirators, a few mentors, and assorted friends, and family. The editors did not try to solicit submissions from past or current clients as they felt that would interfere with the sanctity of their relationship with Bob. Undoubtedly there are many wonderful stories left out.

The editors and the contributors would like to especially thank Bob for allowing us to celebrate our relationships with him. It occurred to us in the midst of this project that it is not easy to be lavished with so much attention and praise. It takes a certain humble aplomb to not shrink or shrug off the efforts of others to compliment and celebrate you, and to put you in the spotlight. Throughout, Bob has been only gracious and generous, giving advice when asked, sharing his obvious delight in the project (which only delighted us further!), but also allowing the project to unfold of its own accord.

In a larger and important way, this book is not strictly speaking about Bob, but about the group and the community of conversation and awareness and movement (of various kinds) that has grown up around him. It aims to be a teaching volume—about groups, about therapy, about balancing work and life, and more. Bob has been but the vehicle—and we are so glad that he has let us ride!

While admittedly we are not Basho, we thought we could end with a creative attempt to summarize at least one aspect of Bob and his office in this haiku.

> Between snowy foothills
> And Broadway's rushing traffic.
> Talk, talk, talk, talk, talk.

Michael M. Dow
Francis J. Kaklauskas
Elizabeth Olson

References

Basho, M. (1686/1960). Old Pond (A. Watts, Trans.). In N. W. Ross (Ed.), *The world of Zen: An east-west anthology* (pp.121-128). New York: Vintage Books. (Original work published 1686)

Sheftel, S. (1991). *Just say everything: A festschrift in honor of Hyman Spotnitz*. New York: Association for Modern Psychoanalysis.

Spotnitz, H. (1961). *The couch and the circle: A story of group psychotherapy*. New York: Knopf.

Statement from Bob Unger

It may seem strange for the recipient of a festschrift to have a say in it, but, why not? Bob usually has something interesting to say, and this occasion is no exception. We asked Bob to reflect on his experience of the festschrift project, and what he thought of it, and this is what he said:

> For a number of years now my professional and personal life have settled into a continuously rewarding rhythm and I have not spent much time considering my own identity. I just do the next thing. This changed considerably when I was told about the Festschrift, as it has made me wonder, "Who am I to receive such profound recognition?"
>
> It is a great blessing to receive this honor. Two of my primary mentors, Hyman Spotnitz and Leslie Rosenthal, had Festschrifts created for them which have served as valuable teaching instruments for me. As I have never been particularly adept at explaining what I do, to myself or others, in an organized theoretical manner, being interviewed in a way that teased out elements of my clinical influences and approaches is incredibly good fortune. And having the opportunity to see how I've been experienced as a therapist and teacher is something that every clinician deserves, as we usually have little opportunity to get feedback about what we actually look and sound like when we work. I can only hope that my feeling of profound gratitude and good fortune for receiving this honor makes its way into my work moving forward.

Interview with Bob Unger

Conducted by Michael Dow and Elizabeth Olson over the course of three sessions at the Brackett House in Boulder, CO, January-March, 2015.

Part One

Michael: It's funny to be interviewing Bob!

Elizabeth: I know (laughs)!

Bob: That makes three of us! I was telling Michael we spend our whole lives interviewing people, basically. So this is quite a deal!

Michael: Now we get to ask you the questions we've always wanted to ask!

Bob: And I get to blab about what I always don't blab about!

Michael: Well, where should we start? Did you have a thought?

Elizabeth: First thought is childhood.

Bob: Of course!

Michael: Do you have any thought about any events or factors that inspired you to become a psychotherapist or psychoanalyst?

Bob: Yes, well, it captured me later. I never had a dream to do so, but it was my father in particular who was a very difficult person. He prided himself on alienating people and it was particularly hard on me because I could watch the whole thing. I was seven and eight and nine and ten and could see how painful it was. I was very self-conscious because of the way he positioned our family in our little town, a little desert town in California. There was a small Jewish community there that was pretty cohesive and that we joined in, but our father alienated us from them, so I was very self-conscious. Along with being very self-conscious in the late 50s and 60s, I was a Jewish boy from the Bronx who wound up in a desert town in California, so I grew up with a lot of social self-consciousness. So when I look back—you either repeat or you compensate—I think a lot of my drive was really towards groups in particular rather than just psychotherapy. It was groups that really got me hooked. Some need to compensate for that, to be able to be in groups and be liked in groups.

And then later I ended up in a therapy group. To my surprise! It all just seemed to evolve quite naturally. Even though you never know how things are evolving naturally back then, I can see now how they evolved. So I think that to this day, like where we live in co-housing, I'm fascinated by the combination of comfort and discomfort of being in a group. There's just nothing like it. It really keeps you alive.

Michael: It's very interesting, Bob, because no one would ever guess that you had a childhood of being alienated from the community. You seem to have mastered that.

Bob: Well, I'm one example of the power of therapy, the power of group therapy! Really, "Exhibit A" of the magic of what it's like, what it is to be an overweight, nonathletic, anemic Jewish kid in a little sports oriented desert town in the 50s and 60s. That's a big jump to where I am now! Friends laughed when I went to college and was in a fraternity, but I always felt a little apart. I always had this uneasy relationship to groups until I found myself in an Ormont group when I was in New York and I was 23.

Michael: *You* were overweight?

Bob: Quite overweight! 203 I think I was in high school. My father was very overweight, and there was a lot of tension in our home. I took the path that was shown to me.

Michael: To eat?

Bob: Yeah.

Michael: I have to see some photographs.

Bob: No, you don't! (Laughs). You have to beg!

Michael: You keep them well hidden.

Bob: Yes, I keep them well hidden!

Elizabeth: It's really an amazing thing that you're speaking to, transformation. When you transform internally, you can transform in an outer way as well. When you channel your unconscious in a way that's more constructive, then you can really make choices about how you want to live.

Bob: Definitely.

Elizabeth: It's wonderful.

Bob: Well, what we do is really helpful for people. You know, it really works!

Elizabeth: I was wondering if there was anyone in your childhood who was really important to you, who helped you. If there's anyone who comes to mind who somehow was a guide.

Bob: So, what immediately came to mind, as soon as you said it . . . I was a paperboy in those days, on my bicycle delivering newspapers. Our little town was about 60 miles from L.A. It's now just a big suburb connected by the freeway, but at the time it was a beautiful little town. Actually it was a feeder town to Edwards Air Force Base where all the famous stuff took place, you know, "The Right Stuff." I was a paperboy and we delivered the Los Angeles Examiner. I would get up on my bicycle in the morning—still a morning person. The fellow who ran the office, our local office, his name was Vic Fritz. I remember there were 15 paper boys. The rest of them were cool desert kids, and I felt a little awkward in that crowd, but I liked delivering papers, and I liked riding my bicycle early on. He took a real liking to me and we developed a lovely bond. He seemed like an older guy then, but he was probably in his mid-30s I would guess. And then he promoted me because I was responsible and always made it to the office in the morning. The papers came in at about three in the morning and I would go to the office on my bicycle and set the bundles up for the routes, the 15 or so paper routes, and I would deliver them to the porches of the kids. And then in the summer I would go and put papers in the stores. We really loved each other, but it was never spoken. I was really attached to him, and he was attached to me. I remember, he was Catholic, and he took me to church one time. It was stepping out, but it was fine. I have to give my father credit. He was a very, very jealous man. He tolerated it. Because it was pretty obvious.

This went on for a year or two probably when I was 14 or 15. And then one day, Vic said, "I'm being transferred back to L.A." I was crushed, really, really crushed. That's what comes to mind. Something that was very special. Whether you call it mentoring, or Robert Bly's thing of having a male figure who is not in the family, it all fit. That really helped get me through a tough, tough, adolescence. My sister, who is four years older, when we moved out there was immediately able to shed the roots and become part of the scene. She was one of the cool girls, the fast girls club. She immediately adapted. She's paid for it in various ways. We're very close my sister and I. Over time there were a lot of family dynamics, and I didn't adapt as readily as she did. I was kind of a squirrely New York kid, sort of out of place, though I have to say I think being raised out there probably saved my life. If I'd have stayed in New York, I'd probably still be there and have grown up a not very embodied young person.

Michael: You say that because the town was more athletic.

Bob: Yeah, you know, Southern California small towns are just athletic. They just are. The heroes of the town are all the athletes.

Michael: Not like the Bronx.

Bob: Not like the Bronx.

Michael: Also hearing about that makes me wonder, how did your relationship with your dad evolve over time? How did he feel about your becoming a therapist?

Bob: Well, he died a long time ago. I finally caught up with my father just a few years ago [in terms of age]—he was 67 when he died. We had tremendous tension always. I came to terms with it in my own mind, which feels like one of the great blessings of my life, during a dathün when I had left New York and was living at Shambhala Mountain Center. I was at the Maitri program up there which included Helena (laughs). At that time it was a three-month program. And I had moved out there and I was just living peacefully, after living in New York. There were only about 15 people, much smaller than now, and then the Naropa program descended on us, about 35 of them and I sat dathün with them.
    And in the middle of it, right in the middle of it with my mind, you know how that goes, racing a million miles an hour, it suddenly hit me—how to surrender to the situation with my father—and I broke out in tears. You know, to the dathün attendees and leaders it was probably, "Oh, there goes someone else crying." (Laughs). And, it let go. It happened. You know, that's the magic. It wasn't "I." "It" let go, you know, whatever the vocabulary is. It was in '82, '83, I think, and my father lived another three years. But after that I was not attached to the history of it and I was fine. I was very lucky that I got that experience before he died. Otherwise, I would've always wondered if I could afford to die while he was still alive,

and all those things, but I was just very lucky that it happened in that sequence, and I was able to be there without holding on. It's one of the great blessings of my life.

Elizabeth: So we've heard about your father, and I find myself wondering about your mother.

Bob: Well, my mother . . . Neither of them were educated. They were both peasant stock, particularly my mother. She grew up with parents who were Russian Jewish immigrants. She was fifth of seven. I think she didn't go past the fifth grade. She grew up on the lower East side. Her father never spoke English. He said prayers in the synagogue, that seems to be what he did. He was 5 feet, and my grandmother was 4 foot six. When I was just in New York for something last May, I went to where they used to live on Avenue C, and First Street. I still remember the address. It was an old tenement. Now that area is booming along. There's some modern building there.

Oh yes, my mother . . . So, my mother was very unsophisticated, and kind of afraid of life in certain ways, while my father was very overpowering. My mother was 4'10" and my father was 5'11", big and heavy, and my mother was also kind of slight, even at a physical level. But in her way she was always doing the best to protect me and I always knew that, even though it couldn't be talked about. There was sort of a pairing with myself and my mother, and my father and my sister. My father was very resentful of me because I was afraid of him and he didn't have the sophistication to be able to say, "Oh, what's happening here?" He took it personally.

So that's where it started, and it just catapulted. My mother, in her way, always did her best to protect me and she was really under the gun with him. She was just afraid. In later years, we just always wished she would've left him, but she never did. Finally when he died, she had already had cancer, and she had about nine months of enjoying her life. She visited us here. Dylan, our first son, had just been born. But she died nine months after my dad died. She didn't really have an opportunity to embrace her life. She would have a lot more if he wouldn't have been around.

Part of whatever I have of soundness, is the feeling that my mother really loved me. However, in the world she didn't know how to manifest very well. She had a kind of integrity in simplicity. I remember one time when I was in college—you know that was a big deal to go to college—and I came home and I had airs about me, and she said something like, "Just because you're in college, don't think you're so smart!" And she just cut it right there, because I was doing that thing.

Michael: It sounds like there was a certain sharpness, but there was something warm there too.

Bob: Yes, it was just right. It was what I needed. It was an intervention you might say. And it was spontaneous with her, because she just had it. She was blessed. She didn't have intellectual sophistication which is a good blessing to be around someone like that. Especially as your mother.

Michael: You really smile when you talk about her.

Bob: Yeah, I do. And you know Helena had the opportunity to know her. When she talks about my father, she still gets the willies. But she and my mother really hit it off in those two or three years that we had.

Michael: Maybe you could talk a little bit about where you went to college and the influence that had on your later development.

Bob: There's a rap here, too! (Laughs.) Well, so I decided to go to college. My parents didn't have the wherewithal. I did it all myself. I think most of us did in those days, much more so. You didn't have various counselors doing computer searches figuring out which college was best and help you do an online application and apply for a million places. So there I was around Southern California, so I went to UCLA. You know it's so hard to get into a California University these days, but I applied and was accepted. My first fantasy was being an architect. That appealed to me. And then I discovered I had no visual memory skills or acuity (laughs), so I switched to civil engineering, a cousin to architecture. Being an engineering student was difficult, because you know it's all math and science, but I'd been a math person more than anything. I couldn't write or read very well, but that's just sort of how I was when I grew up. I went to UCLA for three years and as I said, joined a fraternity, a Jewish fraternity, tried to be a cool Jewish person. That was another group situation where I always felt awkward, even though I thought, "I've made it! I'm in the Jewish fraternity!" But they were very slick L.A. people, because that's the way it was. So I always felt very funny there.

So then a real blessing happened. They have an All-Cal weekend. I think they still do, which is the UCLA/Berkeley football game. They have a whole weekend of a bunch of stuff. So I went up to Berkeley to go to the All-Cal weekend, and there's something about Berkeley... But I didn't think too much of it after my junior year. UCLA's engineering program is a general engineering program and Berkeley had civil engineering specifically, the best in the country at the time. So I transferred to Berkeley just for my last year to do civil engineering. When I got up there which was 1966 I stepped right into the big student strike right after the free speech movement. It was just politically intense. We used to make fun of them in L.A. at that time, but Berkeley was just ahead of everything.

It was just electric and freaked me out, because I was still a very somewhat sheltered conservative kid. I just wanted to get by and do my engineering, and be like, normal. I just wanted to be normal.

During that year, I did go to see a counselor at the student counseling center. I was just trying to think about this. I can't remember exactly what made me go in those days. For an engineering student to go to see the counselor wasn't that usual, something internally uncomfortable must have driven me to try it. I went for a few times. I can almost get a picture of the guy's face. That was my first experience talking to someone—that whole world.

Inside and outside things were very tumultuous, but I graduated. I applied to graduate school in civil engineering and was accepted by both Cal, and Cornell. I thought I'd go to Cornell.

I got a summer internship at a civil engineering company and then I was going to go off to Cornell for graduate school. One of their contracts was to build barracks in Vietnam. It didn't feel right, and then in the middle of the summer something clicked and I was like, "Oh it's something about Vietnam." I had a realization and I thought if I'm drafted I will go, because otherwise I would've been a draft dodger.

And then, one of those miracles happened where you don't know why it happened, but it happened, and it was now August, and I decided to go to Berkeley instead. So I called up Berkeley, and I said, "Can I still go back to grad school? Is my application still in?" and they said yes. I was very happy to be staying there and to start a Masters program in civil engineering.

And then the next thing that happened was really a profound experience. The engineering building is this big building. I was just there this summer. I was on my bicycle and I rode up and looked at these places. At the time, the student placement center was a small building below the engineering tower and I was in the lounge, and we were at a coffee break. I can picture it that particular day, Dow Chemical was recruiting on campus. And Dow made napalm. So there was a huge protest and a bunch of the engineering students were at coffee break, you know everyone milling around, and they were laughing and making fun of the protestors, and I said to myself, "I don't belong here." So I went to see my advisor, boy, so many things just fall into place. He was English. He was British, and the English were not really pro-Vietnam at that time. This was now '67 and I said, "My mind is just tumultuous about this, but I really don't know if I can continue with engineering right now." And he said, "Well, what if you just take whatever courses you want and I'll leave you in the engineering school so you don't have to leave school and get drafted?" Because I would've gotten drafted right away. That was a blessing! And up until then, in my whole undergrad I think I had six non-science courses. Everything was math, science, chemistry, physics, and engineering. So I took a drama class. I took an English class. I took liberal arts classes for the first time, and I became more involved. I never became heavy duty radicalized, but I became more involved in stuff on campus and that was when I first started making the breakaway.

Michael: The breakaway?

Bob: The breakaway from engineering, and all it meant. Then Martin Luther King came to speak at campus and it was elevating. It was not that long before he was assassinated. So it came to the end of the year, and I had to figure out what to do and I signed up for VISTA, which I don't think exists anymore. It's sort of like the domestic Peace Corps and it was a way to stay out of the draft. So, I signed up for that and I told them I wanted to go to the city, but I wound up in this little place in South Carolina. I lasted about three weeks and realized I couldn't do it.

By then, my whole insides were exploding. I didn't know who I was. I was in total transition. I had no idea. I was just not settled. So I left and I moved to New York. I had a close friend from college, and he said, "Come to New York! We'll find you a therapist." So that's where I went.

Michael and Elizabeth: (Laughing).

Bob: So that would've been the spring of '68, something like that. So I went to New York, and he found me a therapist, who was an analyst in training somewhere. So then I got a job. Everyone could get a job for the welfare department, any college grad. It paid $6,450 a year and it was a job with benefits. I was a welfare worker. I would go around and check on people and stuff like that, an easy job.

Elizabeth: And that would save you from the draft?

Bob: No, no it didn't. So, then they had the lottery. You may have heard of the lottery. The lottery was the game changer for everybody. They put 356 birthdays in the thing and then they drew one at a time. This birthday was number one, then number two, then number three. And they figured they would take about the first 150 birthdays. And my number was 60. So I would've been a goner, but thanks to a letter from Lou Ormont I got a psychological deferment.

Elizabeth: What else happened in New York?

Bob: Well, then there's the famous, how-it-all-began story. So I was sitting in therapy, not really thinking of being a therapist, just going to therapy and talking. So then one day I'm driving my taxicab which I was doing part-time. I picked up this young woman about my age at 65th and Central Park West and started driving her across town. "Oh," she said, "I just got out of group therapy with this phenomenal group therapist. You should see him," because she did that with everybody and I was her age. Don't ask me why, but I took his number, and I called. My idea was that it would be a good way to meet girls.

Elizabeth: (Laughs).

Bob: I had no idea what it was really all about. So I go to see Lou Ormont. I call him up. And he said, "Come in for an interview." He interviews you for about 20 minutes and he asks you questions. So I'm thinking, this sounds pretty interesting. He gives me this group to go to, he says, "Tuesday at 2:15."

Michael: Amazing that you can remember that!

Bob: Oh, absolutely! And so he says, "There's this and there's that and you pay, Oh, and there's no socializing outside the group." And my whole insides dropped. I said, "Wait a minute! This is the whole reason I'm doing this right?" But I was too embarrassed to say, "Then well, forget it!" So I went! (Laughter). I still remember the first day. This was the late 60s. I was young. Well, the whole group was in their 20s and very intense as only 60s New York people can be and I was just beyond terrified! I remember after the first session and near the end he said, "Well, what do you think of your first session?" I hadn't said a word for the whole session, and I go, I stutter, "I can't believe how easy it is for these people to talk this way!' and Lou said something like, "Well, it's not that easy."

And then I spent the next two years, pretty much, just in total terror. I could not open my mouth. I had no words. I did not have that language. The group was Tuesday and I would be freaked out until about Saturday and then Saturday was okay. Sunday I started anticipating the next Tuesday and I would start getting very anxious again. It was just so painful. Eventually, the group would not let me get away with my silence. "I have nothing to say. I don't have any words." "Oh, what do you mean, you don't have any words and nothing to say?! You have plenty to say!!" They were not going to allow me to get away with that.

Michael: They worked on you.

Bob: They worked on me! They did not indulge me at all! I remember it took the better part of two years. Finally, one day I just broke out crying out of frustration and that moved it. And I remember leaving that day and my body felt like it had let go of the tension of my whole life. I was about 24. And so then it started moving on and I just found words. Then I stopped seeing that analyst. I got very obstreperous with him, the analyst in training. He was a very nice guy, but I was just maybe too much for him at that time. He moved to Staten Island to continue his practice and that's how he got rid of me. It worked out well.

Elizabeth: He wasn't trained.

Bob: Not with the moderns, no.

So in group I said I needed a new therapist and someone in the group was seeing Phyllis Meadow and said, "Oh, you should try her," and I said, "Oh, okay." I started seeing her, and that's its own story. So that was really my beginning... In the meantime, I stopped working for the welfare department and I got a job in city planning, sort of in my engineering field, but then I found dance. I was in New York. It was the 60s. I was just doing stuff. I got very involved in modern dance and I actually spent a couple of years doing that. I left my job, cut to halftime at the city planning job and I was an understudy in this improv dance group. I didn't have any talent whatsoever, but I just did it, and it was a real eye-opener to be in that world. It is such a world that I would have never been anywhere around.

Michael: What a change! From civil engineering to modern dance.

Bob: Go figure! It was great for me, you know. It was really great for me. It really introduced me to the arts, and the world of gays and straights, artists, and people I hadn't been around before. It was just a broadening thing. But then I finally—you know, after seeing Meadow for a while—I finally took a class at the modern analytic school. It was just starting, '71 or '72, and I took a class right after that. She was very pushy about things— "Take a class!" "Study!" you know—I liked it, but I also got interested in dance therapy and I applied and was accepted into the Hunter College Dance Therapy Program. I deferred my application for a year and then I got accepted the next year. And there was a pull to go to social work school and become more of the analyst type. I was talking about it in analysis, with the wrong person of course, because you know where Meadow's bias was (laughter). I said, I'll never forget it—this is just an example of what you can do with words—I said, "Well, I can't decide whether to go toward psychoanalysis or dance therapy," and she said, "Who said psychoanalysis isn't dance therapy?" (Laughter). There you go! Shall we say, the rest is history . . .

Elizabeth: I've always remembered that, because I did dance therapy for my undergrad and I considered going to Hunter before I met you actually. But I was wondering what kept you in the group when it was so difficult to go for two years?

Bob: I've asked myself that too, because it was so difficult. It's one of those wonderful unanswerable questions. Something. I must have had some instinct that this was the right thing for me to do because it was so difficult. It wasn't rational. Whether I was afraid to leave because of what they would say? That might have been part of it. But you always find a way to leave. There was something. I don't tend to leave things so easily, so that was part of it, but there was something that felt—if I left— of cutting something off. I felt I just should stick it out.

Elizabeth: It's wonderful that there was something in you that could stay with it even though it was so difficult.

Bob: Yeah.

Elizabeth: Like something in you knew.

Bob: Yeah, like something in me knew. I think one of the richnesses of being around the Naropa community all these years is the way I've learned to be able to articulate to myself that there is no "I" about it. It's not like "I" decided! That this is really good for me, so I'm going to stay. It was just something that happened.

Michael: It sounds like the group almost really decided to work on you.

Bob: Oh yeah, they worked on everybody!

All: (Laughter).

Bob: But there were little markers. Like I remember, for example, I spent a lot of time at the beginning thinking, "Well, the reason they can do that is because they know each other so well," but then I would think, "Well, it is true that everybody leaves this group and they don't socialize." It was pretty rigid in those days—they didn't even take the bus together. So I couldn't find an excuse to justify my alienation. If I would've found an excuse, I might have done something, but I just couldn't find one. In other words, there was nothing to do but stay.

Elizabeth: People didn't subgroup outside the group.

Bob: No, exactly. It all happened right there. It really just happened right there, and I couldn't deny it. It was obvious, so I couldn't find a way out, actually. There was no real reason to leave.

Michael: And it wasn't just mildly difficult—it was really noticeable how difficult it was.

Bob: Oh yeah. So I wound up in the group just about 10 years, and once I got over that that bridge, then words really started to come. And it became—not that it wasn't painful sometimes—but it became really rewarding. Suddenly, words, words, words. They were there and I could find them. You know, I became a real mainstay in the group. Most people stayed a long time but by the time I left, there were only two or three who were there as long as I was. So I gradually built up seniority, but it's still a wonder to me that I stayed. It's a wonder to me that I went! (Laughter).

Elizabeth: That's what I was thinking. How difficult it must have been! But something really connected you.

Bob: Well, one of my favorite Bob Dylan quotes, one of my favorite 30 or 40, goes, "The highway is for gamblers. Better use your sense. Take what you have gathered from coincidence." There are so many things that look like coincidence and you just have to appreciate whatever they teach you. These days I think of it more as serendipity. When serendipity happens it's like losing the chains of this world that we live in that are so painful, and serendipity are like these bright lights.

Michael: Are you in touch with anyone from that group from those days?

Bob: One person, maybe two. Lucy Holmes was in my group. She really went on. She's a PhD and she's written. Do you know her?

Elizabeth: Yeah, I think she's amazing. I love what she writes about.

Bob: She's a real sweetheart. I see her at AGPA (American Group Psychotherapy Association) and then Dan Hill who started PsyBC. He's a really early pioneer of online trainings and conferences and stuff like that. That's been his baby for years. Whenever I go to New York I usually say hello to him. Those are the people from the group itself that I have contact with.

Elizabeth: Would you say that was kind of like your doorway into modern psychoanalysis, or, what got you going in that way?

Bob: Well, the NPAP which was the Theodore Reik Institute wouldn't let Spotnitz supervise people because he was too radical and Phyllis Meadow said, "Oh, then we'll start our own school!" So that's how the Center for Modern Psychoanalytic Studies (CMPS) started right around 1970/71 when they gathered that original group. Meadow is really the one who started the Center for Modern Psychoanalysis. It was just in its first year or two when I had started seeing her. And so she, depending on how you look at it, transferentially coerced me into taking a class. At that time they just let anyone take classes. They were just getting going. The classes were very process oriented. And so I took a class. It was taught by Jack Kirman. And in that first class I just went "Ah!" There was some feeling of just coming home. I just loved the way he taught, the whole thing. So I just took classes for another semester to decide what to do and that's when the whole decision to go to social work school came about. That was stimulating, and Ormont was a student of Spotnitz, so even though Ormont didn't affiliate with that specific institute, it was all part of that closeness. So then I think after a year of classes that's when I decided to go to social work school.

One of Spotnitz's brilliances was that he never formally associated with any psychoanalytic institute. He's a teaching entity, so he would never tie himself down. He was honorary head of every modern psychoanalytic Institute. All he did was serve to mediate between people who worked with each other.

Elizabeth: What was social work school like for you?

Bob: Those of us who wanted to be clinicians in social work school kept that to ourselves (laughter). Because social work school was to become a social worker. But social work was the path because there wasn't any MA psychology path at that time. Social work was the Master's level path towards being a clinician, but you didn't talk about it. I think in my social work class at Hunter I was one of only three men. The New York female social work world had a certain culture that I only partly fit with, but it was fine. I just kept it to myself, but I really got a lot out of it.

My first placement was at the Bowery Men's Shelter which was just incredible. After four weeks my supervisor said, "Are you sure you picked the right field?" (laughter). She was just kind of this old fart lady and it was a very difficult placement, but I did it. The next year I got a stipend placement at an alcoholism program, part of the Cabrini hospital. So I got to do real nice clinical work there and that's sort of what got me into the alcoholism thing since I was taking classes at the center and all that. And so I was finally in the field. After school I was able to get jobs and worked hard at them.

Michael: I'm interested in what the scene was like around CMPS back then and that whole sort of psychoanalytic community. Can you describe a bit about it?

Bob: Well, CMPS was very lively because it was new, and it was a breakaway. It liked to pride itself in saying it was. I just think it's so typical of religious types of organizations. One of the classic papers that one of the people wrote early on was comparing classical versus modern psychoanalysis: "Well the classicals do this, but the moderns do this." You could just look at it all from the perspective of developmental theory, and the child individuating. You know, just the feeling of it—"We're different! Not just different, but better, you know."

You know, just like my kids! (laughter). And it's true in a certain way.

So every Friday Spotnitz would give a lecture and they were like, you know, Friday night synagogue services. There'd be 300 people there.

Michael: That many?

Bob: Oh, you know he really had a following. They were at a high school in the village, and they filled the auditorium, just filled it. And people were very lively and chatty. He had a big following, because all those analysts had their minions and brought them there.

I remember having a class on Friday afternoons just beforehand. And the classes at the center, there were always 30 people in them and they were very lively. I remember walking over from the center a few blocks, talking away. And then there'd be the Spotnitz lecture. It was very lively. Just great, you know.

Michael: And psychoanalysis was sort of hot back then, right? Not just Spotnitz and the modern analytic world, but there were others too, right?

Bob: It was still very robust. There were lots of analytic institutes in New York. There'd be these warring lectures you know, the object relations versus the moderns. I mean they didn't say "versus", but ... I still remember some of the classics with Spotnitz and then there'd be somebody else, you know, two people demonstrating working with the same patient. They would have their people there and we would have our people there (laughter).

Everyone would sort of lay claim to their egos, but Spotnitz towered above them all just in the brilliance of the way he was nuanced and the way he used language. It was just amazing.

In this one lecture at the Dalton school, a big auditorium with high ceilings and there's all these people around. It could've been the Roman Coliseum, you know! That night they brought a kind of a walking schizophrenic, an ambulatory guy really severely suffering. So whoever the other therapist was interviews him, this sort of standard interview. And this guy does a good therapeutic interview of him and afterwards the patient goes off the stage and then this guy gives a diagnostic impression that had a lot of sophistication to it and everything. And then Spotnitz gets up and he looks at the guy and he says, "Hello, how are you?" and then he says, "I don't know if you realize this, but this audience is out to kill you." The guy laughs. And everybody starts murmuring in the audience, and it goes on and on, and he goes on and on about this until people in the audience start yelling, "What are you talking about?! Shut up!" And then Spotnitz says just enough to the audience to reduce their tension.

And Spotnitz starts this very casual conversation with the guy and the guy just sounds normal. They just talk about this and that and that and this, and the guy is coherent and more uplifted. Some people didn't get it, but Spotnitz had a way of connecting with everyone in a way that helped them feel better and do better. It was beyond flash.

And there was a similar thing, a big deal in Boston with some group therapist in Boston. And they did a demo, also with a big audience, and the demo was a mock group with students from local colleges. The guy goes around in the group, the first guy—Spotnitz always seemed to go last in these things—and the guy goes around and he asks everyone to introduce themselves and say what they want to get out of the group, sort of a little check in kind of thing, and they kind of go along very proper. And then Spotnitz gets up there with a group, the same kind of make up but a different group of people and he says, "You know, this audience is out for blood." And he goes on and on, and the group spontaneously becomes a group! It was just classic cohesion when there's an outside force.

Michael: He turned it from this thing where everyone's observing and there's this group on stage to where everyone's part of the group.

Bob: Everyone's part of the group. Exactly! It was the in group and the out group. Whenever things got too tense in the audience, he would give some kernel of education, just enough to quiet people down, just enough feeding of the audience, and the group just became a group. They were great. It was just brilliant and we would leave there going, "Wow!" Those imprints, those kinds of experiences were just so valuable for me. That was the climate then. It was very lively, in the early days.

I know since I've left and just through contacts I have back there, that it's gotten more rigid. One of the things I'm so grateful for coming out here. Back in New York there is lot of ego—with smart people we have it—but there was just a lot of ego. So that intelligence laced with a lot of ego is brilliant, but at the same time it can be toxic.

Elizabeth: One thing I've always liked about modern psychoanalysis, at least in my mind anyway, is that it really works on people's narcissism, and their egos, and I don't know, maybe that didn't happen with some people. I guess I think about Spotnitz, the way you describe him, it just sounds like he somehow didn't let his ego get in the way of what he had to offer.

Bob: That's my feeling about him. And if you look at that famous Spotnitz video, he's laughing at himself. I showed it to one of my colleagues, and she said, "I don't know what's so good about this. He sounds like a buffoon!'

And I said, "Well, that's exactly it!" She said, "He doesn't believe anything he says," as though there was a problem with that! And I said, "Right!"

Elizabeth: He's attuned with the client, but detached from his ego, his desire to be a good therapist.

Bob: But that first level of students, a lot of them weren't so detached, so that is subtle but very powerful. When you do what looks like what he does but you're attached, you can feel it in the body, you can feel it in the voice. That's when I think I started my own questioning of that.

Michael: Which started your own questioning?

Bob: Well, I didn't have the words for it at first. When you can work with that kind of intelligence but you're attached, it's not that helpful. You're more invested in yourself than the client. For example, I remember John Bradshaw would be doing these things, and I talked to somebody who went to see him and they said, "Oh he's so brilliant! He's amazing! But I felt so badly because I just couldn't do what he does."

Michael & Elizabeth: Yeah.

Bob: Because the ego gets in the way. That's also one of the really, profound internal teachings I've gotten from Dr. Rosenthal up there (points to picture on bookshelf). He also had little or no ego about the way he worked. Lou had a fair amount of ego about the way he worked and Lou was so charismatic. It was the same thing. You'd say, "I can't do Ormont. What's wrong with me? That's what I should be doing." But Rosenthal, since he didn't have ego attached, it just instilled into everyday life. So that's the real take away that I've been able to articulate.

Michael: That when you work with people like Rosenthal or Spotnitz, you not only come away feeling impressed, but you actually come away with the sense that you can do it, as opposed to feeling like, "Oh, he's just a brilliant person."

Bob: Yeah, I always tell that to students, "Don't think that you have to be charismatic to lead groups!" And the last paper I give them in the semester is called "The Charismatic Leader: Asset or Liability?" (Rutan & Rice, 1981) because a lot of students think, "Well, I can't do groups because I don't have that." You don't have to have that. You just do groups.

Elizabeth: Be yourself.

Bob: You just be yourself, yeah.

Elizabeth: And as spontaneous as you can be. It just comes.

Bob: Exactly, exactly. I think that's one of the main takeaways, but it took me half my time here at Naropa to start to be able to articulate that in a way, because I think when I first came out, I was compelled to try to be charismatic, to do those kinds of things. It just came out as aggression—not only aggression— but a lot of it came out as aggression.

Elizabeth: It seemed like Spotnitz had a way where he really was trying to make the aggression overt. So let's just accept that it's here and allow it to be here and if it's out in the open where we can work with it rather than pretend that that's not really what's happening here, but that actually is what's happening here . . .

Bob: But he did it in the most humorous ways. If you'd have said for example, "You are all experiencing aggression," that wouldn't work. He just did it in these ways that were just so brilliant.

Elizabeth: So pure to the unconscious.

Michael: Also really breaking down this barrier where the audience wants to observe and not be involved. And he's sort of pointing out, well that doesn't actually work that way. You are involved.

Bob: Yeah, like in the first demo I do in the group class. I just did it a few weeks ago in the group class, because you know they do all the little practice groups. I said, "Okay I'll do a demo. Eight people come into the center of the circle." So eight people come in the center of the circle and the rest of the class is sitting out there and we just start talking and I'll usually say something like, "Oh, did you notice that when you were saying that, Joe over there (who's outside the circle) flinched (or something like that)?" Just to call attention to the fact that just because you're in the middle of the circle doesn't mean that's all that's happening in the room. And before you know it, they're talking, the internal group is talking, everyone's talking, without you having to say, "Well this is a group and you watch," or whatever. And they get into it, become part of it, and have an experience beyond just watching.

Michael: This is kind of a larger question Bob, but you left New York a long time ago. In what ways do you think you've done things differently from Spotnitz? In what ways have you sort of evolved different ways of doing things?

Bob: Well, it's a good question. If there's one thing I've learned over time, it's that you actually have an unconscious. It's not just a concept, you know. So I have an unconscious. I've come to realize that I don't even guess at what I do, or I guess at what I think I do. So I don't really know. There were circumstances at the time for why I left, situational circumstances, but in the end I left and I moved to Shambhala Mountain Center because basically I just couldn't do New York. My body does not have enough defenses to do New York.

Michael: All the stimulation?

Bob: All the stimulation. I couldn't get comfortable ever. I just couldn't get comfortable. I always thought there was something wrong with me psychologically, and that enough therapy would take care of it. But fortunately, enough bad circumstances happened so I bolted! (Laughter).

Then more serendipity—this is a roundabout way of getting to your question—I wound up at Shambhala Mountain Center because I had come in contact with the Buddhist community and then on a trip I visited it and I said, "I'm going to leave." I had wanted to leave for a while. It just wasn't working for me to be there. My life was sort of going okay. I had a practice going and I had a good stature at the Center and I had been there for many years already, but it just wasn't quite right.

And then it was serendipity to move here to Boulder. I came down here because I hooked up with Helena because she was in the Maitri program with her M.A. Naropa class. And I was waiting for her to finish school and I thought I could work somewhere, and I was making bowls for a while. I really didn't want to be a therapist. New York left a very bad taste in my mouth. But then Miriam Bloom, who had moved to Boulder a few years previous, had started a local modern analytic school and somehow we got in touch with each other and she referred two people to me. And by then I had gotten a job at the A.R.C. (the Addiction Recovery Center) in Boulder because we didn't really know what to do, so I wound up staying. So there's serendipity again, but I think one of the things that's different is just that my body really likes it here. When I ride my bike to Jamestown and back, I just feel at home.

About once every year or two I have a dream. It's almost the same dream with just slightly different circumstances. For some reason I have to move back to New York and work there and live there. They're very painful dreams of claustrophobia. Why am I here? How can I get out? Did I really choose to come here? Why did I have to come back here? When you're claustrophobic you do this (moves hands rapidly in jerky motion) your mind moves, you're staccato. But here, I can breathe. Between that, and the quality of transparency that is in the culture of Naropa, I gradually realized I didn't have to be so New York analytic. I don't do it very well. I'm not disciplined enough to do it anyway. I didn't do it well, and something about being here got me embodied more. And I think my work is just more embodied, if that answers your question. It's not so conceptual. So I feel very fortunate. It just works for me here. The light air here, for example, it's like the air I grew up with in the desert in California. I'm just really comfortable here. So, since I'm more comfortable with myself, I'm more comfortable working and I think a lot of it has to do with that.

Michael: It sounds like what you're saying is that you've relaxed a lot, relaxed into yourself, and into your body.

Bob: Yeah, for a guy who's not fundamentally relaxed, yes, I've really relaxed! And I've found the physical activities that match my sort of inherent anxiety. You know they're good sublimations, because that whole cycling culture, for instance, we're all a bunch of ADD people. So it works! So that's even a culture of like people, you know, that's the way we would joke about it, you know, "It works!" So I think the combination of a high level of intelligence and academia here plus the high level of physical stuff is just a great combination. Can't beat it.

Elizabeth: I was wondering, can you say more about your relationship with Rosenthal and how you connected with him?

Bob: Yes, it's going to make me cry. So I had Rosenthal for a class at the Center in New York, a group class. Even though Ormont was sort of the superstar of groups, he actually didn't teach at the center. Rosenthal did and he was considered the other group guy. I liked him very much, so when I moved here after I got settled and was back doing clinical work, I called him and asked him if he could work with me. By then I was sort of aware of working on the phone and asked him if he had supervision groups that I could phone into and he said he was sorry he didn't have any at the time. Some months later he called me and said, "Well, I'm starting a new group. Would you like to be in it on the phone?" So I said yes. So that's how it started, around 25 years ago.

So that group started and like any group, some people came and went and it took several years to stabilize. One person in the group was a close friend of mine in New York who was at my second year social work school placement who's still in the group to this day. We're the senior people. So that group stabilized. For years every other week I was in that group, and I saw him a number of times when I went back to New York and AGPA (American Group Psychotherapy Association). And he's just wonderful. His interventions were both brilliant and pedestrian. His intelligence was not to be denied, but he worked from craft and not from charisma. And I think that's the real lesson I got from him: really settle in and be yourself.

Several years ago some students of his made a Festschrift, the Rosenthal Festschrift. So what I said in my piece for his festschrift basically is that he gives you the feeling that you can do it. Because he's doing it out of craft, very simple craft. He was just great. And then about five years ago, his wife of 60 years died. And he was an orphan. He really had a tough go of it at the very beginning. They were married for 60 years and she died and then within a year he really deteriorated. He really started losing his mind, and then he died. However that happens. I think he was 88 when he died, so he worked a long time. So then we've continued the group as a peer group since then. One person has left. Oh, and then we're doing an interesting thing. One person in the group is getting dementia, quite severely and we realized it was happening. And then one day recently last year, when she wasn't there, we decided, since we're all in my age range, that one of our tasks with each other as a group is to be able to be upfront with each other as we age and see what happens as we age which is quite an experiment. So were going to do that. So we're still going every other week. So we're at about 25 years now. But there's something about his temperament.

Even when you knew he was doing craft, it was so him that it was still effective. It's hard to explain, but that's what I can say about it. I think about him and his interventions. We refer to him all the time in the group, "I was thinking about Dr. Rosenthal when I was working with so-and-so," stuff like that. It's just there, the blessings of a lineage.

Michael: It's like this perfect integration of craft and himself.

Bob: Yes.

Michael: It was artificial, you could see the design of it, but it also didn't feel like just charisma.

Bob: I was very, very, very, very lucky. So I'll mention also when we first moved here, I felt I still needed to have a therapist. I contacted one person after I left Dr. Meadow— which was not an easy thing to do, but Meadow was just too toxic for me. I got a lot of shit about leaving her. I heard from one of my friends that she brought me up in a class as a good example of being suicidal.

Elizabeth: That you were suicidal?! Brought up by her?

Bob: By her! But if this is rebirth, hey! So then I saw another modern analyst, but I was too angry, and it didn't work. So I thought after I was out here for a while, I thought I really needed someone and one of the teachers that I really liked was Dr. Hayden, so I called him and he said, "Oh, Mr. Unger, I'd be very happy to work with you!"

So I've been working with him for almost 30 years. He's 88. He's totally relaxed. He remembers everything I say, virtually everything I've ever said and really, it's amazing. He plays doubles tennis and he goes up to Central Park in the winter time and ice skates. He's a very relaxed guy and so, between he and Rosenthal, I think what I really got are males in my life that really taught me a way to be that my father couldn't do.

My father, by the way, was abandoned by his mother on the dining room table when he was six months old in the Bronx. I have a newspaper article from the Bronx News at home that talks about it. It's really interesting. It was the old days of Jewish immigrants in New York and I think my grandfather—he died when I was 16, but he was a very intense, charismatic guy—I think he got sort of one of those arranged Jewish child brides who was only 16 or 17. It was way too much for her and she just left. They had a friend living with them and the friend came home and found my father, just a baby, on the kitchen table. And then my grandfather got set up with this other woman, married her and she became the evil stepmother. So my father did not have an easy time. That was that.

So, I was very lucky to find two males who were very strong males and who have been very kind to me and good examples of how you can be a strong male and without aggression. Because neither of them really manifested as aggressive though both of them had very confident personalities. So I was very, very fortunate.

Elizabeth: I noticed that I'm getting emotional as you're talking, and part of it is that I feel like, I really feel like you've been that for me.

Bob: Well, that's lineage (crying). It works.

Elizabeth: It really feels like an honor to have you in my life. Just more than an honor, but so much...

Bob: (softly) Thank you.

Elizabeth: Hearing these stories of your father, Rosenthal, and Spotnitz, it's just really emotional.

Michael: Let me get you guys some Kleenex!

Bob: I'm running low. Helena steals them! We'll have to go to Costco! (Laughter).

Bob: Well, Spotnitz, you know, I worked with him just about the time that I started the group with Rosenthal, maybe late 80s early 90s. I called Spotnitz to see if I could be in one of his groups and that was before the really easy to use conference call do-hickeys. He actually set up a line in order for me to be able to call into the group!

And so I call into this group... Well, there must've been 30 people in the group. They'd been with him for 100 years. It was a supervision group technically, but all they did was bicker and act like they wanted to impress Spotnitz and he wasn't saying too much by that stage of his career, but I did get the opportunity to be in that group. It went about a year I think and then he stopped the group.

The story is that one of his groups Rosenthal took over and of course they all took out their aggression on Rosenthal because they had been with Spotnitz for 30 or 40 years before he died. And so then Rosenthal would say things like, "Now, what would Dr. Spotnitz say here?" (Laughter).

Elizabeth: I've always appreciated that intervention when I've taken someone's group over.

Bob: Oh, sure, sure! It's such a great intervention.

Elizabeth: It's so helpful. I love that.

Bob: It's such a great intervention. That's what Rosenthal did. I had that opportunity to work with Spotnitz in some direct way so I've really had the benefit of you know, Meadow, Ormont, Rosenthal, Hayden, Spotnitz, so I really got the core of that first group, of that original group of the modern analysts. There's not too many of them left.

Michael: Who else is left?

Bob: Dr. Hayden is left. Let's see. I think Evelyn Abrams died at over a hundred. Arnold Bernstein and Harold Davis recently died. Evelyn Liegner is still alive. I think she's well into her 90s. There's a couple of others. But it's been a long time. And then there's a whole new group of course you know.

Elizabeth: To carry the lineage.

Bob: Yeah, as best we can... At one point Dr. Meadow got fascinated with Lacan. Suddenly everything was Lacan before she died. Lacan, Lacan, Lacan. I don't know what that means, but to me, you know, it's just Spotnitz.

Elizabeth: One of the memories I was having, was when I was in a supervision group with you once and I wanted to know developmentally how you work. I wanted to know what's the developmental way that people progress in treatment. Your response to me was so strong, "I don't work that way. I do not do that!" I don't remember exactly what you said. But you were like, "No! I don't think like that." And I was like, "What do you mean you don't think like that?! Of course you think like that! It has to be!" "Nope, nope! That's not what I do!" (Laughter).

Bob: Well, Elliot Zeisel said it really nicely, at one of his talks in AGPA like five or six years ago. "Modern psychoanalysis, and modern group analysis is actually a theory of the technique." So that I could talk about forever. I don't think developmentally, but the theory of the technique makes much more sense to me, because it's about what you do. My life is about movement, you know, so that makes sense to me because I just move.

Michael: What does that mean, the theory of the technique?

Bob: So it's not a theory, a developmental life theory. It's about why you do what you do in the moment, the effect. You know I've been thinking about this. Helena and I went to Bhutan on a bike trip a few years ago—it was a really good group. There were about 15 people. Helena and I were really the only people who had been around Buddhism a lot. So everybody else was asking a lot of questions, really good questions, you know. It was a good group. Our cultural guide, Palden, he was a small guy, a lovely sweet man, in the wonderful Bhutanese national clothes that everyone wears. Everyone's asking questions about, what this temple means, what the iconography means, you know, they were just wanting to know and understand. He would talk about it a little bit, and then he'd smile his wonderful wise smile and say, "You know the only thing you really have to know about Buddhism is that the essence of Buddhism is just being kind to people." "Oh!" (Laughter). So therapy is like that too. It's just being kind to people.

Elizabeth: I can see that more now and really appreciate it, but at the time it really frustrated me because I was in school and I was learning all these developmental theories. Something that I really appreciate about you and I think I'm still trying to learn from in your approach, is this sense of fluidity. You know, you were speaking about nonattachment, but there's such a fluidity to how you think that I really appreciate. And I've been thinking about how you talk about groups lately. I just really appreciate how you talk about it as one of the ways to have a community experience. Therapy has this fluidity, where we are really having real relationships with people. It's more about what's actually happening between people.

Michael: Yeah, I've heard you talk about it when you don't even think of it as therapy. It's community.

Bob: Yeah, exactly. That's just how it's happened. I don't know how it's got there. It's just how it happened.

Michael: You're not trying to therapize or fix people, or even heal them necessarily. You're trying to connect people, to create a community that works, where it's flowing and stuff is happening.

Bob: Yeah, where people can really talk with each other in a culture that doesn't support that. It just seems important. I'm also biased here, but it seems to me you can take most diagnoses out there and distill them into manifestations of anxiety. You know, it's a really anxious time and there's too much electrical stimulation in the world, in the culture. There's no role models, especially for young men. And sure, you develop symptoms, but they're all manifestations of anxiety and confusion.

(Pointing to Elizabeth) The fellow I called you about for the DBT group... Well, he's diagnosed with Asperger's/Autism. He manifests everything that goes along with it in terms of those categories. So I just talk with him as if he's a regular guy. And we were starting to forget the fact that he's autistic just a little bit because he was talking like a regular guy. Then he gets into this legal issue and his family mounts the autism defense. And I was like, "Fuck!" All that work to just treat him like a regular person and have him manifest better in the world, and suddenly there's all this secondary gain in him being "autistic."

Elizabeth: And there is the repetition. He's doing well, and then the system needs to pull him back. You've got to play a role for us.

Bob: Yeah, but I get very anxious about diagnosis. It just feels so superior somehow. And I think the residue of that is from that aspect of the early modern analysts who felt so superior. And when you try to buy into that, to feeling superior, it creates so much anxiety. It's just easier not to feel superior.

Michael: So I'm curious, it sounds like on the one hand when you were in New York the modern analytic world was so exciting and so vibrant with these great mentors, but then you left, and you said something about feeling burnt out from that whole scene, and the piece about feeling that people were superior. How did those things fit together?

Bob: Well, the culmination was in my first brief marriage to another very smart modern analytic student. I had a modern psychoanalytic marriage, I'd say. We met at a Spotnitz lecture I believe actually, and we sort of hit it off. It was a little iffy for the first year, but then we got very involved. It was like a church with a couple, the way those things are.

Elizabeth: I remember you telling us about Meadow and there was some pressure involved.

Bob: Too much influence. There was a funny dating thing, but we both were seeing Dr. Meadow and she became a matchmaker and there was a lot of transference pressure. The marriage was never going to happen. We were not a good mix at the marriage level. I wasn't struggling. I was considered one of the smart guys there, and she was too. But there was a certain pressure to cooperate. And also, there was something about the competition in New York, and the way people could embody the culture of the city that I just couldn't. I always felt inadequate and I just couldn't. There was this fantasy that with enough analysis I could get comfortable, which was sort of the hook, and when the whole thing really fell apart, when the marriage didn't work and, you know, all the gory details...

I had basically been attacked. Dr. Meadow said something in a couples group I was in that pushed me in a way I didn't like. I just didn't show up at the next group. I just didn't go. And that was not me. I was so compliant. And then I heard, through my almost ex-wife, that because I didn't show up that I was acting out and I was kicked out of treatment! So she went that far. And it just opened up everything to me, in spite of my transference to her. I just knew this was over the top.

Elizabeth: Way over the top!

Bob: Way over the top! It actually freed me. So then I called her up and I said, "Can I come to the group?" and she said, "Oh, yeah," thinking that I was giving in. So I went to the group, and I said, "I wanted to tell you all, I'm leaving. This is it!"

Elizabeth: Nice!

Bob: And they all attacked me. One of the women said, "You do not leave Dr. Meadow!"

Elizabeth: Yes, I do!

Michael: And then later when she called you suicidal—It's like the biggest modern psychoanalytic insult.

Bob: Yeah. You're suicidal! (in taunting tone).

Elizabeth: Really what I am is homicidal! And I'm going to kill off this group and you, Dr. Meadow! Goodbye !

Bob: So, I left the group. I've learned so much about the danger of charisma. It's really dangerous. You have to be so careful about the way you influence people. I think one of the things I've learned is that we take for granted how powerful transference is a lot of times and it really is powerful. And if you happen to have a strong personality, it's really powerful. And, so when I look back, that's sort of what happened. As I look back—you can think about it interpersonally—but I just couldn't do New York. My boundaries just aren't good enough to handle the stimulation.

After the marriage ended, I was really afloat. By then I was doing some work, in a wonderful little EAP (Employee Assistance Program) that a fellow I met started. Joel, he's such a wonderful friend to this day. I started connecting more with the Shambhala community and I came out here to visit Shambhala Mountain Center. I had wanted to leave for a while, but thought I would just visit Colorado. My life was sort of going okay. I had a practice going and I had a good stature at the center and I had been there for many years already. Who leaves New York when you're a successful psychoanalyst? But basically when I came back, I said, "I'm leaving New York." I left, but still, I brought it all with me.

Maybe next time we can do the next chapter and I can

tell you about my initial contact with Naropa. I was still in New York when that happened and how it came to be that I ended up teaching here at Naropa and what I learned. Naropa, in a nutshell, got into me as much as I got into it. For that I feel so grateful. It was very subtle the way it happened and it took time. It got into me. So that's what happened (crying).

Elizabeth: Looks like it's bringing up some feelings! Any words that go with those feelings?

Bob: Such gratefulness, such gratefulness, such gratefulness.

Michael: We definitely have to continue.

Bob: Okay! If we gotta, we gotta!

Michael: This is wonderful and there's a whole other chapter here, a whole series of chapters...

Part Two

Michael: So what shall we talk about? Where were we last time?

Elizabeth: I was counting on your memory, Michael!

Bob: Well, I hope you weren't counting on mine!

Michael: Well, it seems like roughly chronologically we had come up to the point of you coming to Boulder which is actually really maybe only part one and there's a whole part two.

Bob: I can't remember if I told you all the details...

Michael: It's OK, you can tell us again! (Laughter).

Bob: Well, basically the pressure of the New York analytic culture became very discordant to me and in the meantime I had discovered Buddhism. I actually discovered it when I went to social work school through Raymon, a very dear friend of mine, a friend of mine to this day. I was in between my two years of social work school and I didn't have anything to do that summer (this is like 1974, 75) and he said, "Oh, I've heard about this meditation center up in Vermont." That was Karme Chöling. And I thought—I was adventurous—"I'll just go up there and check it out," which I did. I spent a week there and was very intrigued. So I returned there in 1981 in the midst of that swirling stretch when my life was upside down and spent a week sitting. The whole time my mind just tortured me about everything.

The car ride back felt like a reprieve and I listened to music and watched how Vermont gradually fades into the New York metropolitan sprawl. After an hour back in the city, my mind was doing the same thing, just torture. Then unexpectedly, for about two seconds, it all let go. Suddenly, it was all just "thinking." And I went, "Oh!"

Just for that to happen once I was hooked. In the midst of such chaos to just go, "Oh!" So that week of practice found itself at that moment. It didn't last long, but all you need is that one hint. The eggshell was cracked. So I knew I was doing the right thing.

Elizabeth: It sounded like you really followed your intuition, that it couldn't be your mind that led you, that it was something wiser in you that said, "I need to do this." But it was hard to do.

Bob: Yeah, hard to do, but then when it breaks for a moment you go, "Oh! That's possible!" It's actually just your mind. When I went up there I knew that conceptually, but it hadn't happened yet, so that was really fortunate.

I continued to be involved in Buddhism in the city, but in the summer of 1981 I decided to do a cross-country motorcycle trip. So I actually threw my motorcycle in a crate and flew it out to California because my parents and sister lived there. I timed it to go across country and stop at this intensive meditation seminar at Shambhala Mountain Center (SMC) that Trungpa was doing for a week.

I timed it and spent the week there. And I met the whole subgroup of the people who are therapists around the Buddhist sangha. I just kind of fell in with them. You know there's like 300 people, it's SMC, the place was pretty barren at the time, but I had a very good time.

As I was finishing, I met Jed Shapiro who is a very welcoming guy, and he said, "Why don't you spend a few days in Boulder? I have a house." He had a house up on Forest Ave. that he lived in at the time and I said, "Okay."

And I was shocked—this is the New Yorker in me— here's a guy, he's a psychiatrist and he dresses just like regular people! I always thought in New York, you know, psychiatrists only wear suits. And they don't have bodies. They just have minds.

And I had a very friendly time with him. He was delightful. So I spent a few days in Boulder and it was just wonderful.

So I go back I get on my motorcycle after a few days out here. It's August. I just muse over it for about a month. Then I say, "I'm going to do it. I'm going to leave." I called up SMC and talked to the director who was Martha Espeset at the time and asked them if they needed a carpenter. Because I used to do a lot of woodworking stuff. They said yes. And I caught my breath. At that time I was out of analysis. I tried one person after I left Meadow. That was not an easy thing to do.

Elizabeth: That was brave!

Bob: I clawed my way out. I say that was the greatest thing that ever happened to me.

Elizabeth: Good for you. Super individuation.

Bob: It was not easy. There was a lot of pressure and I cannot tell you what a hard decision that was.

So, then I started closing up shop. I left New York the day after Thanksgiving. I had bought a pickup truck. I never had a car in New York, even though I always drove since I was 16, but I bought a pickup truck because that's what you do. I loaded it up, and headed west. I stopped at Jed's house and changed my driver's license. I mean in New York if you want to change your driver's license you have to get in line at five in the morning and you get out by three or four in the afternoon if you are lucky. Here I did everything to change everything and I'm done by noon!

And I get out here, and I'm worried because you can't find bagels at night. To leave New York is a big deal, especially when you're in a New York culture like the psychoanalytic culture, you know. I had no idea really what I was getting into. It's like a different life!

I spent a couple of days in Boulder and then I headed up to SMC. I'll never forget the date, December 8, because it was the first anniversary of John Lennon's assassination. It always stuck with me. I get up there in this cold night in December, and I walk in and they expected me. Martha introduces me to a few people and then she says to me, "Here's your new crew boss, Bob Hastie, on maintenance." And I said, "Oh, ah, um… I thought I was doing carpentry," and, "Oh," she said, "The money didn't come through for that job. You're on maintenance." I had a lot of ego about being a carpenter, but that's the path.

So there I was at SMC, doing maintenance. At that time, it was nothing compared to what it's like now. There was hardly anything, just the building where the kitchen is now. Then there were these little huts around. Also there was that building that I think since has burned down, Prajna, which is where Rinpoche would stay when he came. And the whole winter was very quiet and there were maybe 15 people there and it was stunningly beautiful. I really think of it as rehab.

Michael: Rehab from psychoanalysis?

Bob: From psychoanalysis.

Elizabeth: And New York City, and overstimulation.

Bob: Yes, I mean I still had a lot going on in my mind, but that environment, you can't deny being there, you know. I exchanged letters with a very close group of friends back in New York. It was our motorcycle club. I would do audiotapes back and forth and that was my way of writing letters. Once you're an analyst, always an analyst. Talk, talk, talk, talk.

And then, that spring the Naropa contemplative program came to do their three month Maitri program. This class of 40 people came up and among them was Helena. And there's all sorts of stories about that, but I just won't bother (laughter). Helena engineered the situation very brilliantly and to this day I'm very grateful to have been so totally manipulated.

So then came the summer after Maitri ended. She stayed up there, because by then we were a couple and she cooked and I was still on staff. And then I applied to seminary, but it was way too soon and I was kind of freaked out about the whole deal. As I put it, one powerful transference in a life is enough. So I never really bonded to Trungpa, in the way people do, but I was in the scene and people liked me, and I had a good mind, so I was very accepted. So I applied to seminary, and even though I was sort of new on the scene, I got accepted. I was having my doubts about going, but Helena and I went on our first trip away. We went out to Utah a week or two at the end of the summer. She then had to go back and finish school, and I said, "Okay, I'm going to go." And I'm glad I did.

Afterward I came down from the center to Boulder because Helena and I were an item. I was waiting for her to finish school and I needed to work. I was making bowls for a while, but that wasn't paying the bills. At that time I really didn't want to be a therapist. New York left a very bad taste in my mouth. But then Miriam Bloom started a local modern analytic school and somehow we got in touch with each other and she referred two people to me. And then I had gotten a job at the Addiction Recovery Center because I didn't really know what to do, and I wound up staying and being a therapist again, and being able to do groups again.

Eventually I again was lucky and was hired to teach at Naropa. So many stories about that.

Here's one of my first memories about Naropa. So I'm teaching this first semester class, and it was a strong class. So it was the next to the last class. So this very bright woman gets up and says, "We're getting up to do something" and a bunch of people in the class get up. It was like a mutiny and I said, "You know, we're supposed to stay in our seats and talk." Something like that. And they ignored me. So I said, "Class dismissed!" I just ended the class (laughter), and they freaked out. Then it turned out what they were preparing to do was some kind of skit that they had prepared the class. So I felt badly of course, but it was a lesson, you know, that if a group is out of control, you end the group. That's what I was trying to demonstrate, you know. But it was like one of those things, where I was really reaching. I was really nervous.

But what was great about that, and I use this as a teaching example, five years or so later in a class, it might've been Jeff Price's class, this woman, does something similar, except there was no plan. She wanted to get up and do something, and a couple of people decided to do it with her and in my mind came that time from five years before. So I actually cogitated around it for some period of time, however long it takes in your mind, I said, "Should I do this? Should I not? Is this the right time? It happened last time." And I finally made a conscious decision to end the class in the same way. But it was a wonderful teaching which I've used as a teaching example of how when you do something spontaneously if you keep the information from it, next time the situation comes up you have more information and you can do it mindfully. So it surprised me that I had this happen again, "Oh, this happened before. Is this the same thing? What does it mean to do this? Is this the best thing for the class?" And this took me all of what, five seconds? You know how fast you process things.

Michael: But you made it a conscious . . .

Bob: I made a conscious decision.

Michael: But maybe felt better about it.

Bob: Yeah, felt much better about. Because it was a conscious decision.

Michael: So, like the first time it was more unconscious, you just did it, but then felt, "Oh, maybe that wasn't the right thing," but the second time you did the same thing . . .

Bob: The first time it was instinctive, but it was still informed by my training, but it was instinctive at that time.

Elizabeth: It was like there was a little more space around it.

Bob: It was more integrated the second time. But even the first time it still came from my training.

Elizabeth: It seems like with a little more space you were able to actually take a little more time with it. It sounds like the first one was a time issue, very quick.

Bob: I probably looked more knee-jerk the first time than the second time when it came out much calmer and more embodied.

Elizabeth: It's really interesting the way that an integrated or embodied intervention is received differently than one that is really quick. You're in your head and you're like, "I should do this."

Michael: I was going to say, those two interventions felt very different for you but looked the same, but they actually might have looked very different.

Bob: They probably looked different. And one of the things I love about Spotnitz, is when he's outrageous, it always feels not impulsive.

Michael: It feels regulated.

Bob: It feels regulated. That's the paradox. You know paradox happens a lot at the content level, but I always think of paradox also when you're saying something but it's embodied in a different way than when you normally hear those things. So when you hear "suicide" and people freak out and then Spotnitz talks about suicide in a way where he's not freaked out. Culturally, the way we're enculturated, that's paradoxical. Why isn't he freaked out? But he says, how are you going to kill yourself? He just goes to the heart of it in real language that the client understands. He isn't talking in terms of a suicide plan, a safety plan. So there's paradox that happens in all sorts of ways.

My teacher these days is Alan Watts and one of the many levels of things I really get from his teachings is the relative truth of words. We use words and hear stories so much. The cultural attachment to certain words and phrases which have their own energy: Suicide, abuse, all those things that have their "Oh!" "Oh!" "Oh!" He talks about language a lot in his talks. One of my favorite ones is he's working with a bunch of kids and he says, "Now describe a dog." And they all keep using words, circular words to describe a dog, and he says, "What's a dog?" And then, "What's a that?" and "what's a that?" until finally there's a little girl and he says, "What's a dog?" and she says, "A noun." (Laughter). And so I think at this stage of the game, I'm just interested in all of my influences and what they are, and they just keep coming.

I'll give you an example of that. This client is a wonderful person to talk about. He's a conductor but hadn't been active professionally for a long time. And then he went to Europe to take a conducting school with this man who was a master conducting teacher. There were various famous people there and he had a lot of anxiety about getting up and leading an orchestra and the teacher said to him, "When you conduct, all you're doing is conducting with your life experience up until that moment." And I thought, what a wonderful teaching. It put everyone at ease. And I think of that and I think at this stage, whatever I do, it's just whatever the influences are. There's the modern analytic influence, and there's the Naropa influence and now I listen to Alan Watts.

Elizabeth: And being a parent, and being a husband and a practitioner.

Bob: And being a cyclist. A lot of my metaphors are movement. I can't sit still, so a lot of my metaphors have to do with movement, because that's how my body is.

Michael: What's great about you saying that, is that that's the way it really is for therapists, but people don't always talk about it that way. You know, people tend to say, "I do this kind of therapy, or I do that kind of therapy," as opposed to realizing that what you're actually doing is just bringing the whole history of who you are up until that moment into your work.

Bob: You can't get too attached to how you think you do it. One of the things I've really gotten from listening to Alan Watts over and over and over is that the way we use and define words is so cultural, and so relative, and once you get real fluidity about what words mean things flow. Words are symbols anyway. They aren't real so it gives you tremendous freedom in doing therapy and using words. Not getting attached to the cultural, literal meaning of them just gives a kind of movement to the way you do the work that makes it much easier and more powerful. For example, what's the current hot button word of the day? Privilege.

Elizabeth: It was coming up in my consultation group. I think my thing was that I wanted there to be freedom, for people to be fluid around it and for it not to be a word that shuts people down.

Bob: There was a show when I was growing up called the Groucho Marx show. It was a TV show. It was just hilarious. He just interviewed people, and it was a chance for him to do his thing. So the show would start, and this little bird would pop down on the string and it would have a word in its mouth and he would say, "Say the secret word." So then he'd interview these people and there was a secret word and if they happened to say the word in the course of the interview, they got 100 bucks. So, say the secret word, and the bird would have a little piece of paper with a word in its mouth and then it would pop up. So I thought about it, because the secret word of this year at Naropa is "privilege." Everything is about privilege. They're fighting about privilege. And groups about privilege. Gosh, should you be guilty about privilege? Privilege, privilege, privilege. It can get absurd. But if you're there, you join in. So all I'm saying is, "Well, if you can just play with it as just symbolic of some energy going on, and you get interested in the energy going on, then one of the things you have to demonstrate is your own comfort with the word." So that was my little message to you.

Elizabeth: That was so helpful. I remember you telling me and I of course tucked it away. It was very helpful.

One of the things I wanted to talk with you about this morning is insulation. And I feel like there is a way that as a supervisor, almost more than anything else, what I feel like you offered me was insulation. So that in the places that I am fragile, the places that I felt ashamed or embarrassed, and the places that I got agitated or irritable or mad or annoyed or the things where I could get hooked or tripped lessened. It was like this way that you had that insulated me. It was like insulation for my reactivity to this work and the way I could get myself in trouble if I am not able to be more fluid in a way with it or not let it have a hold on me in that way. And I feel like you could kind of see the spots where I get kind of stuck and then help me through insulation, not by saying, "Oh, Elizabeth you really shouldn't do this," or "Here's what can happen to you if you do this or that." It's more this way of almost protecting me from myself, in a way that helps me to feel like, I can tolerate that and then work more productively.

Bob: Well, that I think is a direct stream from Spotnitz. To me even though all those under Spotnitz people all had their brilliance and I learned so much from all of them to this day, there is a way that Spotnitz was not attached to very provocative interpersonal situations and words that was just in his body. You just got it when you were at his lectures. He'd talk about these things and you'd get very uncomfortable, because he wasn't embodying them in the way you habitually expected them to be embodied. Over and over again that just starts to have an effect, a teaching effect that's so profound.

In one of Alan Watts' talks he said something like, "Well, if you really think this teaching is good, it's because you already know it." It's just great. So the reason I connect with him is because he's just doing more of something I've already learned some of and when you hear more of it, it's just, "Oh, dessert!" He really articulates words as symbols and ideas as symbols rather than anything solid. That's an ecological approach because it's really just a body in nature then. You know when I started to realize that, I realized that, me and my cats, there is no language barrier. You've all had your animals, and you know that there's no language barrier because you don't speak the same content language, but it's total communication anyway.

Elizabeth: From the heart.

Bob: It's... what's our favorite word? The Dalai Lama's word— "interdependence." Bing! It's just interdependence. So that's what I think the insulation is. The whole idea is to work with people so as not to do anything different necessarily. You're insulated when you don't get seduced into literalness. It's just a bunch of bodies doing this. At my age it makes it so much easier to work. The only thing that wears me out at work is just that I've worked for the day. I've spent the day working. It's concentrated work, you know, and you can't pick your nose, except for in between sessions so (laughter) . . . So you get tired, but just from the simple fact of having worked. Now if I had your practice (to Elizabeth) I might get really tired.

Elizabeth: (Laughter). I sleep better these days, but I had some rough ones this fall. I'm trying to be more careful about who I take, because it does take a toll. But you've just really helped me, and one of the reasons I've loved having you as a supervisor and just a person in my life is that I just feel I could tell you anything and you'd help me find a way to metabolize it. I just feel like it really, really makes me comfortable with myself and when I get scared or have an old feeling, like I'm in trouble in my work I just feel like I can come to you and you help me find a way to take it in in a way that's not going to damage me. I just appreciate that so much.

Bob: Well, what a wonderful thing to say. Thank you.

Elizabeth: For me it's just been really, really helpful. And I still need it. Less of the time do I feel like I'm in trouble, but every now and then . . . It's just helpful for me to have that. I was thinking about what I'm going to write for the Festschrift, and I was thinking about Winnicott and how he talks about a way of holding, a sort of holding environment, and for me that's something you've done with insulation. Through the insulation I feel held in a way so I know you're out there (and you're in here), so even though I'm not in a room with you I can think of you. Oh, I'm sitting in Bob's chair! I think about that almost every day. I'm sitting in Bob's chair. [When Bob got a new office chair, Elizabeth inherited his old one that he worked in for twenty years.]

Michael: You actually are sitting in Bob's chair?

Elizabeth: Yes, I am. I was like, "I want that chair! Please get rid of it because I want it!"

Bob: You know, here I am almost 70, and I am still in five supervisory situations and I'm in two therapies. It really is lineage and I get to draw on everyone's experience. Recently some psychoanalytic friends out here and I started a new group. We chew the fat about all this stuff. Sometimes we present cases and sometimes we talk theory. I need it. It keeps me connected. I was happy to be have been able to create an Evolutions Class years ago at Naropa because I constructed that class just to be about lineage. It's just lineage. You learn, and you learn, and it just goes that way.

Elizabeth: But it really is important. I think what you get in the lineage is a certain way of being held and insulated and taught. It's like a holding that helps you be able to practice if you have this community or this way of being . . . I don't know exactly what it is but there's something about it that just really helps you.

Bob: Anytime I see or read about someone who's invented a new form of psychotherapy, I go, "Uh-oh!" because as the Buddha was alleged to have said, "There's nothing new under the sun," and even if you think you're doing something different, if you really study your influences . . . you're just a combination of your influences anyway if you think about it. You can't be anything else but that.

Elizabeth: I really think Spotnitz did do something in the way he broke off and individuated. I think there's a way that even what he was doing back then and what you've taught me and what I've learned, it's actually what is now kind of getting documented and researched in recent advances in neurobiology. What he was doing, what you've done for years, is emotional communication and that is speaking right to the limbic brain and bypassing the cognitive in a way to really interrupt these patterns. The way to interrupt these patterns is by interrupting limbic repetition and the way to do that is emotional communication. I still think, even with current neurobiology, people still aren't quite yet where Spotnitz was.

Bob: Yeah, there are seminal people, who really are creative. Freud was obviously one of them. Einstein was one of them and Spotnitz was one of them. I'm not saying Spotnitz was just like Freud or Einstein, but there have been some people who were really innovative. For me in my professional life, Spotnitz is still the most innovative influence.

Elizabeth: Yeah the way he did it is just mind blowing.

Bob: Yeah, yeah.

Elizabeth: And I think you really hold it, too. The way I've experienced it is you being surprising. Like you're talking about that paradox, that the effect of it is confusion. The effect of it is surprise and sometimes even though it sounds terrible to others to hear what you might have just said to someone's character, the person themselves is like, "Though I don't all like it, some deep part of me really likes what you just said to me."

Bob: In Spotnitz's Festschrift, Harold Davis mentions how some people talk about Spotnitz being outrageous, but he's not really. It's more that what he says is *unexpected*. Davis was a physicist turned analyst so he thinks this way. He quotes Claude Shannon, who invented the mathematical theory of information and says that the amount of information contained in the message is directly proportional to the degree it's unexpected. Isn't that just a wonderful way to put it? So that's what Spotnitz was doing, by surprising us he's going right to the unconscious.

Elizabeth: Yeah and even with all the advances in neurobiology I still don't think they are where Spotnitz was 40, 50 years ago and people are still afraid of working with the unconscious in that direct way.

Bob: Yeah, I don't know of anyone else in any other lineage who does that. Now the first generation of modern analytic students were very smart. But if you didn't really, really get it, a lot of it comes out as aggression. All those surprise interventions, as soon as you have ego in it, they are experienced as aggression, as I see it, because it's so seductive, the secondary gain of being able to do things like that and act out on your aggression unconsciously.

Michael: But just being surprising—if that's just what you're trying to do—that can't be in itself helpful. That's just aggressive.

Bob: Yes. Without an understanding of what Spotnitz was really doing, moving the unconscious by accurately engaging it, without some embodiment of that, you're going to come off as aggressive. And I think that when I came out here, that really was me. First of all I had a lot of aggression, just from the way I ended New York. And I think I was a bit uncomfortable. I was new here. I was such a New Yorker. There's a lot of aggression in the way I did it. That's why I'm so grateful to Naropa and the climate of it all, just the whole thing, the practice climate. It took, let's see, it's been 25 years. It took probably about 10 to 15 years to actually soften me up, to where I could even articulate it to myself that I didn't need to do that. I could start to converse with myself about that, that you have to do it in an integrated empathic way. There has to be a smile about it. Otherwise it's just going to be experienced as aggression.

Elizabeth: With these surprising interventions, my hope is that my clients experience it as being loved by me actually. The feeling behind me saying this unexpected or confrontational thing is really a feeling of love. Of wanting the best for them.

Bob: Exactly.

Elizabeth: Sometimes when I do a group, I do an intervention like that with one person and other people in the group are like, "What?! How dare you talk to him that way. I don't want you to talk to me like that!" They sometimes see it that way, but for the person who received the intervention the hope is that it might be disruptive for them, but they actually really think, "You really understand me and care about me. Thank you for saying this horrible thing about me that is interfering in my life."

Bob: One of the ways I've really learned to integrate such interventions or one of the tests is if I'm very comfortable in the situation and not feeling any aggression towards the client. I can tell because I've worked with people for so many years and if my heart is open to them I feel pretty free to say anything. But if I feel any edge with the person, if I'm not liking them at the moment, anything that has some edge of conflict in it, then I really watch what I'm formulating and watch what I'm saying, and how I'm saying it, much more than if I'm just having positive regard or love or however we say it.

Elizabeth: Yes, because it can be kind of dangerous. It's such a different way of working.

Bob: In the male lineage of my family there are harsh Eastern European Jews to this day, so I really do have to be careful because that is inside of me. It's been really important for me to spend a lot of time just watching what is arising in me. You're always trying to find out about your unconscious. But you only get it by inference. I'm very aware of how much I learned by being in the Buddhist community and Naropa environment. It really has had a profound effect on my personality and how I work. As has age, and experience.

Michael: It sounds like you've really thought a lot about your own aggression and how to use it. You've had to be careful with it and you see it in your own family lineage.

Bob: My two male mentors Rosenthal and Hayden have been so influential. They're really soft men. For a man who doesn't come from a soft male environment and in a culture that doesn't really support soft men, the blessing of having stumbled into this level of intimacy of working with soft men is just beyond priceless.

Michael: But soft men—and I experience you in this way, too—I would imagine they're not just soft.

Bob: Oh no! Rosenthal is really capable of—I'm still speaking of him in the present tense.

Elizabeth: He's alive for you.

Bob: Yes he's alive for me. Really, really, very, very right there. Just right there (pointing to his heart).

Michael: And they have boundaries and structure and they can be sharp, but they don't lead with that.

Bob: Exactly, they don't lead with aggression. In our culture it's so valuable to find men like that. For young men in our culture right now it's just a tough time.

Elizabeth: What's been helpful for me as a woman in this culture is to know I can be actually assertive or aggressive and spontaneous and free to say things. I was talking to a client recently and the dad is an unbelievably aggressive business man. A total boss. And he was furious with me for something I did with his daughter that was totally appropriate, the best thing for her. And I got on the phone with him and he said, "What did you do!!" He went on and on and I said, "I did this!" And I did feel aggressive towards him, but I didn't feel like I was going to attack him or try to destroy him. I just felt like, this is unhelpful the way you are talking to me right now and it's not going to be helpful for me to give you the feeling that you can make me scared.

Bob: Elizabeth, you are so wonderful! You're a fearless role-model for me. We have talked about the families you have dealt with, those families . . . You've had a lot of tough customers, but none tougher than you!

Elizabeth: But it's been very freeing to use that energy sometimes to help the situation. He calmed right down. I could hear his voice change and we could talk with each other.

Bob: Well, when I've heard you do it, I'd calm right down too.

Michael: You really met him. He got to learn that he can't just throw that aggressive energy around.

Elizabeth: And I wasn't even expecting it. I thought he was going to be like, "Well, what happened with my daughter? Is she okay?" When he started in this way, I was like, what is this?

Bob: You do it and people can always tell if you're not doing it impulsively. People can always tell, no matter how intense you are, if you're thinking at the same time. You're making the choice. You're making the choice, that's the embodied thing.

Elizabeth: Maybe how they perceive it is different. It's not reactive. It's purposeful. I think a lot of people in the world have the view of the modern technique as being impulsive. "It's just wild. It's crazy. It's super aggressive."

Bob: And with some people who just haven't worked with it, it is, because it's so gratifying. So it's very tricky.

Elizabeth: It's so interesting to see how some people in the psychoanalytic world who don't really work directly with aggression tend to pooh-pooh what the modern folks do. But in actuality there's a way sometimes that they themselves are extraordinarily aggressive, all in the name of, "Well I am doing an interpretation."

Bob: Oh yeah, extraordinarily so. Well, interpretations. It's the kindest way to be aggressive.

Elizabeth: Yeah, well it looks good supposedly, but how it feels to the recipient can be pretty crappy.

Michael: Bob, could you talk about how your practice has evolved over the years? We talked a little bit about that, that you had gotten softer, or that you had sort of gotten the New York out of you.

Bob: Just recently Dr. Hayden told me, "I don't really think about technique anymore. I've done enough of that. I just talk." And he does! What we do is very conversational, but somehow I feel like I'm working and getting to stuff. One of the things that I have realized that's freed me up is that the form itself takes care of 80 to 90% of the whole deal.

Michael: Yes, I think about that a lot. You've talked to me about that a lot. And that's really relaxing for me, to remember it's just the setup, just the talking, just the hierarchy.

Bob: The set up makes the transference. You don't really have to do much about making something happen, because someone's coming in and in that form, it's there. I know when I call Dr. Hayden, what happens is, I look at my calendar and I see that the session is coming up and I have to prepare my speakerphone, prepare my couch. I have to get ready to write a check and a bunch of stuff, so by the time we start, I'm in therapy. I'm in therapy, that's that. It's been on my mind. I am thinking, "Next week, what do I want to talk about?" You know how it is. I'll muse. I don't know even if I'll ever talk about some of those things, but you put energy into it. So that takes care of so much. And you know, he listens and reflects, but it's all just very conversational.

Elizabeth: It has a lot of fluidity. I just feel like I've felt that in you. I think I met you in the late 90s and there's just been such a fluidity that I've experienced in you over the years. A quality that's very relaxing, comfortable, and it is soft and open and I think it's helped me be softer. Because I could be very rigid and righteous, "And this is how this is going to go . . ."

Bob: When I speak with clients, I just talk with them about their lives, what they're thinking about, their experiences. We just talk, you know. I have seen a lot of popular diagnoses come and go, bipolar, borderline, autism, ADHD, but regardless it helps everyone to talk and connect.

Elizabeth: You talk sometimes about how therapists like to help people. They want to work hard, to work on this or that. That's how sometimes people approach it and one of the paradoxes you brought in sometimes is, well this isn't really work or this isn't about working hard or helping people. Could you say more about that?

Bob: Well something's coming to mind. I lost a patient a few years ago. A very isolated, but very bright and brilliant young man. He loved therapy and loved talking. Our sessions were so conversational, yet so about him and his experience, and he loved it so much because there was no sense of trying to get him out of anything, forcing him to be one way or another, but it was the first time that he could really go out of his own world. He came from a family of artists, and if you've ever worked with people who are really artistic, it's a real treat, because the whole conversation is just so playful and artistic.

It was such a treat to talk to somebody who was so psychological and just loved talking about himself and the other people in his life. So often in our work we have to discipline ourselves about where we go because we have to match where they go. But I just got interested in him and he began to understand many things about himself especially when it became apparent that he had a drinking problem. He went to rehab for a month and when he got out he immediately started drinking. You know how when you don't have a drink for a while your tolerance goes down. His mother knew it would be a hard transition for him to return to the world, and she was flying out to spend time with him. But she just missed it and he died. So it was really, really difficult.

The way it happened, I'm not holding, "I should've done something different." He was very loved by his mother and he had a brother. It was a perfect storm of how his life wound up this way. So it's very painful to lose him

Michael: So the treatment was actually going pretty well.

Bob: The treatment was going really well. I knew that to get to the point where the treatment would convert into helping him function well in the world might take 10 years, but the treatment was going well. He quoted it. He remembered what we talked about. It was just this real tough one.

Michael: You weren't trying to fix him, just letting him be.

Bob: But the treatment was fixing him. He was coming to stuff just from our talking and his life was getting better. The whole story is very sad. It really wasn't a purposeful suicide. He never quite walked the earth, so there was some karmic thing about it. When I've been talking to people about it, I heard myself saying, "Oh, I really loved him." And one of my colleagues said, in my little peer supervisory thing, "What do you mean, loved a patient?" Like she couldn't quite get that. And I think, five years ago, I would've said the same thing she said, but I feel like at this stage in my career I so appreciate it, and I've settled into it so well. I really think of it as—they're all relationships. And they're relationships in a form, which is psychotherapy and it's purposeful, but it feels so natural to me now, that I can actually realize I really do love a lot of the people that I work with.
You're shaking your head (looks at Elizabeth).

Elizabeth: I know. I started admitting it a couple of years ago! (Laughter).

Bob: Isn't that funny? You have to admit it!

Bob: The word has just come to me naturally, whereas a few years ago I would've said, "Huh?" So basically it's just fruitionally doing it. And the love has to do with just appreciating people. I appreciate that they come in, always revealing themselves even if their defenses are as tight as a drum. Just by coming in you're revealing yourself you know. And the supervisory situation—it's so exposing to be supervised and present your work. I just have tremendous appreciation for the whole thing that we do.

The setting produces such powerful experiences. When I'm on this couch talking to Dr. Hayden, I'm aware of what I'm saying, and of what I'm not saying. I'm aware of my pressured voice. I'm aware of thinking, "Do I want to tell him how much I've masturbated in my life?" It just goes on and on and on and on. So, this is me! It's magic. This form that Freud invented is incredible. I mean the form has existed in various ways throughout history, but the way it's been formalized in this last period of time is just amazing.

Elizabeth: And you are doing something by holding that process for that person. You're part of it. You're part of that form.

Michael: It's interesting because I do analysis on the phone. As you guys do.

Bob: We all do.

Michael: And I think there's an interesting paper in there about the neuroscience of it. Because everyone's into the face and empathy, but of course on the phone there's no face.

Bob: When you're not doing the face, it's all in the voice. I can tell when Dr. Hayden falls asleep. (Laughter). And it has happened more than once. And this is our tool, the voice. And it's highlighted when the other senses are blocked. I think for the analytic approach the phone really has its value.

Michael: I wanted to ask you about an experience I had with you. The first encounter I had with you was as a Windhorse housemate and you were a supervisor on the Windhorse team. And that was my introduction to Naropa and therapy and we had this weekly supervision group. And there was this one moment that really stands out. The whole situation would just get super intense at times and all this aggression would come into the system. And as the roommate, I was just in the middle of all this intensity. And I was just freaking out at one time and it just felt like no one on the team was paying any attention to what I had to go through. And you offered to do phone supervision with me. I was just out of my gourd at that time. And the next day we had the supervision group, this big supervision group of 13 or 14 people, and you just said the most provocative thing, which I can't repeat here, and I almost jumped out of my seat. I felt like, "He's saying that for me!" And everyone was getting anxious and shifting in their seats, like, "Why is he saying that?" And I still think about it. I guess that's still a question for me, like how you have the capacity find the courage to say things like that.

Bob: Dr. Spotnitz!

Michael: I had the feeling that you were doing it for me, but you didn't say that. You didn't have to say it. And so there was this very special feeling of "Bob's doing it for me." He's doing it for me, and no one even knows.

Part Three

Michael: What do we want to talk about for the last time? The thing I had in mind was, so what now? What are your goals for yourself going forward? What do you see as being important in the next chapter for you?

Bob: Well, I can ramble about that, because I do think of a couple of things. I was getting really tired and then we decided, "we" meaning myself and Helena, that I would stop doing clinical work on Fridays. And work four days. It's been about two and a half years now. And I think I told you how that happened. So we went on this bicycling trip to Peru with the group, it was a couple of years ago now and again we had a wonderful local guide. I was very taken with Peru, the creativity of people. Just because you don't have written language doesn't mean you don't have phenomenal minds. You know those kinds of things really open your eyes.

And we were up at 12,000 feet, because that's where you are. And we were visiting this weaving co-op and here's this beautiful lawn with the mountains around. And they were doing these wonderful weavings. Now if you've ever seen them, the weavers are maybe this far apart (holds out hands) and they're throwing the weaving thing back and forth between them, working along, weaving beautiful blankets and all the while they're chatting away. It's all totally social. I had a great time, and somehow it struck me. I said to Helena, "My life has to change." And every now and then that happens.

And you know Helena has been elbowing me for a long time to work less, so she said, "Oh, I'll hold you to that." Because you know Helena, she does that sort of thing. And so she said, "What are you thinking?" And I said, "I've got to cut back to four days a week." Because you know, you work five days a week, and now the kids are out of the house, but still it takes at least one day of the weekend to do the paperwork of life and you barely catch your breath on Sunday and then you're getting ready to go to work again. I was getting tired. By then I was 64, 65 or so. It took me a few months to do it, but I gave up Fridays. And that really relaxed me even more. But then this past year the same thing started to happen. Because of the flotsam and jetsam and paper and emails. It just keeps increasing and I was just always stressed, and Helena said, "You're working as much as you did 10 years ago, but you're 10 years older!" She didn't like it. And she has a habit of saying what she thinks, you know Helena. So, I said, "Okay, what we can do?"

I looked at everything and the thing I didn't like the most was the administrative aspect of Naropa. More and more silly emails from mothership Naropa. I said, "Okay, I'm going to stop teaching." I don't want to grade papers. Or electronically take attendance! I always made an attendance sheet and kept track of people who didn't come, but everyone almost always comes all the time. It's graduate school. Really, they're adults. I get these nasty notes from Naropa because they make you start taking attendance online like everything fucking else! So they can see it. I just wasn't doing it for a couple weeks and I started to get these emails, "You haven't taken attendance!" At my age, I'm getting these notes? It's ridiculous. I so love working with young people. I forget my age while I'm working. But when I get stuff like that, I remember how old I am!

So finally I decided to stop, and that was a big decision. I love being in the classroom still. I could do that forever. They're groups you know. So I made the decision in November and it's just naturally repurposed me. And the way it's repurposed me is with just more enthusiasm for what I'm doing. I just love coming to the office and seeing people. I love doing supervision and supervision groups. And as my mind gets looser, you know, (laughs), in psychodynamic work that's often a good thing. You know, more free associative, more flexible. Because I can't go here (holds hand up high), I can't go here (holds hand down low), it's more...

Elizabeth: It's more the present moment.

Bob: Exactly, it's more present moment. As my psychoanalyst friend Neil says, "Psychodynamic psychotherapy is the province of the ADD."

Elizabeth: Or the elders (laughter).

Bob: My analyst said to me one day—he's 87 and he remembers everything I've ever said—he was saying to me one day very casually, "Oh, I don't think about technique. I just do what I do." Total presence you know. And that's sort of what it feels like to me. I really enjoy the work more.

So it's just what I want to do more of. I mean, what else do you do, other than do it? So that's kind of what I see. I really like it. It takes the energy of work, you know going to work and working all day . . . Most people have jobs that are exhausting, but you know our work . . . For those 50 minutes you're not calling your friend up, you're not going to the bathroom, so there is an arduousness just to the intensity of it and the focus of it, but I'm not worn out by doing it. So it's just seems like a wonderful time to work. And there're drawbacks. Because we can't travel quite as much as we'd like. Somewhere two to three weeks is about as long as I'm comfortable being gone. I couldn't do what Ormont did and take the whole summer off. However he did that. People were also more attached to therapy in those days. Everyone I talk to has more in and out in their practices these days, even the New Yorkers. In the old days people just came and they just kind of stayed. The whole culture just moves more.

Our son Julian, I just spent a lot of time with him in San Francisco. He just got a high-tech job. He'd been working part-time. It's his first real job and he's got benefits, and he says, "This is a good resume job for when I start looking around." And this is after three weeks! I laughed. Well, everyone's like that. It's just movement. So anyway, that's my answer.

Michael: You really just love your work.

Bob: And I never loved it this much. It's a very odd thing in life to not be looking forward to when X happens, or you know, "When I accomplish this . . . " It puts you much more in touch with your anxiety when you're not looking for, you know, the fantasy of, "When I do this then I can relax," and "When I do that, then I've arrived." The next thing to do is die really, it seems like. Because I have everything I want and I'm doing everything I want. We could always travel more. And there are questions like, do I get another car? And when should I get another motorcycle or trade one in? I've had this bike for five years . . . But I just play with those ideas. I have everything really. Our family's doing really well at this point. We have a lot of contact with our sons. They're doing well. And Helena and I just have a great time. We're just at a stage in our marriage where we just enjoy each other. And I like the work. So it does put you in touch with your core anxieties because you're not ever totally settled . . . And I have core anxieties, because I'm an angst kind of person so it makes it interesting to not have anything to be anxious about. I feel anxious about the world. Michael and I were talking this morning about it. I'm very attached to the whole Snowden thing. I followed it very closely and I watched the movie about him, "Citizenfour," this week and wrote a big letter to the paper. He has one of the clearest minds of any mind I've ever experienced. What do you think?

Elizabeth: I appreciated him. I found the movie to be really impactful and he predicted what the media was going to do and then the media did it. They tried to organize the media against his character, saying all these things about him. And I thought, gosh, when you hear him talk, he sounds pretty reasonable and thoughtful.

Bob: Yeah. We couldn't sleep the night afterwards. So I'm certainly affected by the fact that we're in a culture that's crashing, and who knows how it's going to play out. People who have younger kids—ours are a little older—are going to be affected, so I think about that.

But in terms of my life, this is . . . Fruition doesn't mean the day before you die! You can actually live in fruition for a while, and for me it's just being grateful.

One thing I've learned from Buddhism that's actually inside, is that there really is no "I." Well, "I" did so and so. Well, "I made a decision to move to Boulder and start a practice . . . " but then when I really think about it, there is no "I." It just sort of happened. Too much Alan Watts in me. (Laughter). So you know when you think of the position of almost everyone in the world—you really have to think of your circumstances—you're in the 99.9%, just sitting in a fancy painted office in fancy-shmancy Boulder talking to you in front of the camera like this. So then, I think, that's why I get so touched by people who really put themselves out there like civil rights people or Snowden. He really put himself out there. A lot more than I ever have!

So anyway, what else do you want to know? I think that's what I want to do. I just want to keep doing more of this!

And enjoy it more!

I have a theory. You have to have a theory to justify the way you think about your work. If you think in terms of the unconscious, that's all anybody is ever really doing. They make up theories in their own minds to justify the way they think they work. So my theory is—I have a couple of articles, though of course you can always find articles to back up what you think. So if you think, "Well, what's therapeutic?" Well, there's a million things that are therapeutic, but one thing that strikes me is therapeutic is if the person you're working with experiences you enjoying them and enjoying being with them. That could be the major part of the picture because most people come into treatment because in various ways they were not enjoyed.

Did I ever tell you my little example of what I saw at the locker room at the health club one day? I went in there one evening around 5 o'clock and you know, it's a men's locker room, there are a lot of people in there after work, etc. And there's this kid—he was maybe four or five—with his dad. And this kid is a total chatterbox of confidence in his talking, just like he knew that he was being listened to. And there was this dad, who was just a young fellow maybe in his mid-30s who just oozed basic goodness and kindness. And he was just smiling at his kid and kind of encouraging the chatter and this kid just knew that he was being listened to and appreciated. It stayed with me and it's been like five years ago and it's always been an example for me, because it was so extreme. This kid was so confident. He could talk because he was being listened to, and enjoyably.

Michael: You could just feel it from the dad.

Bob: You could feel it. He was interacting some, but the dad was just with him. And I've seen any number of kids dragged into the locker room because dad's working out. And you know, they're nice to their kid. They sit them down. They haul them into the shower. You know, it's all fine. You don't see anything mean happen. But this one really caught me. And this kid is going to grow up with just such confidence in their ability to talk and have the sense that they're being seen and listened to. And of course when you have that sense, then you are, because it's the repetition, you know. You induce it so that people listen. And then you feel more confident, so you talk more. It's a positive loop rather than a negative loop. So that's one of the things that it seems to me as a practitioner, you find a way.

I think maybe that's Spotnitz's notion of the anaclitic countertransference, that after a while you have the feelings for the person. And I've only ever had one or two people in my whole practice that I never developed an anaclitic countertransference to. One person who I worked with for over 10 years, it always bothered me. Sometimes I could manufacture it by getting them to talk about certain things. They were from the East Coast, wealthy, very cold, you could just feel it. And I could never find a way to have compassion for them, except sometimes when I would get them to talk about their mother. Then sometimes I could find it. I could find a way. Because I was trying to find it. But it always plagued me. And then they finally left, and found something else to do.

Elizabeth: I'm remembering an AGPA supervision group we were in together on the difficult patient.

Bob: What a memory!

Elizabeth: You know what it was, Bob? It was an association!

Bob: Right! And then the leader he attacked me for admitting I felt this way towards the patient. What a strange duck he was. All brain with little heart. Actually not that in touch with human feelings. He couldn't tolerate what I had to say. He says bring up difficult cases? Okay, I'll bring up a difficult case. Then it's Fuck you with your difficult case! (Laughter).

Elizabeth: I know, you were like, what just happened here? Watching you go through that, being scapegoated by the leader with all these credentials, gave me such respect for you that you prevent that from happening in your groups, and you have the resilience and self-knowledge to not let it damage you. You can laugh it off. It is okay if some people don't like you, and you don't like some people.

Michael: I have such a strong sense of listening to you Bob of how therapeutic just being a therapist has been for you.

Bob: Oh, absolutely.

Michael: It's like it's almost been a practice for you. And how listening to people and enjoying them, how much you enjoy that.

Bob: Oh yes! I feel so privileged because I really struggled as a kid socially in our little desert town we had moved to from the Bronx in the 50s.

Michael: It's so hard to imagine you struggling socially.

Bob: Yes, it was tough. My father was so difficult. And then I was a fat and non-athletic kid in a little town in Southern California. That doesn't get you too far. But when I've been back to my high school reunions, a couple of them, I did better than I thought I did. Which is a lot of people's experience. In high school, you're so self-conscious, but actually people didn't think you were as bad as you thought you were. But still I was something of a misfit, even though I don't regret it at all. It was the right place for me. If I had stayed in the Bronx, I don't think I would've survived. God! You know, working-class Jewish Bronx was just horrible. Brooklyn has character, but the Bronx! I hear the Bronx is finally starting to gentrify, but God!

Michael: It was pretty tough.

Bob: It was always tough. Our apartment building in 1951, which was Jewish, it cleared out in two years. Everyone moved either to California or Florida. Boom! Or further north in the Bronx. There were some co-ops up there. And then, my father was so antisocial. I was very conscious of trying to make it happen. Which is okay. I started off as an engineer, but when I stumbled into this field, I still remember, I was thinking of this, it was just serendipity. I don't know if I've mentioned this, I got waylaid into Ormont's group when I was a taxi driver, by Deborah Bershatsky. Pure luck. And then there were various twists and turns, which we've talked about, but I just feel so fortunate, so privileged to have had the particular journey I've had (and continue to have). I've found a way, or "it's" found a way, you know, life's found it's way with me, you could say. And that's what we do as practitioners with our patients. We find a way. We just keep finding a way.

References

Rutan, J. S., & Rice, C. A. (1981). Charismatic leader: Asset or liability? *Psychotherapy: Theory, Research & Practice, 18*, 487-492.

Photographs

Bob and Dr. Leslie Rosenthal, New York, NY, 2000, at the
dinner celebrating the publication of the Rosenthal Festschrift.

Bob and sister, Lenore Unger, Catskills, NY,
ca. summer, 1950.

Bob and his mother, Ann Unger, Santa Monica, CA, 1982.

Rhinebeck, NY, 1976.

Raymon Elozua, Bob Unger, David Gross and Don Blair. Day after Thanksgiving, 1981, New York City. Moving to SMC.

David Gross, Bob Unger, Steve Sanders, Sarah Smith, Ed James, & Don Blair, Daytona Beach, FL, 1980.

Bob racing his Ducati Supersport at the 1980 Daytona "Battle of the Twins" Amateur Road Race.

Bob (right) and Mark Singer, Cleveland Heights, OH, ca. 1973.

Bob and his dear friend, Raymon Elozua, in his New York studio, 1995.

Helena and Bob camping in Canyonlands, Utah, 1982.

Bob and Helena just leaving their marriage ceremony
performed by Judge Torke on the bike path outside of the
Justice Center, Boulder, CO, June 6, 1983.

L to R: Dylan, Bob, Helena, and Julian, 1991, Boulder, CO.

Bob receiving his PhD, May, 1993. L to R: Tim Wian (brother-in law), Helena, Lenore Wian (sister), Bob Unger.

Note: All photos copyright of Bob and Helena Unger, 2015

Introduction to the Tributes

So what have we learned from Dr. Bob Unger? What has he uniquely brought to the field of psychotherapy worth celebrating? In the following pages, 115 different authors hold forth, offering their tribute. While a simple summary is not possible, a number of themes and lessons emerge. And importantly, while Bob is the source and inspiration for these tributes, the impact of our interactions with him ripples outward and beyond our individual relationships. As you read these encomiums, we encourage you to reflect upon the larger lessons to be drawn here.

Blake Baily discusses how Bob brings to the therapeutic endeavor an encouragement to "not take ourselves so seriously." This is at least partly because, as Bailey points to in his piece, who we think we are, and our memories of important events themselves may be inaccurate. In a similar vein, Paul Bialek illustrates how, contrary to predominant trends in the psychotherapy world, Bob has encouraged an attention to the self-aggressive aspects of self-improvement, leading to a "crazy view of basic goodness that could prove contagious." This is therapy as play, rather than therapy as task. Indeed, as Maureen Dummigan says in her contribution, Bob has taught us to "notice and play with everything." Michael Dow also discusses the way Bob uses humor and lightness themselves as primary interventions; silliness as both means and end. Adrianne Holloran writes of the shift that happened for her when she stopped trying to help people and focused more on having fun with clients. Bob suggested that rather than help a client with their stated goal of being less intense, that she say, "Who told you you were too intense?" He encouraged her to "Be intense with her." In this way, Bob manages to join the modern analytic technique of "joining resistance" with the Buddhist principle of basic goodness and radical acceptance in a unique and seamless way.

What is perhaps even more impressive about Bob's use of humor is his use of it as a tool to open further into conflict and tension. Many of our authors speak about this lesson from Bob, of relaxing further under tension. Michelle Fields discusses Bob's ability "to be spacious and playful and curious during even the seemingly tightest and darkest of situations." Dan Fox talks about Bob's "comfort with tension," Stacy Boston of Bob's "opening under tension" and Wendy Buhner of Bob's ability to sit through and play with the hurricanes of emotions. Clearly, Bob's ability to work with aggression, whether with humor or otherwise, is a key learning point for many of our writers. But how did he do that? What did he actually do? Lodi Siefer describes a specific example of Bob working in this domain, concluding,

> He metabolized my aggression. He didn't take it personally, but held his role, willingly stepping into my attack, unthreatened (seemingly anyway) by my anger toward him.

Some combination of welcoming anger while holding one's seat is in evidence here; giving space with a light, jocular touch. In her poem, "The Anger Whisperer," Suzanne Smith uses the interesting phrase, "he holds it so dear"—not one we tend to associate with anger. The anger is imagined as a ball thrown to Bob who catches it, and then bouncing around a large room (one imagines Bob's therapy office), until at the very end, "it was you all along." Bob never seems to ask people to "own their anger," though an awareness of one's part (arrived at by oneself) is somehow where his spacious approach ends up leading.

Teri Dillion writes about learning not only the point of welcoming aggression but a sort of larger point that even difficult emotional communication can "be studied as opposed to being manipulated in some way." Study as antidote to defense. This is a different posture in a sense—study, curiosity, wonder—which itself subtly but powerful counteracts the reactive crouch of aggression.

Jeannie Little writes of Bob's use of "radical neutrality" which allows him to pose provocative questions which lean into the tension of the moment, such as, "How do you know I'm a man?" Isha Lucas similarly writes about how Bob is able to get away with challenging statements—"You're a curmudgeon"—perhaps through his playful tone which engages rather than alienates.

In Elizabeth Olson's piece, she explains why such a stance of leaning into and welcoming aggression is key to successful treatment. Welcoming and studying all feelings, thoughts and impulses is essential because

> These inductions inform the emotional understanding and mental conceptualization of what a person is experiencing, especially the ways that they repeat their early experiences in the transferential relationship.

To understand our clients, one has to feel it all. And then, in crafting interventions, Bob taught her to use a "range of different vocal tones" in order to communicate subtly and directly to the unconscious.

But it is not that Bob has taught us to join or lean in as some sort of default setting. Chuck Knapp writes that it:

> takes a disciplined and sensitivity to nuance to eventually master discriminating between taking matters prematurely to a painful point, as opposed to leaning into emotional energy when its overt recognition is timely.

One feels the induced feelings, but studies them before deciding what to do.

But, interestingly and importantly, as MacAndrew Jack points out, Bob has also taught us the importance of not being aggressive. Of "creating a pause" and "listening to one's impulses" so as to purify aggression "before it pops out in words or deed." Bob is consistently concerned with ethical comportment, and boundaries. MacAndrew also writes of Bob's deep listening, how he listens to the tones more than the words:

Bob is listening to so much. For so much. He is following the trail, and the echoes, the undertones and the overtones. He tracks history, trajectory, and turn of phrase. Master listening from one whose professional life has included enough listening to hear harmonics among the notes of conversations.

Somehow related to this stance of welcoming aggression, yet being careful to not act aggressively, is Bob's use of paradox, which is another theme that emerges here. Bob not only uses paradox, but has a view of therapy and human nature that perhaps, a la Alan Watts, sees paradox as coincident with truth. If it's not paradoxical, then something might be a bit off. Deb Bopsie discusses his use of paradoxical injunctions in his Naropa classes—"I don't care if you learn. It's up to you"—and how they opened up boundaries and possibilities. Angelo Ciliberti speaks to this further. How this paradoxical injunction led to classes alive with discussion and dissension: "He seems to orchestrate an ongoing conversation where ideas could be questioned, appreciated and dissolved back into the larger context from which they had arisen."

Winding its way through probably nearly every piece here, is a sense of deep acceptance that many of our authors felt from Bob. This is no ordinary acceptance but some sense of acceptance despite or even because of contradiction and conflict. Ciliberti writes, "I felt my totality—contradictions and all were welcome." Wendy Buhner writes of his willingness to "take me in any form and nothing less." Sabrina Neu writes about the "atmosphere of total acceptance," that Bob is able to create, which manages to encourage the "full range of feelings" as Susan Nimmanheminda elaborates. As Andrea Dugan writes eloquently, it is as if Bob is making a soup in which all ingredients are welcome.

Matthew Holloran describes what he has learned from Bob about generosity and disappointment, and their unlikely link. That perhaps what is most generous is to allow others to be disappointed in you. As he explains in various clinical examples, he learned to turn towards his clients and his own actual experience, including profound disappointment, and examine it closely.

Neil Rosen appreciates Bob's thorough embodiment of the notion that talking itself is curative, his faith in mutual dialogue, conversation and a "libidinously alive way of talking." This is also essentially the theme of Justin Bogardus' entertaining and brief anecdote—that for Bob, talking is the thing, over and above a concern about "connecting" or "helping" someone. The real juice, the real movement forward is in talking, which is, after all, a form of movement. Jason Carpenter writes of Bob's willingness to give his mind "free reign," and how this communicates a sort of trust in his own and others "basic goodness and ability to learn from experience." Staff of the Harm Reduction Center seem to echo this theme.

In a related vein, many authors talk about Bob's inspired use of movement, and his transmutation of movement into words, and vice versa. The poems of Brooke and Gabriel Fortuna speak to this, as does David Chrislip's piece highlighting Bob's "schpilkas."

And then, also, in good paradoxical fashion, from Bob we have learned the power of doing nothing. Ashley Eyre's piece beautifully illustrates the clinical power of simple presence, of holding, of not-doing, perhaps even especially when the induction to act and "do" can be so strong. Gil Spielberg appreciates how his decades long close collaboration with Bob has been made more intimate and delightful by the fact that Bob never tried to "teach" him anything:

> I can safely say that I have not learned a single thing about group therapy technique or theory. Not a single thing. And this has been Bob's greatest gift.

Francis Kaklauskas speaks to how Bob manages to be both confident and unabashedly himself, while also somehow not putting himself up and others down, "Bob does not champion himself. He champions everyone. He doesn't take sides. He is on everyone's side."

A number of authors use the word "intertwined," as in Jed Shapiro's article, or a synonym of it, like "tangled up," from Chuck Knapp's piece. And this seems to be another lesson from Dr. Bob. In a world that is getting faster and more disconnected, Bob's therapy practice speaks to the power of long-term relationships, the wisdom of getting yourself tangled up in the lives of your colleagues and your students. His "powerful intelligence" as Chuck Knapp writes "towards maintaining healthy relationships with individuals and groups." As Marc Jalbert writes, in Bob you can see that the opposite of addiction is not necessarily sobriety, but human connection.

And this speaks to Bob's evolving and perhaps unique approach to groups. In Bob's view, group therapy is ultimately not about curing, but about relating, not about creating a container for therapy as much as simply creating community. Paul Gitterman writes on this theme, of the continually impressive "attachment function" that the group serves, over many years, how it allows both affiliation and autonomy, meeting both early needs and furthering professional development. Going even further, Wong contends that quite contrary to the notion that group therapy is an artificial setting which works, when it does, by re-playing "real" problems that are occurring in the outside world, that the situation is in fact the exact opposite:

> I often wonder if what I'm walking back into as I descend the stairs out the door and off of that green painted porch at 8:30AM each Wednesday is some fake world—a dream or an imaginary horror. A surreal world which only exists in the context of the more tangible group. Group is the reality. Ninety minutes becomes a little larger than the entire universe (as Pessoa would say (Pessoa & Zenith, 2006)).

And this is perhaps what Bob has shown us more than anything else: that therapy is play, an art form, the creation of a world at times more real than real. Love and hate are both welcomed, and in fact required. Lean in, have fun, feel it all, especially the hard stuff, and don't forget to smile.

Michael M. Dow

Tributes

Anonymous

(in conversation with Michael M. Dow)

When you think about Bob, what do you think about?

I was thinking about it and I think it came down to something very simple. Not really knowing for sure if Bob cared, but then when things got really difficult for me, Bob was really there. In important times, when things were rocky. He was just there for me when it mattered. And somehow he knew when I needed that. I don't know how he did that, but he knew.

I feel more warmth from him since I left the [supervision] group. Individual sessions with him were more powerful.

Group was frustrating. Groups were hard with Bob. That's probably true for a lot of us. I just want to say that and put that out there. I lead them well, but it's just so hard being a group member. Always hard to find my voice in there; there were always a lot of strong people in there! Jesus, it could be hard! I don't know why I stayed in it for so long. (laughter).

Why did you stay in it for so long?

It's hard for me to leave things that I commit to. I don't leave difficult situations really.

Observations of Bob Unger

Bob Backerman

For the past thirteen years my office has been next door to "Doctor Bob's." This has given me many short contacts with him frequently throughout each week. From these contacts, what stands out most clearly for me is how much enjoyment Bob gets from his work. He appears to look forward to each individual, couple, or group that he sees, and rather than appearing enervated from a long day of other people's problems, he only seems to gain energy from this.

Certainly Bob also appears excited when he is carrying his bike downstairs for a quick ride up Flagstaff, but excitement at exercise is more common around here. I think that Bob's enthusiasm for his work and his clients, a less common commodity, has no doubt been transmitted to these clients through the years and been one more healing factor in their work. It makes a huge difference when a therapist likes their work, puts effort into it, and enjoys seeing the incredible depth and complexity in all the lives he touches. Bob's former clients and students will no doubt attest to this energy and enthusiasm in their views of this remarkable healer.

Blake Baily

Since graduating from the Contemplative program at Naropa in 2003, I have held rather firmly to the memory that Bob gave me an "A" on a paper I'd written for his Evolution of Central Concepts in Western Psychology class about a psychological condition called paruresis, a social phobia that renders the sufferer unable to pee in front of others. There is a story behind this "paper," but that story is not about Bob. It's about me, of course, which reminds me of one of the best things about Bob: that he is willing to listen to what you have to say with a genuineness and affection that never really leaves you. In fact, it's quite a rare thing and wonderful to experience first hand. I recommend it. But I digress . . .

I was once a sufferer of this annoying paruresis condition, and as it happened, mindfulness-based meditation combined with the simple fact of growing older and becoming less concerned with the considerations and judgments of other men and women about the precision of my arc or the stability and grace of my stance, or the quality and prestige of my membership, had, by the time of the paper's writing (ca. 2001), effectively cured me of the condition. A personal triumph, I might add. So I wrote this paper with all of the passion and academic inquiry of a good contemplative and aspiring therapist, and to be sure, with an eye toward Bob's approval.

This evening I went to the garage and searched for the paper in the deep trove of my old Naropa materials, and after a short time was able to locate Bob's class folder, complete with syllabus and records of the archival searches I'd done up at Norlin library on the subject. But paruresis wasn't the subject at all. Nor was it the subject of the paper, which I was also able to locate. It was on Irritable Bowel Syndrome. What the fuck? Bob wrote, "Nice work. You have a clear and orderly writing style. A."

My God, I thought, alone in the garage with the full record of my Naropa days neatly filed away in front of me. All of that bashful bladder business must have been nothing but a sort-of-embarrassing-yet-compelling and maybe textbook Freudian sort of false memory. What unsettling part of me wanted Bob involved in my glorious march toward micturition liberation? Troubling still, I have no recollection of suffering IBS. Bob, I'm sorry to say this, but I'm afraid that you are one of the few teachers who encouraged me to think deeply about such matters. You always placed a high value on your students' personal and intellectual investigations, and always seemed to tell us in one way or another not to take ourselves too seriously. Good teachings. Lifelong teachings. I think so, anyway. At least that's what my memory tells me.

Helen Balis & Barton Balis

Curious, passionate, reflective, intense, teacher, sincerity, conscience, integrity, community, super dad, bicycles, and all things Dylan, are a few of the words that come to mind when we think about Robert (Bob) Unger.

Our family has had the pleasure of knowing Bob since 1983 when he came to Boulder. We met at a class at the Colorado Center for Modern Psychoanalytic Studies. He was eager to share his knowledge and his enthusiasm for learning. He taught his colleagues, students, and friends about transference, counter-transference, resistance and aggression in a uniquely personal way.

Above all Bob has been a dear friend with a big heart and caring spirit.

Bob Unger's Eyes

Sue Bell

For a man who enjoys everything being put into words, his eyes say so much. They twinkle.

His eyes tell everyone whether they be a student, client, friend or supervisee that they are welcome. That they have a place to feel and say what they really mean.

His eyes have a way of rolling up to the right or left while he nods and lets you know that your question or comment has merit and is being taken in fully.

They close while he falls asleep in group. Not sure what he is saying here. Could be that he is tired as anyone who listens all day might be. They could be saying other things as well. This is left to your imagination and certainly your transference tendencies.

Though he is a masterful manager of anger and aggression, Bob's eyes always betray how deeply sincere and kind he is.

Yes, Bob has great intellectual prowess and enjoys his academic pursuits.

But, for me, the best part of what he communicates is through his eyes.

Paul Bialek

I have had the good fortune to know Bob over the past twelve years as teacher, mentor, colleague, and friend. For the past couple years we have worked together as Clinical Tutors for Naropa University students in their internship year. The students generally begin the year earnestly seeking to become better, kinder and smarter therapists. One of the pleasures of co-leading this small group with Bob has been watching his outright refusal to add any fuel to this fire of aggressive self-improvement. Earlier this year I watched the following exchange:

Student: I need to be more confident with him and improve my attunement skills.

Bob: [Laughing] Improve? [Turning towards me] I don't see anything wrong with her, do you? Maybe you should try giving up all attempts at self-improvement.

Student: [Laughing nervously] But I have so much to learn!

Bob: [Singing in a Dylanesque voice]: I've got so much to learn, and so little time.

Student: [Laughing] No, but really, this client needs help.

Bob: What do you mean when you say the word "help"?

After a moment like this there is often an awkward feeling in the room, as if something is happening here but we can't say just what it is. Something improvisational, unfixed, and alive is happening. It tends to wake us up.

Both in working and studying with Bob I have felt an invitation to join in this improvisation, to come out and play. As if there was fundamentally no problem at all with me, with him, with the students, and with the clients. A crazy view of basic goodness that could prove contagious . . . Of course this invitation and this view is often met by me, or by the students, with serious resistance. And Bob meets our resistance with continued irreverence and radical encouragement.

Thanks, Bob.

Marsha S. Block

Dear Bob,

I am remembering your early days when you were first joining the American Group Psychotherapy Association and how cumbersome the application was then and how you stuck with the process to join the group. Your subsequent participation on the Annual Meeting Committee and as faculty, the Membership Committee and the International Board for the Certification of Group Psychotherapists has always been in the service of getting people on board and welcoming them in the process. I am sure this is also true as you developed the Colorado Group Psychotherapy Society and brought that group to AGPA.

Thank you for all you have done and continue to do to welcome people into AGPA, for your wise counsel to the organizations and for your warm sense of humor.

With much admiration and respect,

Marsha S. Block

Mike Block

We at the Boulder Shelter for the Homeless are eternally grateful for the generosity and support Bob has offered us over the years. For as long as anyone can remember, 15 years at least, Bob has donated his time to our twice monthly staff process groups. These groups assist us in navigating the tragedies we witness and dealing with the lack of resources committed to addressing them, while not losing sight of our personal need to stay healthy within this landscape in order to thrive as both providers and people. Recently, Bob extended his service to us by offering support and wisdom to our Case Manager Team in order to elevate our skill set in working with a community that often faces great obstacles to safety and stability.

On more than one occasion, colleagues in the community and beyond have inquired about the Shelter's commitment to our staff's emotional wellbeing. When I mention that we have a regular process group led by a clinician named Bob Unger, they stop me and say, "There is no need to explain further. If you work with Bob, then you understand support."

Indeed. Thank you, Bob. Words cannot express how lucky we feel to have you on our side in this challenge to serve the most needy.

Justin Bogardus

In clinical tutorial (a small group supervision which is part of the Master's in Contemplative Psychotherapy program at Naropa University) we had the following exchange:

Me: I've tried a few different things, but don't think I'm connecting to this client."

Bob: Why do you need to connect to them? Just keep them talking.

Me: About what?

Bob: Oh, you know, any old thing will do.

Bob Unger: Teacher, Mentor, Supervisor, Jewish Brother, Friend, Community Organizer

Deb Bopsie

I remember the first time I encountered Bob Unger. I was beginning the second semester of my first year in Naropa's Contemplative Psychotherapy program (referred to at that time as MACP) and Bob was assigned to teach my cohort about group theory. Immediate perceptions and fantasies of boredom and even bodily nausea preceded my entrance into class. I was aware of my nervousness about the irritation I might feel and the possibility that I might actually fall asleep in class. As I am writing this and thinking about Bob reading it, I am aware of my wild mind and keen imagination, which Bob would eventually help me appreciate and take care of.

At the beginning of class Bob gave a few instructions. He said, more or less, what you learn in this class is up to you or was it, "I don't care if you learn or not, it's up to you," and added that there would be no note taking. Then there was a silent pause accompanied by Bob's easeful smile and open gaze. My whole body relaxed and I sang a version of "Glory, Hallelujah!" internally, while my classmates came unglued and started to act out, giving Bob plenty of material to help us understand group theory.

I remember sitting outside at Paramita's [Naropa's North Campus building] green a few weeks before graduating from the MACP program, and I asked Bob if he would be my supervisor. Bob's response was direct. He said he couldn't talk with me about this until I graduated. I walked away from that brief encounter with feelings of being held by the boundary Bob set, as well as the feeling of possibility. I'm not sure how he transmitted both of these ideas/feelings alongside one another, but this experience of equanimity and possibility is always present when I speak with Bob.

I remember sometime after a supervision session coming to this description of Bob: Bob Unger has the rare and beautiful gift of guiding people to their brilliant sanity and infusing the feelings of confidence and goodness in all whom he touches.

Bob is a transmitter of basic goodness, which is something the world is starving for, and I am blessed to know and love him.

I bow to you, Bob Unger. Happy 70th Birthday! May we celebrate many more years together in laughter and light.

WWBD (What Would Bob Do?)

Stacy Boston

Bob Unger is a professional at holding his seat. I had the privilege of learning from Bob when I was a Contemplative Psychotherapy graduate student at Naropa University from 2005-2008. I learned how to hold my seat as a therapist by observing Bob model how he held his, especially as an object of negative transference. In my private practice today, I sometimes experience being an object of negative transference, and I do my best to hold my seat as I learned it from Bob. I like to call it my "WWBD" skill.

The first time I remember practicing "WWBD" was during my internship year when a client sat across from me in great distress. Through tears of sadness and anger, she blamed me, she said, because I "wasn't a real therapist." I had an immediate impulse to defend myself because who likes to be blamed? Then I thought of Bob and asked myself, "What would Bob do?" I thought of how Bob would simply take the blame. Instead of defending myself, I took a breath and asked my client, "If I were a *real* therapist, what would be different?" I learned a lot that day about myself, my budding ability to hold my seat as a therapist, and about my client's needs and beliefs.

Over the years I have had many opportunities to practice holding my seat. Frequently, I consider "WWBD" and always I do so with gratitude for Bob. Bob Unger has been my teacher, my Clinical Tutor, my supervisor, my mentor, and my friend, and whether he knows it or not (I hope he knows), Bob also gets my "good dad" transference. I am a better therapist, and I believe a better person, because Bob helped teach me how to be one by modeling being Bob. I am grateful.

Fond Memories of Bob

Annie Brier

Fond memories of Bob . . . Thinking about him brings tears to my eyes. What a wonderful guy!

It is almost 4 years since I graduated from Naropa's MACP, and they have been challenging years. In the midst of these turbulent transitional times, I have been grateful for the path I am on, although I often forget that the path is the point, and to live it wisely and with compassion makes all the difference, because we can't know the outcome anyway.

Last week, scrambling anxiously around in my mind for something to grasp, I woke from a dream about Bob. The dream was a simple one in which we spoke for a few minutes and he asked me about my life. Yet, there was something powerful about that dream because his presence brought me back to understanding the importance of the Buddhist path, and I loved him for it. Thanks for being there, or here. Thanks for being, Bob.

Another short story. It was the first day of "Western Concepts" (The Evolution of Central Concepts of Western Psychology) class with Bob. I listened, without doodling as I might have because no desks were allowed and no paper or writing utensils either. I listened as my classmates carried on about Freud and his theories. I had nary a clue what they were talking about. Towards the end of the class, I expressed my feelings of frustration and how I felt I had nothing to offer and Bob said something to me that has stayed with me, and I have offered to others since, which was simply, "That's what you have to offer, then, that you have nothing to offer!"

Happy retirement Bob! Best wishes. Thanks for being part of my life.

Love,

Annie Brier

For Bob on His 70th Solar Return

Brooke

Masterful movements, wise with laughter
Oh-so-skilled facilitation, compassionate neighbor
Treasure of being lit with delight
Authentic presence, practitioner on bike
Genuine heart, mountainous mind
Humble and humorous, and routinely kind

Bob, I wish you continuous delight while you wend your way on a road of blessings.

With love,

Brooke

Wendy Buhner

I met Bob back in 1993 as a student of the then Naropa Institute. He was a clinical supervisor at two of the agencies I worked for in those early years: Boulder County Mental Health's Friendship House and Alternatives to Family Violence in Commerce City. It was in those places that I quickly saw Bob's ability to sit through hurricanes.

Being originally from Miami, Florida, hurricanes have a particular significance for me. But for Bob, the hurricanes had special qualities and could be given names like Hurricane Anger, Hurricane Confusion, or Hurricane Sadness.

Where I first saw his ability was in the Group Theory class he taught, in the form of 3 x 5 note cards on which Bob would have us write our thoughts, musings or questions at the end of class. At the beginning of the next class, he would read some of them aloud. Get any group together, let alone a group of 20 or so and winds will blow. You could feel the hurricane in those cards! But he would read them apparently unperturbed, with his smile and a simple "Oh!" Bob seemed able to meet any wind, soft or gale.

Then, as a young, aspiring student, I was mystified. Here's this man, asking for it, telling us to put it into words . . . taking these winds on, no matter how strong . . . and having fun! I witnessed him do this, just like the idiots who go out there on Miami Beach at the news of a Hurricane approaching and get on their surf boards. Is this man crazy?

So I joined one of his supervision groups. Here I stand now 22 years later. Most of our work has been over the telephone or Skype. The last time I saw him, in person, was 9 years ago when my first daughter was two for a Naropa Anniversary Celebration. He's coached me to ride my surfboard in the form of my life, and taught me how to ride the waves of my mind and the waves of others' minds.

What's amazing is that Bob was and is still willing to take me in any form, and nothing less. I left the psychotherapy field temporarily because I burned out at the young age of 26 or so. I left Boulder for New York City and found the executives I worked for crazier than my clients at Friendship House. But I paid off my school loans, met my husband and we traveled to India to study yoga. I returned to Bob with an idea: "Bob, I'm teaching yoga. Can I present my clients in group?" "Sure," Bob said, without one hint of hesitation. My work continued to unfold. The hurricanes came and we got our boards. I got the crazy idea to return to Miami with my husband when we were starting our family. Five years of living in Miami, falling off my board, flipping in the water, the currents almost drowning me, and finally, I got steady on my board. Bob, with his "Oh!" and ability to laugh with me, was there.

Now, my husband and I live in Vermont with our three beautiful children. No more hurricanes, but the wind can still blow up on the hill where we live. We are building a farm where we raise goats for milk and make cheese and grow medicinal herbs. I work five hours a week at a local mental health center. I see Bob via telephone for monthly supervision.

My life is precious, every moment. I've had the good fortune to have Bob in my life, through my life, to sit, bit by bit through it all. And no, he's not crazy. Through his relentlessly kind ways of seeing me, he has taught me how to see myself, love myself and thus how better to serve others. He's still teaching me and I love him deeply. For Bob, I am eternally grateful.

Bob of the Group

Casey Burnett

Under a winter star, rising high above a crowded eastern city, an angel appeared before a young Jewish woman. "Behold, God has shown you favor. Your prayers have been heard. You shall bear a son, and name him, Robert." She was struck with awe but also with a fear for her son and she replied, "But why me? There are plenty of other scapegoats in our community." The Angel of Adonai said, "He will be known as Immanuel, wonderful counselor." Left alone in the dark, she wondered about all these things. "Why me? I just was sitting here, a gentle member of our tribe. I didn't do anything. Why did I get targeted?" The community leader bridged her concern and isolation with others in the community so she would be able to tolerate all things unknown and stay in relationship as her mysterious child grew inside.

An edict went out from Roosevelt stating a draft would be called and all people should report to their home cities. The young lady and her betrothed left for their tribal home. Overcome with pains of birth, they were forced to stop to seek shelter. No place was available for them at any inns. Finding shelter at 25 East 21st Street, Sixth Floor in New York City among encircling chairs, young Robert entered with a role and a task at hand. Guided by tradition, and a divine star, three wise men bearing gifts visited the child. These were known as Spotnitz, Ormont and Trungpa. They came carrying gifts of an ash tray, a circle of chairs, and a bottle of sake.

Robert grew with the favor of his tribe and leaders. He studied and worked. He journeyed inward and outward to a relational center that grew in accordance with his destiny and ethos. Disciplined and practiced, with 111,111 pedal strokes his heart-mind was strengthened and purified and after many years, Robert became Bob of the Group. With clarity of a crystal in sunlight, his teachings free-associated to every facet of his mind. With uncertainty and discomfort, mixed with confrontation and structure, Bob went about sharing the good news of groups with all who would listen. Students of all ilks approached him to follow. Many would leave shaking their heads, saddened. He knew they'd be back when they grew. "It's all relationship," Bob was heard to have said. With what, to whom, or when or how was unclear. He worked to elucidate the implicitness of one's projective processes in the game room of transference and object relations. Many who met him were changed. No words could express what the encounter meant. It was enough to call it an experience and allow it to sit.

I write these things to you people of Boulder so that you might know what has been said and done in these recent days. Bob of the Group has performed many miracles recorded elsewhere. Might you have had an encounter with the Bob of Group? Do tell. The lessons keep bearing fruit beyond season, and the freshness of an artisan spring might burst upon your mind without warning. Bob was an orchestrator of change and facilitator of the acceptance of the impermanence of life. That intimacy and frustrations were equal players in all moments. No preference, but an engagement with life itself. Bob is still about the town and worth listening to—if you can pedal fast enough!

Hilary Callan

Thank you to Bob for being my surrogate father. Bob said, "Let me know if I should be worried about you," as I stumbled through the end of my marriage, scared as hell but knowing that I had Bob's metered and safe eye on me when I needed it.

Bob asked AGPA to grant me a scholarship based on the financial difficulties of being a single mother, something I didn't actually realize until I was well into the conference.

When I was financially indebted to him for a significant sum, Bob made the brilliant intervention of raising his rate, stimulating me to figure out how to settle our debts and create safety for me and my children.

And when my father was dying, Bob was available by email and phone, present with me and offering whatever bits of perspective that were useful.

Bob teaches me about natural hierarchy, emptiness, and the coincidence of position, reminding me that if he were paying me, I'd be the analyst.

I feel very lucky to have ended up with the opportunity to train my mind this directly and precisely, and with such humor. Bob is an inspiration to the craft of psychotherapy. And a great pleasure to have in my life.

Jason Carpenter

It feels difficult to condense my experience of Bob in that whatever I begin to write tells only a portion of my feelings. Perhaps I should say that what I write here can only begin to touch on the entirety of my thoughts of such a warm and generous man. Bob has always seemed to me genuine, assured, but not at rest, in both his view of himself and his willingness to play and learn with others. As a student, a teaching assistant, and in other contexts with Bob, I have always felt equally at ease and anxiously curious about what to expect next. He has the most delightful way of keeping you on your toes. Being his Teaching Assistant was a thrill because his mind is nimble and associative and he's willing to give it free reign in an unapologetic manner, while trusting in his own and others' basic goodness and ability to learn from experience.

To be more specific, Bob was a revelation for me. I arrived at Naropa with an unverbalized and hard to verbalize feeling about what being a psychotherapist meant, but no real clue as to what a psychotherapist might actually look like. Sitting in Bob's class this internal, inchoate idea met up with something, someone resembling it in the external world. It was thrilling and satisfying. I felt I was given permission to be myself. He conducted his classroom as a potential space in which thoughts could be explored, developed, and made use of. Through my time with Bob, I gained a concept of not only what it meant to be a psychotherapist, but a way to articulate it. Though the idea has grown and developed since, the experience of being with Bob at that time remains the central concept I hold of what being a psychotherapist could be like.

Finally, while recognizing the incompleteness of this description, I want to add that a wise man, also named Bob, once said, "To live outside the law, one must be honest." I don't think I've ever met someone more capable of living outside the law than Bob. He is an original, a culmination, and an inspiration.

Lauren Casalino

Here's the thing: many times when I am laboring uphill on a bike, wishing I was free-rolling downhill instead, I think of Bob. I think of how he likes the long hard climbs, relishes them one might almost say, and the animation that overcomes his body when he speaks of them. As soon as I think of him all lit up about climbing, I am charged with energy and I huff uphill with, if not exactly enjoyment, then at least a smile on my face from remembering Bob at such a time.

And that's the thing: Bob is energy. Bob is matured passion. Bob is skill and craft and artistry. He is fearless free association. He is generosity in relationship.

The first time I met Bob he was teaching a group class in which I was a graduate student in a way that was bringing out many forms of rebellion and aggression. He seemed to thrive on placing himself as the lightning rod for the charge in the air which was circulating with unpredictable velocity and zapping power amongst 40 students. Wow! He could take the charge, the charge of all of our unprocessed emotions, privileged expectations, fearful wants and needs couched as rightful demands, and all the rest of the cumulative unconscious expressions at play. I knew immediately that he was manifesting a way of relating and a mastery of group facilitation that I had never experienced before. This was definitely worth the price of tuition!

That was 28 years ago and our relationship is now also one of colleagues and friends. Bob does not cling to hierarchy and power. He relates in whatever form the situation may present, bringing out the best in people, believing in and encouraging people to believe in themselves and to be their best. He inspires. I believe I would be a facilitator of groups without him in my life, but would I be as inspired and dedicated and skillful a facilitator without him? Certainly not.

Now, as Bob enters a new decade, he is still biking uphill faster than racers decades younger than him. He is still allowing people their gyrations. He is still taking the charge, and often bringing humor to it all. He is still expanding the possibilities within relationship for himself and for others.

May all this continue and may you be healthy and happy for many years to come, Bob, whatever the uphill challenges of living may be.

With love and gratitude, I wish you a Happy Birthday!

The Center for Harm Reduction Therapy: Jamie Lavender, Justin Castello, Celia Sampayo Perez, Maurice Byrd, Melissa Eaton, Monica Massaro, Abigail Dembo, & Diana Valentine

Bob has been co-leading a group supervision group with Jeannie Little at the Center for Harm Reduction Therapy since 2003. By some mystery, the group immediately became a here-and-now oriented training group, much to the discomfiture of several members. In the early days, many sessions were taken up with questions of "What is this group for, anyway?" The old process vs. content focus debate was alive and kicking.

Now, more than eleven years later, the current group, which still has some vestiges of the original, met in an hour long free associative session focused on Bob. This is what transpired, as best as could be transcribed at the time:

Yoda

Before Skype, he was Black Box Bob, or sometimes The Voice of God.

On one occasion, Jeannie was out of town and both joined the group by phone. The group wondered what it meant when Bob said, "Are Jeannie and I in the same room? Would the group want us or not want us to be in the same room?" This was the first psychoanalytic group co-leader intervention the group had ever heard, and a rather concrete interpretation followed. It blew up into years of angst, questions of boundaries and "What is the purpose of this group anyway?"

It's OK . . . as long as you have your shoes on . . .

Bob takes the group places it didn't expect to go, and seemingly comes out of left field.

What do you like about Bob?

Sense of humor

He seems excited to talk to us. Except when he falls asleep.

In his paper, "Buddhism and psychoanalysis: Paths of disappointment," (Unger, 2008) he reinforces the importance of not having an agenda and being fully present in the moment. This is so critical for our work as harm reductionists.

How does he hold all these people in his mind anyway? What's the word for that? He's not a taskmaster, that would be Jeannie, but . . . a sage!

If Bob were a recipe, he would contain:

> The force
> Laughter
> Wisdom
> Timing
> Intuition
> Experience
> Authenticity
> Presence
> Enjoyment
> Penetrating questions (and . . . we circled back to the first issue)
> Whatever the dish, it would be served family style!

What else do we think about Bob?

> Bob is teachable.
> Bob is fresh.
> Thank you.
> Bob really sees the group itself as a living breathing thing, as an entity.
> He is very skillful at taking us to a journey of transformation where we can take higher risks in a very nonjudgmental and mindful way. He gives the lesson and you have to take the risk. 'Speak your mind' seems to overcome the mind's warning not to talk.
> Don't be afraid of your mind.

He really has an understanding of our clients, and does not minimize them.

He gets the group to talk to each other.

Bob is the opposite of the Northern California Group Psychotherapy Society—he really respects and appreciates the work we do in community programs.

What have we learned from Bob?

The group leader has to form a relationship first to help members bind to the group.

Co-facilitators talking to each other as way of speaking to the client—it's high-level stuff.

A group is a group is a group—I really got groups in a way that I never had when I understood that.

A group is a learning process. It's hard to not have an agenda. We have to learn the group.

It's OK to be wrong, really OK.

Drawing responsibility to self for the experience of group members when the group can't tolerate the tension.

The strategic back and forth of co-leaders.

Anything else we want to say about Bob?

Strategic

Provocative

Slippery—you can't really pin him down. He'll wriggle right out of any tight spot. If he were an animal, he'd be a snake. It always comes back at you with Bob. He absorbs the blow. He doesn't really. He turns it back. There is no Bob.
He doesn't really DO anything.

He shines the light into a corner you haven't been looking in.

He was reflecting my deepest fears.

Master of? Aikido. Of course, he's Yoda!

Genuinely interested. When he's awake . . .

What are the merits and realities of the therapist falling asleep? Is it or is it not permissible? What makes it permissible? Can it be useful?

The S&M discussion about the group that Jeremy and Maurice led went into our Race, Power, Privilege meeting. It became a thing!

This discussion is like a history of this group. Many things have gone down over the last 11+ years. During this hour, we have demonstrated our deep ability to free associate, and a good time was had by all!

References

Unger, R. (2008). Psychoanalysis and Buddhism: Paths of disappointment. In F. Kaklauskas, L. Hoffman, S. Nimmanheminda, & M. Jack, (Eds.). *Brilliant Sanity: Buddhism and psychotherapy* (pp. 347-353). Colorado Springs, CO: University of the Rockies Press.

David Chrislip

I first met Bob at speed in the middle of a bike race on the rough dirt roads north of Boulder. He, of course, was very competitive and eventually came out the winner of the race. I had flatted and sat out a lap fixing the tire. What amazed me about connecting in these circumstances was how quickly we found a meeting of interests during those hectic moments. We've been friends, fellow cyclists, and professional colleagues since that encounter.

In part, this reflects Bob's nimble mind that encompasses his varied and eccentric interests ranging from group psychology to the make of the carburetors on a vintage flat track BSA racing motorcycle. Which brings me to one of my favorite words that Bob uses to describe himself which is "schpilkas," meaning "ants in your pants" in Yiddish. Perfect! Anyone who meets Bob quickly learns that he can't sit still. And one also learns how well he uses this restless energy with great compassion for the benefit of others. In these ways, Bob is *sui generis,* of his own kind, in a class by himself.

Angelo Ciliberti

"It's an odd thing to call this a 'class'. Typically, in a class you learn something, but in here you really aren't going to actually learn anything." Bob said all of this with a smile as he thumbed through the Evolution of Central Concepts of Western Psychology syllabus that had just been passed out. This was my first encounter with Dr. Bob Unger and I was already feeling a dizzying combination of confusion, excitement and shock.

"What do you mean we aren't going to learn anything?! Isn't that the whole point of this class?" a student in my cohort angrily questioned. "Naropa is charging us enough! You think we would have the opportunity to learn something!" Then, from across the room, another classmate chimed in, "Before this semester started I calculated with our tuition how much each class is actually costing us. If I were to pay at the door, I would have to hand over $50 per hour for each class in each section all semester long. And basically you are saying that we are going to have nothing to show for it?!"

Bob then said, "Oh, and you remind me of a good point. Since the T.A.s (teaching assistants) and I really don't teach anything, as a part of this class you are asked not to even take notes." As the class sat stunned, pens paused on in mid-air, Bob looked at both of his T.A.s flanking him on either side and said, "Now, how did that chant go at my high school football games? One of the guys would catch the ball and the cheerleaders would sing out, 'Here we go...Hey!'" I sat in stunned silence, trying to digest the idea that this man I had heard so much about, actually had nothing to teach.

Instead, what actually occurred in that class and others that I took with him changed everything that I knew or thought I knew about the psyche, group dynamics, and human interactions. The classes were alive with discussion, dissension, and discovery. That is not to say any of it was coming from Bob per se. Rather, he seemed to orchestrate an ongoing conversation where any given story, idea, or theory could be questioned, appreciated, and dissolved back into the larger context from which it had arisen. As we each would share, challenge, and contradict him and each other, Bob would smile, nod, and encourage whatever was unfolding. I would leave his classes feeling a quality of acceptance that was as fortifying as it was unfamiliar. I felt like my totality, contradictions and all, was welcome.

In the 10 years since those first moments with Bob, I have been incredibly fortunate to study with him both as a student and a supervisee. To study with Bob is to sit on the edge where conceptual thought and expectation meets open space and unpredictability. Academic and cerebral by nature, I have often showed up to his classroom and consultation office wanting to nail down ideas around "transference", "ego", and "resistance". Instead, I walk away thinking in terms of Bob Dylan lyrics, cycling metaphors, and children's stories like *Tacky the Penguin* (Lester & Munsinger, 1990). I often can't remember a single, prescriptive intervention that has been suggested. Instead, I leave feeling a curious and powerful trust in my self, the intelligence of the body, and the associative function of my unconscious. I feel grateful beyond words to have had the opportunity to study with such an inimitable man.

References

Lester, H. & Munsingser, L. (1990). *Tacky the penguin.* New York: Houghton Mifflin Harcourt.

Michael Cohn-Geltner

At some point near the end of my time in college, I decided I wanted to learn to be a bicycle mechanic. I had ridden bikes on and off as a kid, but mostly off. However, the work appealed to me. It was a skilled job in an industry on the rise.

My parents discovered a bike repair class in Colorado Springs. To help me get a grasp on all things bike related, my dad asked his friend Bob to show me the ropes. I stayed with Bob for only a few days, but he treated me with profound kindness. He showed me all his various bikes and let me ride many of them, including a unicycle. He brought me to his favorite bike shop and helped size me for a bike that would fit. When it was time to take the class, he drove me to Denver so I could catch the bus to Colorado Springs.

Afterwards, biking became a huge part of my life. When I lived in New Orleans I biked every day. I worked as a mechanic and salesmen for a year, and have used my skills to fix hundreds of bikes. I'm not sure if taking the class would have had as much meaning if I had not spent the first few days with Bob. Though it was only a few days, it ended up having a disproportionally large impact on my life.

Susan M. Cooper

As I have watched Bob conduct groups over the years and have also participated in a supervision group he conducted for group therapists, I have learned two lessons from Bob that stand out among many. The first is that it is natural for both group members and group leaders to space out or lose focus from time to time during group sessions. This reality relieved a lot of my guilt as a group leader and helped me to be more gentle with group members who obviously "went away" during the group process. The most important lesson I have learned from Bob, however, is how important it is to have fun conducting groups—to really enjoy the process—as it was so obviously what he was doing throughout his facilitation. At the same time, he could be penetrating and extremely authentic. Because of Bob's impact in this regard, I have enjoyed group facilitation more than any other psychological process I have engaged in and still joyfully run groups to this day.

Happy Birthday, Bob, and thank you for your many contributions to the field of group therapy and to my growth as a group leader.

Gratefully,

Sue Cooper

Michelle DeCola

Here's to you, Bob!

I first met you at COGPS dinner in a city (I can't remember which one) where we were having our AGPA annual conference. I was living in Chicago at the time, but attended the dinner as I was planning to move to Denver in a few years.

The next year I was thrilled to be in your two year Institute group which you co-led with Gil. My fantasy was that I could bond with another Colorado therapist, and that you would be the "supportive father-figure," as I navigated an upcoming move and an impending divorce.

This two-year Institute group was a challenge for both members and leaders. I didn't get my fantasy father! I experienced frustration and loneliness in the group and during our quarterly phone sessions in between the two years. I wanted both you (the dad) and Gil (the mom) to fix this mess! There were many men in this group, and much testosterone and fierce competition were present. On the last day of our two-year Institute, I watched how you and Gil gave of yourselves in our group, in ways that brought our anxiety down, and allowed us to be softer and more vulnerable with each other. I learned a lot from both of you and a lot about myself.

This past Fall, I had the pleasure and joy of getting to be an assistant teacher with you in your Group Psychotherapy class at Naropa. Well guess what? My anxiety went up again!! I was aware of my transference (again) with you. I wanted to be seen as smart, witty, fun and knowledgeable as a group therapist and teacher. You were always warm and engaging with me. You encouraged Teri and me both to join with you and share our experiences. You helped me feel comfortable in a setting that was completely new to me, and I learned so much from you. I grew a lot from experiencing myself in this environment.

One of my favorite moments with you was on that Saturday class where you graciously had to make up lost hours by meeting with the class for a day. You and I had the chance to have lunch together at Whole Foods. I had you all to myself and wanted to get some "expert" advice about someone new I was dating. I explained that I had found myself highly attracted and drawn to a man who was very different from me in two ways. Politically we were opposites. Spiritually as well, we saw things from completely different perspectives.

You listened to me state all the ways in which we were very good matches. I looked at you with big eyes waiting to hear your response. You said, "Michelle, is he kind? Is he open-minded?"

I said, "Yes." "Well," you said, "There is your answer."

Bob, thank you for your kindness, your openness, your wisdom and your support.

Our Fearless Leader

Abigail Dembo

What is within *us*—
We are a midden.

One lens, two lens.
A constellation.

Layers of dust, a matrix, a focus.

Puff, powder, puff.
Ray, laser, ray!

Name the group's dynamics, Bob!

Teri Dillion

I'll never forget the day when, in the MACP class on Western Psychology, one of my classmates very brazenly challenged Bob Unger's competence as a teacher. I was expecting that Bob would immediately cut him off, get defensive, or fight back in some way, and instead, he was unflappable. It was as if this communication of the student's was just like any other—and definitely nothing to get concerned about.

While I aspire to that level of non-defensiveness and have yet to find it, I have learned nonetheless how to take Bob's spirit of delight with group dynamics into my work. In fact, thanks to Bob, I have come to love studying group dynamics in a way I never would have imagined.

Not only have I learned the value of welcoming aggression, hostility, and disappointment in my work with groups and individual clients, I have also learned on a more basic level that any sort of emotional communication can exist really to be studied as opposed to being manipulated in some way. Perhaps this speaks to the psychoanalytic approach, which Bob makes quite accessible to his mentees and students. Either way, it seems to complement the contemplative approach of practicing inquiry and acceptance instead of some sort of psychological materialism that encourages people toward self-improvement projects.

Recently, I brought Bob's spirit with me when presenting on group dynamics to a group of about 60 senior teachers and practitioners in my meditation lineage. I spoke about the importance of welcoming feelings of hostility, paranoia and fear in meditation discussion groups. Countless people shared how helpful it was to have these basic drives and group dynamics named. I was reminded of the power (and the novelty) of naming difficult feelings and welcoming their expression in a group format.

Bob has a way of touching on the human situation with humor and heart, and for that I carry immense gratitude. Not only have I learned to be a better group leader thanks to him, but a better therapist in general— who now knows a bit about how to meet people in a fresh and welcoming way.

Elizabeth Dining

(in conversation with Michael M. Dow)

I nannied for Bob and Helena's son, Dylan, when he was eight months old. I was 19, and having just turned 48 this year, that's a long time. So what I can say about that is that while I'm more in contact with Helena by far, what they have meant to me is really as a couple. There has been a consistency and "unconditionalness" with them that I never had with any one. I never had anyone, parents, partners, anyone for that long, and whether I was in college, doing drugs, getting married, it didn't matter. They were just there. It was formative and amazing as a person, and as a parent myself.

But the story I have about Bob happened back when Dylan was very young. When they were pregnant with Julian I was the one who was supposed to be "on call" to care for Dylan when Julian arrived. We didn't have cell phones back then. I got home to my answering machine one night after going to Perkin's for late night food (Bob to this day doesn't believe that's actually where I was, I think). There were three voicemails from Bob. The first one, was, you know, that voice, "Hello, Elizabeth! It's time!" The second one was a lot more intense, "Elizabeth, we need you to come over—now." And then the third one, was, "Elizabeth?! Where are you?!!" Not angry, but Bob, stressed. By the time I arrived at their house on Floral Drive Helena and Julian had been transported to the hospital, having had the actual birth at home. That was not the plan. She had gone into labor quickly. The story I was told of the events immediately preceding my arrival were something like this: Bob was on the phone with 911. "Tell her not to push," they said, and so Bob says, "They said not to push," and Helena says, "Tell them to fuck off!" And then Julian was born right there at home, into Bob's arms. I'll never forget arriving in the aftermath of all of that and I'll never forget Bob's voice in those voicemails.

The thing about Bob is that he's just so there. Maybe he doesn't know that I feel that way about both of them. As much as I chitter chatter with Helena, seeing him is an important part of that equation.

It's easily nine months at a time that we don't see each other and then I text Helena, "I miss you, " and we get together for tea. But just walking into their house, it never doesn't feel like it was just yesterday. Even if it's been a year, or whatever, it never doesn't feel like they are family.

What We Talk About When We Talk About Psychotherapy: Stories and Lessons From Dr. Bob

Michael M. Dow

Like one of Lorenz's goslings, I had my first imprint of what a therapist is from Bob. The imprint runs deep. Sometimes I can still feel it there beneath my conscious attempts at original interventions, in my "Oh!s", and in my "What makes you think..." or my "Which would you rather feel?" I've grown a lot, done many other therapy trainings, but still, it would seem I can hear echoes of Bob speaking through my voice, my words.

In my first encounter with Bob, he was a supervisor on a Windhorse team, a community based model of mental health care pioneered at Naropa in Boulder. I was newly employed as a therapeutic housemate, and super green. Straight from living off the grid in Northern California, I had been stuck in a 1970s time warp for some years, farming and practicing Zen Buddhism.

It quickly became apparent that I was in way over my head. Periodically, the client would decompensate into a pretty extreme state of mind which is hard to describe. Despite the presence of a team, I was struggling.

Bob offered to do phone supervision with me. I can't remember the content of that phone call, but I do remember our group supervision with the team the very next day. Bob began by swearing up a storm, putting words to the feelings of frustration I had been having. As others in the room squirmed, I felt the strange, exquisite pleasure of knowing simultaneously that Bob had taken a big emotional risk for me, and that no one else could possibly know that he had done so.

Bob had spoken for me (and perhaps, by extension, the client), and in doing so, had helped to give voice to the difficult, nearly intolerable feelings which seemed to be holding all of us back in moving forward. He both voiced, and in a sense, attracted towards himself the aggression in the system. Afterwards, as I found often to be the case with supervision with Bob, everything seemed just a bit easier and more workable.

A few months later, I was sitting in one of my first Naropa classes, Bob's class which he structured as a group with no agenda and open to anything. I felt both challenged to show up as my whole self, and also more exposed than I quite ever remember. I was intimidated and nearly paralyzed. No lectures and no notes! Just open space . . .

Each week we were to write a card with our experience of the class. I remember a sort of aching to have Bob read my card. And for like 7 or 8 weeks in a row, my card happened to be read. Bob would respond in a way that felt like he was speaking to the deepest part of me, while also challenging me, and somehow speaking oracularly to the group-as-a-whole. A sort of speaking I hadn't really heard before.

The last week of class we watched a controversial Spotnitz video. A student walked out horribly upset, offended, and the class froze. I was in fight or flight, my heart beating rapidly. I had seen this sort of thing before and I knew how it went. The student walked back in and said something like, "I'm so pissed off and upset. I'm just not sure if this is my stuff or if it's just you." Bob turned red, just nodded his head and said softly with all sincerity, looking her in the eye, "I think you can just assume it's me."

That was not what I had expected. I couldn't quite assimilate it. I count that as one of the first moments in my life observing someone respond with non-aggression in a highly conflictual moment. It was something I hadn't experienced before, and have seen repeated many times: A willingness and uncanny ability, surely Spotnitz-inspired, but still impressive, to be unapologetically, outrageously oneself and simultaneously without defense, without counter-attack. I wonder still about how exactly Bob manages to do this.

Later, I was applying for my first internship position and I needed references. I was inexperienced in the field and felt insecure about asking people. I asked Bob and two others, and was especially nervous about asking Bob. What would he say? Would he be OK with it? Would he even respond? And while all three said yes, the others took a few days to get back to me. Bob called me within the hour and left a message and with just the right combination of glee and limit said, "Yes, I'd be delighted to write you a recommendation! Why don't you write a letter and tell me what you want me to say." I felt completely met, mirrored, and also thrown back on myself.

I joined one of Bob's weekly consultation groups with excitement and trepidation. I was a new graduate, and most other members were pretty seasoned veterans. I had a very hard time talking. I'd often sit next to him, often too terrified to share my cases in any depth, and Bob would just be there with that smile, a humorous question here or there thrown in my directions and absolutely no sense of pressure at all. I gradually grew more bold, and ended up spending nearly ten years in that group, becoming a senior member.

Years later, I was sitting at AGPA in New York at one of the plenaries and listening to Judith Wallerstein talk about the legacy of divorce, how the legacy is not often felt until later in adulthood when those children are having relationships and how they lack the template of a secure relationship to rely on. I started to have a visceral reaction to hearing her, as I am a child of divorce who has experienced exactly such effects. I generally see myself as being contained, but I must have started to show some signs of something, because I looked over and there was Bob, sitting four or five seats away but somehow uncannily attuned to what I was going through, nodding his head in the most sympathetic way. It was only after seeing him nod that I realized there were tears streaming down my face or perhaps it was seeing Bob nod that triggered the tears. There was the strange and very supportive sense that Bob seemed to know what I was feeling almost before I did.

There are many more stories and behind the stories, many lessons. I thought of making a "Ten Lessons from Dr. Bob" list but there were so many. Characteristic of all of them was that they were the opposite of what I had been trying very hard to do as a therapist.

First there was the eye opening lesson about joining resistance rather than fighting it. Support people's reasons for not changing! Help them understand their "defenses" before moving to change them. Encourage and welcome anger towards the therapist (at times). And how patients responded!

And then of course the joint modern analytic and contemplative insight that what you feel with patients, especially even the difficult "I'm a failure as a therapist feelings", are more often a replay of something from the patients' life than purely yours.

I started work at the Mental Health Center in Boulder, and Bob's instruction to me was that I needed to learn to manage and support my supervisor "from below," as it were, rather than getting supported by them. This was not what I was doing at all. And not what I wanted to hear! But it made all the difference, and played a big part in my being able to keep my job.

The nearly constant lesson about humor and lightness! Bob seemed to use joking around as his main therapeutic intervention. This seemed ridiculous, but with some clients (and I include myself here), not only helped ease the ground for other interventions, but in a sense was the main intervention. When I first heard Ferenczi's quote, "Remaining serious is successful repression," (1913/2002) I knew the truth of that because of Bob.

Then there is the lesson, more recent for me, but familiar to anyone who has spent time with Bob outside the office, of the helpfulness of talking, talking and more talking. It can be jarring, given how disciplined at listening he is in the office, to experience Bob in "real life" and see that this is a man who not only "walks his talk" but quite literally "talks his talk"! The way in which he seems to so deeply trust his unconscious and impulses, while also being thoroughly committed to self-control and managing his aggression. The transmission of being with Bob is truly that you can (and he will!) say anything. And that you and he have a special bond that he values, and will never give up on despite distance or time.

And then the lesson of relationships. The festschrift itself is evidence of this: Bob stays in close contact with a staggering number of people. Much of his life is structured around various groups, many of them meeting for decades, relationships woven into the fabric of his days. And there is the constant sense of invitation with Bob—when are we meeting next, what are we doing together next? Months can go by, even years, and yet, Bob despite the scores of people with whom he is contact, Bob somehow keeps you in mind.

Psychoanalysis as a Form of Love

Lately, in the process of doing the festschrift, I've had another perhaps larger insight or lesson from Bob, perhaps unlikely from the analyst who's interested in aggression and disappointment, which is that psychoanalysis, if it is about anything, is basically about love.

At the same time, I've learned from Bob that psychoanalysis is also basically about the form, and perhaps strangely, that these two things are not in conflict. In a very concrete way, as Bob says, it's the form of analysis which does the healing work. The patient comes, talks. The analyst listens, responds. There's a basic hierarchical situation, the payment, the healing properties of a regular schedule, coming on time. It's not commonly understood or accepted, but it's arguably the form itself that is healing. There's not a lot, in a certain way, as the analyst that you have to do. The form, if you put yourself in it, and if patients put themselves in it, does the work.

And love too, real relationships, it could be argued are much more about the form than one typically suspects. Stan Tatkin's (2012) and the Gottmans' (1999) work gets at this, the laws or the form of love, so to speak. Certain postures, rules of engagement, allow for certain things to happen. Love is a form and a practice, more than simply a feeling.

And then, combining these two, you could say not only that psychoanalysis is a form of love, but perhaps even the truest form of love. "To love is to listen deeply," says Thich Nhat Hanh (2006), and who listens more deeply than the analyst? In fact, might the analyst, even the most enlightened analyst, perhaps listen more deeply, more "un-reactively" to his patients than to his spouse or his children? Of course it's easier to listen for 50 minutes a few times a week than at any hour of day or night over a lifetime, but I'm arguing here, and Bob has taught me this, that to practice psychoanalysis is to practice love. Not in the mushy, sentimental sense, but in the deep listening/feeling/digesting, 'putting your own needs aside' sense. In other words, psychoanalysis is not less loving because it's "artificial"; it's precisely its artificial or formal nature which allows it to more fully manifest love.

It's been interesting to watch myself in the course of this project look for the ways in which Bob is an imperfect person, to find the real man behind the wizard of Oz. And naturally, Bob has his failings, and there can be a sense of disappointment (as in all relationships) when you see the person for who they are. But so what? In fact, isn't it possible to read this in the other direction?

Rather than seeing the discrepancies between an "ideal" man or therapist (whatever that would be), and the reality of who Bob is as a sign of something wrong, couldn't the reverse be true? That the existence of this discrepancy is in fact the definition of mastery, a sign that in one's work one has surpassed oneself, has truly gone beyond what one is capable in everyday life?

In this way, this latest "lesson" from Bob, I have been able to relax more deeply into my work. I can be imperfect as a person, and still, and even because of that, excel as a therapist. Things will take care of themselves. Come back to the form. Listen deeply. Talk. Breathe. Therapy is a practice of love. And there's not a thing you can do about it.

References

Ferenczi, S. (2002). Laughter. In E. Mobasher (Trans.), *Final contributions to the problems and methods of psycho-analysis* (pp. 321). London: Karnac. (Original work published 1913)

Gottman, J. & Silver, N. (1999). *The seven principles for making your marriage work: A practical guide from the nation's foremost relationship expert.* New York: Harmony.

Nhat Hanh, T. (2006). *True love: A practice for awakening the heart.* Boston, MA: Shambhala.

Tatkin, S. (2012). *Wired for love: How understanding your partner's brain and attachment style can help you defuse conflict and build a secure relationship.* New York: New Harbinger.

Karen Drucker

I met Bob in COGPS and Naropa in the early 2000's. I was intrigued by his mind, his manner, and his humor and later joined his supervision group for a few years. There was never a dull moment. I was often surprised by his comments or approach, and sometimes dared to disagree with him, which led to lively discussions, and usually gave me a perspective I had not considered.

Thank you, Bob, for your brilliance, your compassion, your directness, and your irreverence!! You are an amazing man and such a gift to us.

More Than Soup

Andrea Dugan

I'm lying on the couch and trying to notice what comes up when I think of Bob. I relax, let the couch hold me, and notice my breath. A simple association comes. Soup. Why a bowl of soup? How did soup and Bob end up in my mind together? Is it hot soup? Cold soup? Is it spicy, or mild? Colorful? Is the bowl of soup half full or half empty? I'm curious.

It's been over twenty years since I first saw Bob standing outside the Café at Naropa's Arapahoe campus, eating a bowl of soup. The second time I saw him he walked into my Evolution of Central Concepts In Western Psychology class, sat down, passed out the syllabus and quietly looked around. Nobody spoke. In the silence, we waited for our teacher to teach. Someone took a bite of a bagel they'd brought into class. Bob looked around the circle and said, "In this class we have a contract and there is no eating or drinking in class."

Bagel Boy sort of laughed nervously, while he considered the next bite and asked, "Why?"

The silence was loud in the room as Bob replied, "Oh, it's part of the contract, as is coming on time, and sharing the talking time."

I could tell Bagel Boy couldn't decide if he should take another bite or not. As the minutes went by, we found out that sitting on the floor and taking notes were also against the contract. We were to call him Bob, rather than Dr. Unger, and he said "Fuck" in class? What kind of teacher was this? What would happen if we decided to eat, drink and sit on the floor anyway?

This was not how I thought I'd learn about Freud, but I kind of liked it. Bob sat in our circle with a T.A. on either side, which highlighted the fact that he was the teacher, and we his students. He stirred the pot with his slightly offensive unwritten contract. Class was unnerving, raw and experiential, and exactly what I needed.

For the first weeks we talked about the reading and the contract, like soup warming on a hot stove, or at least I think that's what we did. In the sixth class a woman stood up and held out her hands to a classmate to demonstrate her understanding of the concept of "Resistance." Evidently standing in class was also against the contract, and we were to put our thoughts and feelings into words rather than actions.

Standing Gal said, "I just want to show what resistance looks like with my body."

Bob responded, "This isn't a body class. In this class we are to put our thoughts and feelings into words."

Standing Gal: "But wait, this will just take a second." She ignored Bob's reminders about the contract and proceeded to engage a student sitting next to her.

Abruptly, Bob ended class and walked out. Our breaths caught, and then a flood of reaction. We exploded with energy, shock, wonder, anger, and curiosity. What just happened? Was he mad? Was he teaching us something?

With this one action he turned up the heat, and shortly after a petition went around to get him fired. How could he stir up those uncomfortable feelings? Bob wasn't going anywhere. The next class he took his teacher seat with a simple "Any questions?" This was when I knew I trusted him to be my teacher. In time, he told me this was not the first time he'd walked out on a class for the sake of education.

Later, I was in my internship working with a court ordered population facilitating anger management groups. Bob was our agency supervisor twice a month. We talked about intense cases, but what Bob's supervision did was teach me how to deal with my impulsive, aggressive supervisor. By this time, I had already completed Bob's group class, and to watch him work with her intensity in a group was like watching a magician. He'd stroke her ego one minute, and titrate her rants the next. I quietly learned and decided to join one of his other supervision groups to throw a little more into the pot of my learning.

I asked if I could be one of his T.A.s. I became one of the people that sat beside Bob, in a room of eager new students, and did this for several years. The air was electric on the day he showed the Spotnitz video, and this day was no different when a woman in the class stormed out in the middle of the video. Like static electricity, my awareness was pulled keen and sharp sitting beside him. I noticed my breath as well as the students checking to see what our reactions were. The woman later returned to confront Bob in front of the class about showing this video that was "racist and demeaning to women". With his Bob-like flavor, he responded skillfully and kindly, without easing the tension in the least.

Afterwards, I talked about the hair on the back of my neck and asked him about it. "Does the hair on the back of your neck stand up too?" With a trickster smile Bob replied, "Let's just say, you're not the only one."

I was around Bob frequently, and saw how he supported students and colleagues, and fellow supervisees equally. He wanted everyone to succeed, and maybe even write a paper about it. In my supervision group, he met everyone where they were, and in his eyes I saw love and appreciation in even the hardest moments.

Bob could apply bike riding metaphors and Bob Dylan lyrics to most any situation. Bob was a cabbie, I think in New York, and started his career by joining a therapy group in order to meet girls. If he hadn't become a psychoanalyst, he might have become a dancer. He took singing lessons for fun, raised his boys, and had a special relationship to a lathe and a block of wood. He studied limiting words like "just", "always" and "interesting" and seemed to have fun doing so. After years of sitting beside him in class, and in his office doing supervision, I learned about Bob the human being and have no doubt he was a one of a kind cabbie, and could have easily ended up a professional dancer instead of a therapist. I suspect he may still have dancing in his future; with Bob anything seems possible.

The energy that Bob created and held with his students drew me to him all those years ago. However, it was his willingness to be deeply present and loving that kept me with him over time. I got my first private practice client, and needed an office. Bob offered me his, and I found myself in his chair with a key to his office. I liked it. He was, and is, generous and discerning.

I've seen Bob nearly fall asleep (at least it seemed that way) while sitting in a group, and I've also seen him tear up. Some people never see past his intelligence and humor, or his willingness to teach through unconventional, yet experiential means. They've missed out. Bob loves beautifully.

I had finished a semester of being his T.A. for the Group Therapy class, when my first son was born. Bob came to visit shortly after, bearing a grandfather smile and sweet baby blue outfit. He was one of the first men besides my husband to hold my newborn son. He invited me to continue in the group, whether I had to call in, or bring my baby or whatever creative means were necessary. He understood the juggling act and my challenges before I did. I brought my infant to group and grew both my babies in Bob's presence. He supported me with his Cheshire smile. I stopped being Bob's T.A. right before my second child was born, and shortly after stopped the supervision group.

I think of Bob as an artist at heart, the kind that feels the form, whether it's in his students or a block of wood, and then does his part to help it become what it's meant to be. He allows for inspiration, much like a soup that's thrown together organically without a recipe. Bob's gift to the world is his willingness to think and feel in equal measure. Besides invigorating the world around him, Bob is almost too kind for words. I am one of the lucky ones to know this. With his birthday coming up, I can hear him sing Bob Dylan lyrics, "I was so much older then, I'm younger than that now."

I wonder about Bob and soup, and how I came to love him. From that first class when I felt the tension build among my classmates, to seeing his generosity sprinkled across a community of therapists, and now meeting for an infrequent bowl of soup between clients, I've witnessed Bob stir the pot of aliveness for all. Bob is like a rich soup, that is spicy, flavorful and stimulating and of course so much more than my simple soup association. It's more accurate to say Bob's the chef, the soup and the bowl.

Raymon Elozua

Bob had given up a career as a highway engineer and was dancing with the Daniel Nagrin Dance Company in New York City when I first met him. Maryanne, my girl friend, also a dancer in the company, introduced me to him in 1972. We first bonded over motorcycles. Bob had a Honda 450 that he wanted painted in a candy apple blue. Being somewhat experienced in auto body work, I agreed to do so and he was pleased with the results. Over the next few years Bob financed his motorcycle addiction by buying and selling motorcycles. Visiting his tiny Elizabeth St. storefront was a treat, since it was always filled with five or six used bikes in various states of repair.

I had several motorcycles as well. I put together a BSA from a box of parts and when it was complete it would not shift into third gear. I called Bob. He took apart the transmission and got it working again. When I crashed my BMW R75, I called Bob and he rebuilt the front end. I was always in debt to his overwhelming generosity in helping not only me but others as well.

Bob soon acquired his dream bike, a Kawasaki Z900, which he detailed and maintained immaculately. Later Bob decided he wanted to race so he bought a Ducati SS 900. I went to Daytona Beach and watched him race as an amateur. All the time I marveled at his mechanical skills, his attention to detail and his devotion to learning as much as he could about motorcycle mechanics and later racing. I was always in awe of his ability and fearlessness in leading the life he chose. All these qualities stood him in good stead as he went on to Hunter College, becoming a psychotherapist, then leaving New York, moving to Naropa, meeting Helena, raising two great sons and building a practice that has counseled and consoled many. In all of his endeavors, his humor, humility, devotion, enthusiasm and intelligence is always personally inspiring to this day.

Sara Emerson

Many years, and definitely decades ago, the annual AGPA conference was in San Antonio, which was when I first met Bob. Actually my first encounter was not a meeting but a following. So I may actually be one of his early "followers." At that time I was relatively new to AGPA and to the Annual meeting. We were both significantly younger then. I was out for an early morning run along the River Walk, and I could see a runner ahead of me, probably a man; he was going at a good clip. The River Walk ended, but a path continued on. He continued on as well, and I kept following. I don't remember when we actually met, but when we did we decided that we could run together and we did. My recollection is that we ran in different cities, talked about ourselves, our lives. Over the miles and the years we got to know one another and developed an enduring friendship which continues to this day.

However, I do recall my upset and disappointment when one year he appeared with his bike informing me that he was now biking (maybe a running injury). I felt like a jilted lover, left to run on my own.

Beyond running together and a deepening personal relationship our professional relationship grew. I have vivid and valued memories of sharing Institute tables, and thus our clinical work. In the times I was not assigned to his table I can recall the disappointment. I have always valued his clinical observations and boundless support he has provided.

Another poignant memory, which does not speak to his brilliance as a clinician or a teacher or a mentor, or to any of his many other professional skills, has to do with a memory from a cab ride in New York City to the airport. I can't quite remember the details of why we were in New York City, but we were leaving at the same time. From my perspective, we had plenty of time to get to LaGuardia Airport and catch our respective planes. From Bob's perspective we were late and in danger of missing our plane. I said, "Bob, calm down. You left New York years ago and now live in Colorado, laid back and chill. So relax.

We'll be fine. He quickly told me, "You can take the boy out of New York, but you can't take New York out of the boy!"

Maybe that tells it all. Bob is a mensch, a teacher, a kind-hearted man, devoted to his family, his work, his students, the mountains, and his bike.

I am so glad to have you in my life and to have traveled some of my professional path with you.

My love,

Sara

Ashley Eyre

I brought my family to Bob after I had worked through a lot of my trauma from my parents' divorce. I was pretty nervous as we had never addressed what happened as a family, let alone sit together after the separation. I wondered what Bob was going to "do." Well, he showed up entirely present and didn't "do" anything and every member of my family had an emotional release and response. I was blown away by how his mere presence moved my family through so much pain. He held the space for each of us to open to what was real by doing nothing. He then asked the right question to each of us.

Michelle L. Fields

When I think of Bob Unger, I think of Bob Dylan. And bicycles. And then also: obscure musical references, non-sequiturs, cultural commentary and funny stories. A generous good-natured laugh that tickles my heart. And him falling asleep while meditating in front of a class full of students. Though initially quite puzzled, I now feel so blessed to know Bob, via Naropa and Windhorse. Bob, thank you for sharing your passion for groups and your willingness to always engage and even be foolish or brilliant. Thank you for your ability to bring spaciousness, playfulness and curiosity to even the seemingly tightest and darkest situations. Thank you for being a bright mirror, a warm heart and clear mind. Thank you for giving of yourself all these years.

Love,

Michelle

Ode to Bob

Gabriel Fortuna

Ask the reader, who is Bob?
Bob is a father and a husband,
The soothsayer to the Unger mob.
Stoic until bikes break green,
And a gleam streams from Bob's wild eyes.
I had interest expressed of wheels and nobs once, and then all
at once (it was at once!)
to the museum.
"This one is for love, this one is for truth, and this one is for
speed!"
As aluminum's dust and steel mixed in humor, cool and warm
with rubber and bolt.
The Eden of grease and valleys filled with tombs of tires;
And he rides through the roads of the shadow of time and fears
no evil.
So he smiles a lot when it comes to love, truth and speed.
A smile so sunlit Apollo is inspired to ride. The dust and steel
are hearts apart from a hair to his mind.
Bob lives, and Bob loves.
Bob rides and Bob teaches.
We've learned a lot.
Ask the reader, who is Bob?
Well fuck, only the road knows.
But I love Bob.

Dan Fox

I've been fortunate to cross paths so many times with Bob since my years in grad school. I will always appreciate his sage advice to me when we had our first child, "Pay your sitters as much as you can. They become like family."

Still, some of my fondest memories are of those years in Bob's classes. Was he deliberately messing with us? It seemed that everything, from the biking shoes to the bobble in his head, was cultivated to create irritation. His was a polarizing, "can't miss" class.

Later, our class hired him to lead us in a large group process. I remember the first day, sitting around trying to look casual, waiting to see what would happen. Eventually, I suggested to Bob that he lead some exercises to give us direction or promote some ice breaking. He quickly chirped, "Oh, that would be a good idea if you were uncomfortable with silence." I was so mad! I couldn't believe my good idea didn't get more deference. After several days and considerable reflection, I decided that he didn't really care at all about my awesome idea, he was just trying to rattle me.

I needed a good rattling.

Valerie Frankfeldt

I was chatting with Bob about a tough couple case, and he commented, "They don't come in for the 411. They wait and come in for the 911," which perfectly summarized my frustration, while helping me laugh at the same time. This was only one of a gazillion unique bon mots over the years that have popped out of Bob's mouth.

I've been friends with Bob since 1978, I think, when I heard him give a fabulous lecture about alcoholism at the alcoholism clinic I worked in and he was the head of the Bellevue Alcoholism Clinic in New York City. He was quite the charismatic one. Then when Paul Geltner and I graduated from the Center for Modern Psychoanalytic Studies almost simultaneously in 1989, we wanted to start a peer supervision group, and Bob immediately came to mind, as he was already a long time Modern Analyst, but had moved to Boulder some years before. I suggested we invite him, even though Paul had never met him, and after the three of us got together (Paul and me on two phones in one or the other of our offices, and Bob out there in his place), we had a perfect triad that has been going strong ever since.

I've always appreciated his advice that if you don't feel guilty about a patient's accusations toward you, you can accept them by attacking yourself or otherwise agreeing. However, if you do feel guilty, it's not a good time to overtly attack yourself. He points out that it's not that helpful to measure one's worth or stuff in terms of whether it's "deserved" or "undeserved." It doesn't really get you anywhere.

Bob is amazingly adept at conceptualizing a patient's dilemma in the whole system in which the person is operating. I think it works well to take the onus off the person for feeling solely responsible for an issue that has a much larger context that is impinging on him (e.g., extended family, multigenerational family, culture, immediate environment, etc.).

Perri Franskoviak

Dear Bob,

You're the master of unmasking, a superb systems thinker, and an inimitable interlocutor. You always got me to think outside the box, and I've taken that experience into my systems-centered work.

Happy birthday! May you continue to ask the question, no matter where and what you are.

Warmly,

Perri

Paul Geltner

Although I'd wanted to choose a particularly emblematic story—a quintessential Bob moment—to illustrate my long relationship with Bob, there are so many threads in this weave that I just can't choose one. There's his proclivity, not matter the situation, to instantly cite a line from Bob Dylan that not only captures the heart of the matter, but deepens and clarifies it while always bringing out the humor in it. There are the scores of cases I've discussed with him over the years, talks in which he inevitably tells me something that I wouldn't have heard anywhere else; his mind and his heart always right in touch with the emotional pulse, never lapsing into cliché or conventional thinking. His uncanny ability to turn an ordinary situation inside out and see something new in it, something unique, something beyond the given.

When I'm struggling with a feeling that I might feel afraid or ashamed of, he is always able to tell me ways in which he has felt it himself, and he always reminds me that no matter what I feel, I'm doing the best I can and it's OK. He is one of those few people in the world to whom I can really say absolutely anything, secure in the knowledge that he can hear it with loving understanding. There are the 25 years that he, Valerie Frankfeldt and I have been meeting, more weeks than not, telling each other about our work and our families and our health and politics and our angst and everything else that we needed to talk about in order to stay half-sane.

And then there are the other things, like how he took my son and me on a bike ride down a mountain in Winter Park, patiently waiting as we crawled along at what must have been a quarter of the speed at which he went, never pushing, always supportive. After we had been riding for about three hours, at which point I was completely exhausted, he said goodbye and went off to ride back up the mountain that we had just descended.

There's the time he came to stay with me and happily took a Bozo spoon to stir his tea. The synchronicity that he and

Val and I all took up singing almost simultaneously, without having discussed it with each other, and then spent some wonderful evenings singing together. There's his wisdom, his humor, his generosity, his commitment, his support, his incredible humbleness, his willingness to accept life's horrors without it dulling his zest for living it. Who else could perform marriages by telling the couples that they are embarking on "the path of disappointment" and have them leave the wedding happy? No, there isn't a single moment that sums it up. Happy Birthday, Bob. And I plan on celebrating many more with you.

Jack Gipple

In the arts, there is a long tradition of painters, writers, and musicians copying the masters of their day, while seeking their own original voice or style. When I met Bob 23 years ago, I was a newly minted psychotherapist and he became the main master I tried to emulate. I couldn't own the title of psychotherapist for myself, but Bob called me a psychotherapist and invited me into the art. I learned to think like a psychotherapist—and learned to use every part of myself, including the things I hated and concealed about myself, in the basic media of oil paints and musical scales I used in my work. Window cleaning, Dylan, push-hands, the Shelter, husband, father, outsider—the elements of my life were all included. Some of my early disasters as a therapist were when I did what I thought Bob would do. I had to learn to use my own voice, not keep copying Bob's. I have only felt encouraged in the fine art of psychotherapy by Bob Unger. The songs I hum are familiar to anyone who has been influenced by Bob too.

Group as Family

Paul Gitterman

I met Bob during the winter of '94/'95 when he facilitated Louis Ormont's visit to Boulder, CO. I was a new member of the American Group Psychotherapy Association and a graduate of the Smith College School for Social Work searching for a group. I spoke to Bob after the talk and he told me about a group he was running for group psychotherapists. 20 years later, I'm still in that group. It's changed and so have I, as well as has my relationship with Bob.

The group is a consultation group and it has expanded from just being for group therapists. Bob runs it as a group. He attends to the dynamics the way he would in any group. As members, we're just more insulated, as it's our professional identities that the group is designed to support. Yet it is this professional relationship of over 20 years that has led to so much personal growth. Bob has stewarded that process through his insight, skillfulness and years of experience, but most importantly through his compassion and unconditional regard.

Group provides an attachment function that continually impresses me. It's more than the sum of its parts: somehow attachment to the group seems to have the capacity to meet early maturational needs. As with any group, the dilemma of membership is a constant tension between the need for affiliation and the need for autonomy. I guess Bob has helped me tolerate that tension so well that I don't need to separate from the group or from him to preserve my autonomy, and yet I still benefit from the affiliation as my career continually develops. It models for me how differentiation from our families of origin and our development of self-in-relation are continual parts of life's journey.

This analogy or experience of group as family is common to most practitioners. This was evident in AGPA's recent annual meeting which had attachment as its theme.

During this meeting I was again reminded of how the family tree of psychotherapy links us practitioners. At AGPA, the Colorado subgroup gathering is the obvious place to meet those linked to Bob as his influence as a therapist, teacher and bike enthusiast permeate many social circles in that community. Yet as we all grow and make life changes, my peers in this group are now spread around the country. I feel fortunate to be a part of such a grouping as I see reflections of Bob in my peers and their own unique way of metabolizing and making use of Bob's influence in their careers and the rest of their lives.

I have been similarly fortunate over the years to introduce others to modern group work, AGPA, and of course Bob. Seeing individuals new to the profession catch a hold of this passion and create their own sense of professional home reminds me of what a privilege it is to have Bob in my life. When first I looked to him to inspire me to be the best professional I could be, I now am grateful that he inspires me to be more fully myself in all of my life.

Thank you, Bob.

David Gross

Sometime around 1973, I got a rather hysterical phone call from a good friend and former lover named Tex. Tex told me that a, hmm, colleague of hers was in jail at Riker's and I needed to go bail her out. I went. It was a woman named Jeanne. I bailed her out and fell in love with her. She moved into my apartment in Brooklyn with me and, after a few months, told me she knew someone from her hometown and thought he lived in the city. That person turned out to be Bob Unger. I had just gotten my first motorcycle and when Jeanne called Bob, she found out that he had a motorcycle as well.

It turned out that we had a lot in common. Motorcycles, cats, Bob Dylan, CBGB's. Bob and I became very, very close. We went on a lot of bike rides together. In fact we once went on a two week trip across New England and through Nova Scotia with another friend of ours named Don. It was a heck of a blast. So, that's how I came to know Bob. I could tell you a lot more, but I'm afraid I'd be like one of those old men who just drones on and on and on about the good old days and how things were different when he was a kid. I'm not going to risk that.

Well, OK, let me drone on just a bit more. Sometime in the late 80's, I had made a decision to fly to Boulder, there to join Unger in his little red pickup truck with his BMW on the back and drive to San Jose, California. We were going to ride down the Pacific Coast Highway to Laguna Seca, there to catch the US GP (Grand Prix) bike race. Our purpose was twofold. First, of course, was to watch the race. Laguna Seca is always a great place to watch the race and back in the day the Americans had taken over the world of Moto GP. Our secondary purpose was to join up with our friend Don Blair and to ride back with him from Laguna Seca to Boulder, there to entertain ourselves with the sights of the city.

Everything went swimmingly at the race. Someone won. I don't remember who. We had met up with Blair. At the end of the weekend, having partied with many of our friends, the three of us took off eastward across California in Unger's little red pickup truck, with the BMW in the back. About an 18 or 20 hour trip. So, we took turns driving. Bob took the first shift getting us a lot of the way through California on Route 6, by which time night had fallen. Being an early-to-bed, early-to-rise kind of man, Bob decided to get some sleep. The only place to do that was in the back of the little red pickup truck, nestled next to his BMW. Blair was driving.

Bob had given us incredibly explicit instructions that when we came to the intersection of Route 93, we were under no circumstances to turn right onto 93, but to stay on Route 6. 93 led directly into Las Vegas, a place Bob then abhorred as much as I and Dr. Hunter S. Thompson. I was in the passenger seat and fell into a wee snooze. When I awakened, I looked at one of the road signs, you know, the ones that tell you what mile marker it is and what route you're on. In any event, I looked at the sign and said to Blair, "Don, did you turn right onto 93?" He said, "Uh, yeah, I guess." "Holy crap!" I said, "We're headed directly into Las Vegas."

Well, I looked at the map and saw that we had passed the "go/no go" point and it would take longer to turn around than to forge onward. I figured that as long as we were headed there, there was nothing to be done but to pull a stunt on Bob. Blair and I talked it over and decided that we should lock Bob in the back of the little red pickup truck, park it in front of the gaudiest casino we could find, go out and take a walk around, and then come back and see what had happened to Bob. Had he been arrested? Destroyed the little red pick up truck trying to escape? Gone over the edge? About 20 miles outside of Vegas, we heard a pounding coming from the back of the truck and realized that Bob had awakened, seen the glow of Las Vegas on the horizon, and realized what happened.

Having been foiled in our plot, we decided to carry on, driving through Nevada without stopping, thence into Arizona. At three or four in the morning, we decided it was time to stop. We were in the desert of Arizona. It was, as I said, three or four in the morning and dark. We decided that, in honor of Dr. Hunter S. Thompson, we should roll up a big fat doobie, lie on the hood of Bob's little red pickup truck and smoke it. We did that. What we didn't realize was that that was the night of the Perseid meteor shower. So there we were, the three of us, lying on the hood of Bob's little red pickup truck in the depths of the Arizona desert, stoned out of our minds, while the night sky exploded above us. There is nothing else I need to say.

How I Met Bob

Stephen Hansen

I first met Bobby Unger at Bridgehampton Racetrack on Long Island, New York in 1979. I had picked up an Italian motorcycle in Italy the year before and decided I needed to race it. These were small club races that happened about once a month during the warm season. I actually drove the thing to the racetrack with a small bag of tools and my girlfriend on the back. Once there and on my own trying to prepare the motorcycle, I needed to borrow a tool, so I walked over to a trailer with three Italian bikes parked behind it more or less ready to race. I was impressed and realized immediately providence had brought me to the right place. These three bikes belonged to David Gross (one of my best friends to this day!), a guy named Ron Roth, and Bob Unger.

Bob's bike was by far the most magnificent, a Ducati 900SS, silver with blue racing stripes, and definitely worth salivating over. Already a classic. I remember walking back over to my bike and telling my girlfriend, "Hey, there are some cool guys over there all with Italian bikes!" Before long Bob and David came over to where I was parked and checked up on me, offering some ideas and suggestions. When the race that I had entered began, Bob was lined up right in front of me on the starting grid. When the flag dropped, Bob just took off and disappeared pretty much by the first corner! I remember being amazed with how quickly it all happened. I mean really, he was gone like a shot! I think Bob won that race. There was one other guy who was pretty fast and the whole thing was really between those two. I got my head down and kept going and after a few laps I think I was fifth or so. I crashed in the sand at the end of the back straight. That night, looking at my once pristine machine now with scratches and dust all over it, I did some soul-searching and wondered if I really wanted to do this to my still relatively new machine. I decided yes, I was going to go back the next day, Sunday, and try again. And it was the same thing: Bob was there, in front of me at the start, and then he just disappeared down the straight. But at least this time I kept it all together and finished second! I was hooked. I also had some new friends.

That was the beginning of my long and lovely friendship with Bob. I learned Bob grew up in California in a town not that far from where I grew up. He was from the high desert. I was from the low desert. Hmmm . . . Maybe that's why he was so much faster than me.

So, that was the start. We ended up going to the track and pitting together. I never got close to beating Bob, but later that year he ended up blowing up his engine during a race. He had decided he was going to try synthetic oil, which was a new thing then, to lubricate his motor. I was wary and I think even Bob wasn't completely certain. But anyway, I'm pretty sure that was Bob's last race. The time and expense of rebuilding that engine pretty much put the kibosh on his racing after that. I did get him to race my bike once however after that. The club had an endurance race Labor Day weekend each year. It was a four hour race where you put together a team of drivers who switch off during the race. I asked Bob to team up on my bike, and another guy Ed James, whom we had met at the racetrack and was a friend of that third guy from before, Ron Roth. We made the podium with a second place finish.

Time went by and Bob's marriage fell apart. At this point, he decided to leave New York and move to Colorado. He didn't know anybody out there, but that's where he wanted to go. He drove himself and what belongings he wanted out there and recorded a couple of tapes of his thoughts as he was driving and sent them back to the gang in New York. He was really putting himself out there . . . going off to a new world and a new life for himself. You could tell it was not the easiest thing for him to do, but it was something he had to do.

When he first got to Boulder he wanted to make a living doing woodworking. He had a small workshop which I visited where he was making wooden bowls on a lathe and wanted to market them. I think that lasted maybe two years. Then he changed his path once more, this time going back into psychotherapy, which is what he had been doing when I met him.

It was at this time that he met the love of his life, Helena. I've always been so happy that he and Helena got together because they are two of the most wonderful people I know. Bobby has always been a joyous, upbeat, positive, thoughtful and smart person, and Helena is the perfect partner. I love them both.

Bob, I just want to say that even though you are much, much, much older than I am, you still look pretty good!

No, really what I want to say is that I've been very lucky with the friends I've made and kept over the years. My life has been happy and so much richer because of them.

Thank you, Bob, and Helena too.

Obviously, the people of Boulder have been very lucky to have had you around for the last 35 years or so as well. Thank you for all you have given by just being who you are.

Oh, and Happy Birthday!

Theresa Harding

Bob and I arrived at Rocky Mountain Dharma Centre the same day in early December 1981. We had both just left untenable, painful situations. I hoped my time at the meditation centre would set me on a path to peace of mind and sound life decisions; he hoped for a good job.

While I have enjoyed telling Bob's aspiration like it was a punch line, it wasn't long until he got the job, the girl, the kids, the house—the whole shebang—and he also got peace of mind and makes sound life decisions. Who's laughing now, eh?

Bob and I have much in common—love of motorcycles, Bob Dylan, and family—and this difference: Bob puts in the time, effort, and discipline to give the best of himself to everything he does and those he meets. He rides 50K as the sun rises, brings family and friends to his debut singing performance, and coaches his sons for success in school and work. On the surface these might seem ordinary, but each is a story with many chapters threaded together with extraordinary care and attention. Similarly, the 100-plus contributors to Bob's Festschrift are the tip of the mountain of those who have been touched by his wisdom and compassion.

We each have many stories about how Bob has made the world a better place and our life more meaningful, or love more radiant. Casting my mind across the decades, I pause to absorb a realization: the moments most eloquent were conversations on life's struggles, when Bob walked me to the water and left me to choose how and when to see my reflection. These were powerful expressions of trust and friendship that inspired profound changes in me.

My grandmother used to say, "Show me your friends and I'll tell you who you are." I don't mean to brag, but Bob's a very, very dear friend. Such a brilliant, penetrating mind and such a kind, gentle heart—our Bob.

Festive Festschrift filled with friends and family, Bob!

Love always, Theresa

Greg Harms

Bob,

Your steadfast commitment to the care and growth of the staff at the Boulder Shelter is laudable. Over the years, you have helped to create a culture of dignity and safety at the Shelter staff meetings. A culture that will endure, I hope, long after both of us have moved on from the Shelter. Thank you again for your generosity, dedication and wisdom in working with the Shelter staff as we serve the less fortunate in our community.

Greg Harms

Mike Harris

In my second year at Naropa, I was confronted by the program administration who became convinced that I didn't have what it takes to be a psychotherapist. Bob learned of my struggle and called me on the phone. He invited me to come to his office that Saturday so we could talk further about the administration's concerns and my reactions. He agreed to shed any light he could. Feeling desperate, I took him up on his offer.

That Saturday I met with Bob. I was struggling to understand why he agreed to meet with me on the weekend and to figure out if I could trust him or not. I was whirling with an array of feelings toward Naropa and toward the MACP's administration. I told Bob that I was thinking about giving up and dropping out of school. I felt like I was too sensitive to be a good psychotherapist. The three years of experience I already had in the field were a mistake. If I could have been somehow emotionally tougher, then I wouldn't have taken the character attacks so personally.

Bob sat back in his chair and listened to me self attack and cave. Then he leaned forward and cut me off (Bob has always cut me off at just the right time.) He started talking to me about how the very traits that were being criticized were exactly the strengths I needed to be a good psychotherapist. I cannot recall exactly what he said to me that Saturday, but eventually I started to relax and looked around his office. I came to the conclusion that I could be a psychotherapist.

I had a FLAG meeting the following week. Bob volunteered to be at that meeting and support me. I still feel deep gratitude toward him for doing that. Bob started the meeting before anyone else could speak with what I now know is a classic Bob "Prognostic" intervention. He told the group, "Let's start by going around the room and saying how uncomfortable we all want this meeting to be on a scale of 1 to 10 with 10 being the most pleasant we can imagine—a day at the beach." He then said that he'd go first, "Of course," and threw out the number 10. That was the first time in my life that

I felt joined. I don't remember much else that transpired in that meeting, but I learned the value I could bring into other people's lives by being available and taking some risk.

I've been meeting with Bob at least every two weeks but often weekly in either an individual or a group setting for supervision/consultation since then. That's been a decade now. Every accomplishment I've made I can look around and see Bob standing there smiling. I have what I have today because of Bob Unger.

Steve Henne

My first reaction upon meeting Bob, then my professor in group psychotherapy in my first year of graduate school, was anger and outrage. 25 years ago he taught me in a series of classes on group psychotherapy at Naropa University. He ran our classes like a large group, weaving in an examination of the group contract, helping members bridge and subgroup, holding the boundaries and amazingly exploring all topics.

This outraged me and my fellow students who demanded a regularly structured class. Where were the lectures?! Where were the videos? Where were the carefully scripted group examples that were the standard for the teaching of group psychotherapy? And how were we, all 40 of us, expected to learn from the "experience"?! We certainly hadn't signed up for this!

Carefully we scoured the assigned readings searching for understanding and meaning. The brave ones challenged him while others defended him and many of us began to dimly understand that something else was happening. Each group he would start on time, weaving the group together, exploring the resistances boldly and helping to resolve them patiently and kindly. Self-destructive behaviours started to emerge in us. Members started arriving late, others skipping class altogether. Others would pout and sulk, some would debate and argue endlessly and still others go on and on about this theory or that. And Bob continued to explore. Carefully focusing first on the group destructive resistances then on other group-as-a-whole themes. He helped members through careful and thoughtful interventions. And all the while he was teaching, if only we could open our understanding to what was happening.

Oh, there were mistakes aplenty! And how gleeful we were when they occurred, running off together after each group to discuss and dissect each one. But Bob faced all of them in group exploring them relentlessly and courageously. I slowly began to see that almost anything could be explored and be a source of learning.

After each class, small groups of us would gather to discuss and debate interventions, explore themes and complain about our very dear narcissistic injuries. But something else was beginning to happen. We were starting to grow. We began to see how others responded to us. My characteristic style of silence and anxiety in groups endlessly failed to give me the nurturance I needed. I initiated some very small and tentative changes and realized to my great surprise that I did not die! With time and Bob's careful guidance, I began establishing myself and saw that there were a variety of reactions to everyone's behavior.

I started running my own groups. I saw how my internal reactions, thoughts and feelings were part of an intersubjective field created by all of us in the group. I saw the value of working though my resistances in my own supervision with Bob and how this made me a better group leader.

As group leader, I was thrown into a variety of situations. At first awkwardly and then more boldly, I started to take my seat as the leader. I first used imitation, mimicking interventions and even Bob's mannerisms with the hope that if that was how Bob did it then it should work for me! However, after many failures during which Bob patiently analyzed my work, I realized that I had my own style and my confidence began to grow.

I began to see what a group could really do. There is a magical power of bringing people together, with a thoughtful contract designed to encourage and explore resistances in words. I also began to see that my resistance as well as others' were protective mechanisms from real or imagined pain. That they were to be worked with gently and kindly and fearlessly. I learned that the first step was developing an awareness of these resistances by putting them into words. I learned that instigating exploration, developing cohesion and encouraging individuation were wonderfully powerful and transformative. And that the kindness and care of both the group leader and the group members allowed new and helpful behaviors to emerge. I and others could practice these behaviors thereby rewriting our past in a new, open and clear manner. And finally I learned that all this was wonderful.

For these precious gifts and the benefit they give, I thank Bob. I have found Bob Unger to be an intelligent, ethical and incredibly brave man. He is an extremely talented group psychotherapist who has generously helped me as a therapist, as a mentor and as a friend. He has brought two powerful worlds together for me, Buddhism and group psychotherapy and shown me that they are really one and the same.

A Biker, the Wedding, and a Superstar Maker

Adrianne Renee Holloran

When I think of Bob, I am always struck by one of my first memories of him: arriving to class having just unsaddled from his bike, wearing shorts, bike shoes, a button down dress shirt, and a tie. I remember feeling a bit thrown off by his attire, feeling both mystified and inspired. This guy was teaching my graduate level class? My preconceived notion of what a graduate school professor's attire would look like was completely thrown—just as I was about to experience in digesting his class materials and class process. I felt liberated and simultaneously challenged by almost everything he said in class and learned quickly that Bob really trusted his students' ability to tolerate frustration and put our impulses into words. I often felt very annoyed by this but ultimately, deeply grateful that anyone could believe that we were mature enough to handle anything that came our way. After all, we were training to be therapists.

Before saying any more about Bob, it seems relevant to mention that I credit him with at least some responsibility in helping me to meet my husband, Matthew. Bob and his lovely wife Helena routinely held their annual garden party at their home in honor of the first year students. I arrived to the party and when I approached the front door, unbeknownst to me, my husband-to-be happened to be inside the house and near the front door. Upon my knock, he swung open the door and we greeted one another. Sparks were surely flying, but it's hard to remember exactly what happened. Later that evening, we spent some time talking and maybe even flirting on the steps in the Unger's living room. Had it not been for those garden parties, would I have ever met my amazing husband?

Bob has been my private practice clinical supervisor for at least a few years. I feel incredibly grateful for his support, his suggestions, his gentle guidance and reminders. At times I've struggled with an idealized father transference with Bob, imagining he knows how to handle any situation. He always seems to know exactly what to say. Due to that transference, I also have a desire to make him think I am brilliant, his brightest and most favorite supervisee. But with my attempts to impress him, I often feel anxious and I think, "It's Bob!" In my mind, I turn him into an icon. But then, I just recall that first image of Bob entering class in his bike shorts and tie and I remember that he's human. When I spoke to him about my anxiety in our sessions he asked me, "Well, are you having fun in our supervision meetings?" Since then, I've stopped trying (and probably failing anyway) to impress him and have realized how much easier and enjoyable it is to make "having fun" my goal. What a relief.

Bob has such a warm presence. I bring him any of my challenging client scenarios, waiting to befuddle him just once but that still hasn't happened. In one client case, I shared about a young woman who was struggling in relationship with her alcoholic boyfriend. She had a belief about herself that she was "too intense" and imagined that this intensity would be the reason her boyfriend would leave her. Bob suggested that I help her to learn to reside in her own intensity and to ask, "Who taught you that you were too intense?" He suggested, "Be intense *with* her." This was such a great example of empathy and compassion: that I could enter into the feeling state with my client to understand her better and help her to accept herself as she was. And, a good reminder of everything we learned at Naropa. Thanks, Bob.

The Generosity of Disappointment

Matthew C. Holloran

The night after hearing about this festschrift, I had a dream about Bob. It went something like this:

> Me and my family were at Bob's home for dinner. We were there for a birthday celebration. I felt awkward in the dream in part because we were planning to have dinner again later. As I was leaving, my children appeared and proceeded to throw Bob's exercise ball out of the window. I also noticed that I had left my mountain bike in his dining room. I grew anxious when suddenly I realized many others had left bikes in the room as well. I relaxed and thought that Bob can accept us leaving our stuff around his house or throwing his stuff out of the window.

While I'll let the dream analysts do what they will with this, the dream points to two themes that I want to touch on in my reflections about Bob. In one sense, these themes correlate with a personal experience of Bob (generosity) and a clinical experience (disappointment). Yet, as I hope to make clear, ultimately these two traits or experiences are intimately connected and can come together in the therapeutic situation and serve as the heart of interpersonal interactions.

Fundamentally what I have learned from Bob's modeling and supervision is that becoming aware of my feelings and risking being viewed as a disappointment could be a manifestation of a clinician's generosity. It seems that disappointment is a part of life. Being a disappointment to others is part of being human and can be a real gift from a clinician. Learning to allow disappointment, to feel it, and to let others have it is fundamentally healing and confirming of our humanity. As with most things: easier said than done. But let me at least offer how I have seen these traits manifest in Bob and how I am trying to incorporate them.

Bob has been unspeakably generous to me and many others. His joyful enthusiasm for all things biking is contagious and has helped me re-enter a world of physical competition and training that had long been dormant. Whether offering to meet with me to help pick out my first road bike or agreeing to help another put their bike together from a mail delivery box, Bob joyfully gives his time to others. His generosity is not limited to scorching me on long hill climbs either. He has donated time to the homeless shelter, graciously offered to supervise staff at a local Vet Center, and taught, tolerated, inspired, nursed, befuddled and infuriated countless Naropa students (and quite a few Naropa staff too).

His generosity is particularly clear in the clinical setting. He has a compassionate knack for making clinicians believe in themselves and their ability to do this work, in spite of their "alleged" failures. And specifically, he has an impressive willingness, which I see more clearly all the time, to tolerate his clients' actual experience and examine his own experience at the same time. I have seen him fearlessly let others see his humanity including finding him a disappointment. If you don't believe me, just ask anyone.

The first time I really had a glimpse into this was at one of Bob's championed events, the American Group Psychotherapy Association's annual conference. I was a member of his two-day institute. One group member did not like Bob or his style. Beyond the typical criticism and complaint about Bob's presence and style, she began to level very personal attacks. She likened him to her "terrible" mother and attacked his physical appearance. I was appalled. However, Bob listened closely and seemed to take her words in. He did not defend or deflect. He did not try to explain his approach or try to make her feel better. Indeed, he did nothing to change her experience or try to soften her words. He was generous in letting her have her experience including her perspective that he was a terrible disappointment to her. What really made this experience stand out was that at the end of the two days this group member said something to the effect that she did not like his style of leadership but had learned a lot in the group.

Through this experience, I began to understand that just being nice or doing familiar things that align with what I think a client "wants" doesn't necessarily benefit that client. Indeed I am starting to consider how it might do the opposite. As summed up by the folk singer Claudia Schmidt, "There is fail in familiar." I tend to believe that everyone who gets into this profession has some unconscious desire to make others feel better. But I have begun to see how this tendency can actually undermine the process of a client learning to trust their actual experience. For example, polite often mechanical acts can accidently serve to cut off a client's chance to feel and express disappointment. When I am running late, I have started to realize that I say, "I'm sorry I was late" before allowing a client a chance to express anything about my lateness. I used to try to stifle yawns to avoid "offending" or fight desperately to hide my heavy, tired eyes.

Perhaps a more substantive facet of this came up recently in an interaction with a recovering opiate addict. As we talked it became apparent that she, like everyone, has other addictions. We described this newly identified addiction as "the Addiction To Approval." As we talked it became clear that this client had a relationship with approval that was very much like using a drug. If she didn't get it, she felt withdrawal and would go to great lengths to find it, even when those lengths were ultimately self-destructive. Have you ever said yes to something when you really wanted to say no? Don't worry, that is only one of the symptoms. If she was able to get the approval, she would receive the rush of safety and satisfaction and for a brief time the anxiety of disapproval (just like the sickness of physical withdrawal) would abate. However, satisfaction, happiness, and peace were always tied to the need to get approval: approval from a boss, a partner, a grocery clerk, a parent, maybe even her therapist. Perhaps the corollary would be that her peace and happiness were tied to avoiding having others feel disappointment.

But this recognition brought up a dilemma for me. I like to be liked too. I don't want to make others feel unpleasant feelings when I think it is avoidable. I was raised to be (or have some character trait to be) likeable . . . though some might quibble with that. I want to be someone who is helpful, not frustrating, a person that makes others feel good, makes them laugh, shows compassion, etc. In this session, I saw that in my own countertransference response to this client, I was likely to consciously or unconsciously be used as the drug and at the same moment at risk for taking my own hit. I wondered internally how she might try to seek my approval and how I might try not to feel or show disappointment.

Without the experience of Bob's tutelage and perhaps more importantly the experience of watching how he lets clients be in their experience, irrespective of whether they approve of him, indeed perhaps in spite of it, I might have just tried to mollify this client. Instead, I tried to be mindful of my urge as well as her need. I tried to remember that this dynamic would arise again and again in our sessions and to consider the notion of letting a client have their full experience including being angry or frustrated at me or feeling like treatment is not "helpful." Too often as humans our so called "negative feelings" are pushed aside. We are shamed for disliking someone, for feeling it and especially for saying it.

None of this is to say that I only see Bob through eyes of disappointment. I have seen him show anger, sadness, ebullience, patience, confusion and of course drowsiness. This modeling has made me more fearless in my own work as a clinician and thus as a person, husband and father too. It has made me ponder my own "failures through [acting] familiar."

I am beginning to learn that my disappointment is my own. It is in my eyes, my experience, and my feelings, as they interact with Bob letting himself show up with little fear of my reaction. And in that way, I have softened in my fear of disappointing him and grown more comfortable with others feeling disappointed in me. I realize that others too have left "bikes in his dining room" or "thrown his goods out the window." Perhaps the dream is a reminder that it is okay to be imperfect, to risk disappointing others so they too can feel their own anxiety of being a disappointment. That holding that possibility might give the client an opportunity for their own insight that someone can tolerate their imperfections, their disappointing habits and love them literally "none the less."

So Bob, here's to you and your generous and unflagging persistence in being yourself and letting me have my disappointment. Dr. Spotnitz would be proud. As a branch on the tree of lineage, I hope to carry this legacy into the uncertain but certainly disappointing future.

Phillip Horner

Bob is a gentle soul whose wisdom comes out just at the moments you need them. He has provided so many learning opportunities for me and has helped my growth as a therapist continue to blossom in the short time I have had the privilege of working with him. His ability to hold space even in non-traditional therapy moments has allowed me to understand dual relationships and enlightened me to my own anxiety around complex relationships in a small town. Small words from him have made large impacts in my life and I am very grateful to continue to work with Bob.

MacAndrew Jack

"Come in," she said, "I'll give you shelter from the storm." (Dylan, 1975a)

I was excited to get an interview for a faculty position at Naropa University. I was particularly excited because I had been told by my contact for the department, "Bring your biking shoes and pedals if you want to ride."

This was to be the first contact, the foreshadowing of Bob Unger's welcoming, generous style which he extended to me like he has to many others, since that first contact. This open handed gesture would be repeated and elaborated with both reliability and freshness as we both aged a decade, working together, riding together, and joking together.

> You used to be so amused
> At Napoleon in rags and the language that he used.
> Go to him now, he calls you, you can't refuse.
> When you got nothing, you got nothing to lose.
> You're invisible now, you got no secrets to conceal.
> (Dylan, 1965)

One elaboration, not obvious at first, lies in the way that Bob listens. Behind squinting eyes, his gaze is not always knowable. With periodic punctuations of mouth clicking, head nodding, or coos, it is clear that he is present with the conversation. Deeply present. In meetings, I got the sense that Bob is listening to so much. For so much. He is following the trail, and the echoes, the undertones and the overtones. He tracks history, trajectory, and turn of phrase. Master listening from one whose professional life has included enough listening to hear harmonics among the notes of conversations.

"I often listen to tones more than words," Bob once told me, not nearly as breathless as I, as we climbed elevation on our mountain bikes, amidst an open pine forest outside Boulder.

While I wished to hear more specifics: what kinds of tones? Strains, sharps and flats, lifts and drops? My oxygen starved brain could barely elaborate my own questions, as Bob, ever fit and lithe, a superb climber on any set of human powered wheels, had said enough for himself, and we continued to climb in silence. The possibility of riding alongside Bob on a climb was a motivation to get stronger, gain more aerobic capacity so as to not be dropped on the uphills while he spritely danced on his pedals when I wanted to stop for a rest but could not ask. He would stop of course, if I actually asked. But, being more than 20 years younger than Bob, I used Bob like the ultimate pacer: if I could keep him in sight, I would grow. And I couldn't always do that on the trail. Few can.

Mama, put my guns in the ground.
I can't shoot them anymore. (Dylan, 1973)

The same holds true of Bob talking about people. If you can keep him in sight, you grow. If you can see where Bob is coming from, you will grow in your humanity. Bob's recognition of motives, vulnerabilities, and his sensitivity to those in his responses show his decades in the field of psychotherapy, in his own therapy, providing therapy to others, and of course his supervision of others. He can point out the exquisite variations of ego's vulnerabilities, strivings, and aggressions. Yet rarely if ever do you hear judgment, disparagement, or criticism of all this ego activity which, in the context of a graduate program training in Buddhist psychology, shows his incredible restraint. As the listener, I would hear the descriptions of ego, and I would fill in the gaps with my own exasperation at the suffering radiating from ego actions of the client or student or colleague being described. Yet Bob's words do not betray such exasperation. There may be a hint in what is not said, but his discipline with such aggression is impeccable.

This leads to another quality that I associate with Bob that is akin to the Hippocratic oath: first do no harm. So often, when a conversation heats up, I see him literally close his mouth and tuck his chin down. I imagine that he is creating a pause, possibly brief or possibly indefinite, in which he is listening to his impulses, and purifying out any of his own aggression before it pops out in words or deed. In a world where so much of our suffering is apparent, and hurt bounces off and amplifies when it springs off another hurt, Bob's contribution to this ricocheting world of suffering is remarkable for following the Hippocratic oath: first do no harm.

Now, I am not always prepared for this in a friend. In fact, I am relieved when, among my friend circle of psychologists and therapists, we can drop the professional role and "shoot straight" with each other. I am used to a certain amount of teasing and horseplay. So with Bob, I am sometimes disarmed at how a friend can be so careful at how much repartee he engages in. It is not that he doesn't reveal his own ego process, defensiveness, and paranoia. It's that he is careful to not direct it at anyone. Like shooting his gun out over the ocean, Bob doesn't give his ego the satisfaction of aggressively "landing" its impulses.

> My pathway led by confusion boats,
> mutiny from stern to bow.
> Ah, but I was so much older then,
> I'm younger than that now. (Dylan, 1964)

This also doesn't mean that Bob stays out of the local dramas. In fact, at one point, he talked to one of his close friends, who was a board member above my boss. When it came out that he had, as far as I could tell, raised a scrutinous eye at some of my boss's behavior to this friend, I was alarmed. I had to work with this person, my boss, and felt that somehow if the hornet's nest was going to be poked, I was going to be the closest person when the hornets came for retribution. I was upset about this, and, trusting our relationship, told him that I was uncomfortable about what he had done. Unfortunately, we were in line together at the campus cafe when I said this to him. He shortly after told me that he was uncomfortable with me raising my concern with him, my upset at him, in a public place, with others around. Here we were, two friends, in conflict. We both had our insecurities about our supervisors' power over us, and how this was going to be used. Even though he was a senior faculty member, in this situation, I was the chair of the department and thus his supervisor, of sorts. Complicated, mixed hierarchies. As we let the situation cool down, we discussed our hurts and fears as well as how much we valued our friendship.

Although it could have been a completely unrelated interaction, I remember this whole interchange ending, as many things happen with Bob, over bikes. He was upgrading his road bike components and thus selling his "old" components, en masse. His "old" components were, of course, several steps up from those on my road bike, so we agreed on a price and I bought them from him. The best part was that he agreed to help me transfer the parts over to my bike, which basically involved several hours in his garage, tinkering with bike parts, using his vast array of tools, ending with a finished product of my bike, now upgraded with the high end components that came off his bike. Along the way I saw how he dismantled and assembled bikes, and felt his generosity and massive peace offering. My bike was now whole again, as was our friendship.

> We live and we die, we know not why
> But I'll be with you when the deal goes down.
> (Dylan, 2006)

There is something about the way that Bob welcomes and is unshaken by conflict and powerful emotions. It allows me and, I think, others, to spend a little more time in my bruises, my paranoia, my petulance and my defensiveness. In spending this time, I come to befriend, understand, and, sometimes, even voluntarily release my hold on these parts of myself. And on the other side I emerge feeling joined, more understood, and even more understandable. In all of my humanness.

So when you see your neighbor carryin' somethin'
help him with his load.
And don't go mistaking Paradise
for that home across the road. (Dylan, 1967)

Who but Bob can turn disappointment into such an uplifted thing? One of Bob's pieces of writing and contributions to the interface of psychotherapy and Buddhism is a paper entitled "Psychoanalysis and Buddhism: Paths of disappointment" (Unger, 2008). I read his chapter as a chapter about liberation. Liberation from the tyranny of one's wishes and expectations, from the oppression of one's ego-driven impulses. All the while, his chapter never falls into the trap of demonizing our humanness, of rejecting or ostracizing our hopes and expectations. Rather he brings us along to look at our actual lives, to look at the way that we are constantly disappointed, and through that experience we naturally let go a bit more.

After spending time with Bob, I naturally feel more where-I-am. I am grateful for his presence in my life, and particularly, for the way that he provides shelter for us all, including our brand new leopard-skin pill-box hat (Dylan, 1975).

References

Dylan, B. (1964). My back pages. On *Another Side of Bob Dylan* [CD]. New York: Columbia.
Dylan, B. (1965). Like a rolling stone. On *Highway 61 Revisited* [CD]. New York: Columbia.
Dylan, B. (1967). The ballad of Frankie Lee and Judas Priest. On *John Wesley Harding* [CD]. New York: Columbia.
Dylan, B. (1973). Knockin' on heaven's door. On *Pat Garrett and Billy The Kid: Soundtrack for the Motion Picture* [CD]. New York: Columbia.
Dylan, B. (1975). Leopard skin pillbox hat. On *Blonde on blonde* [CD]. New York: Columbia.

Dylan, B. (1975a). Shelter from the storm. On *Blood on the Tracks* [CD]. New York: Columbia.

Dylan, B. (2006). When the deal goes down. On *Modern Times* [CD]. New York: Sony Music

Unger, R. (2008). Psychoanalysis and Buddhism: Paths of disappointment. In F. Kaklauskas, L. Hoffman, S. Nimmanheminda, & M. Jack (Eds.). *Brilliant Sanity: Buddhist Approaches to Psychotherapy*. Colorado Springs, CO: University of the Rockies Press.

Marc Jalbert

I've known Bob for over 25 years. We met near Boulder and have spent literally thousands of hours together, mostly side-by-side on several generations of bicycles. I can tell you a lot about his likes, dislikes, successes, failures, and more minutia then you care to know, such as what the perimeter of his mouth looks like after a two hour road bike climb up some local canyon. Hint: it's not pretty. It has to do with his ability to talk non-stop while exercising at maximum capacity, which is a rare skill.

Lately, I've been thinking about something I read in the Huffington Post about a scientific experiment using rats and something called a "rat park." The experiment involved giving rats unlimited water laced with heroin or cocaine, and then later introducing the rats into a fabulous rat park with all kinds of rat amenities, such as colorful balls, great rat-food, fun tunnels, and plenty of rat friends. In other words, Boulder for rats.

Surprisingly, these addicted Boulder rats mostly shunned the drugged water in their new rat park and went on to live happy lives, while their counterparts in crappy rat cages became very heavy drug users. Some even died. Other studies were done with people with similar results, but I prefer to discuss rats, because I think they are easier for me to understand.

The moral of the story was this: Addiction is a well-known concept. However, the opposite of addiction is not sobriety (and Bob is mostly sober), but is, instead, human connection. Bob connects on a deep level with more people then I can count, and yes, I can still count. It's a marvelous quality, and one that very, very few people can lay claim to. Right now, Bob is probably having his third or fourth social coffee of the day with someone that will walk away from the encounter with a big smile on his or her face. I know I'm smiling now. Thanks for being you, Bubka!! And . . . I'm glad you chose Boulder over Newark.

Bob and the "F Word"

Gretchen Kahre

I met Bob long ago in the late 1980's at Naropa where he led some workshops on large groups. Fast forward to 2002. I had been working for over 10 years at an agency in Boulder and had said the "F word" to a very disturbed, entitled and irritating psychotic client. I was sent to Bob by my supervisor. To date, my work with Bob has been the best "punishment" ever. When I first met with him individually about joining a supervision group I felt I had to tell him why I was there. It was a confession of sorts. I humbly told him I was sent by my supervisor and I had said the "F word" to a client. Bob, in his Bob-like way, said that one of the things I might learn in a group is how to, for all practical purposes, say "f you" with out saying "f you". He didn't suggest that I clean up my act, but explore my impulses to say "f you", for instance, and have it be of benefit rather than get me in trouble. That sounded great to me! In the words of his wife, Helena, "I was having the right feelings," but I was impulsively acting on those feelings and getting in trouble.

My time with Bob in his supervision group has been the single most effective tool to make my work easier and actually enjoyable. When with a client, or anyone actually, I often hear Bob's voice and tone in my mind. I don't hear an actual phrase but more of a tone of playful curiosity. That tone has a hint of naughtiness to it. I've learned how to say things that will land an "f you" when necessary and not get in trouble over it but actually be an effective intervention.

My training with Bob dovetails with my understanding of Buddhist principles, mainly that of non-violence. How does learning to effectively use "f you" relate to non-violence? It is a way of being inclusive and not rejecting anything that comes up in the mind. The mind, especially the unconscious, is not politically correct and doesn't limit itself to only soothing thoughts or feelings.

Bob's supervision has helped me to be curious and inclusive of everything that arises in my mind in the context of a therapy session, not just the things that make me look good or feel good. I'm not certain that I would still be in the field of psychotherapy without Bob's insistent confidence and support. He has never given me the impression that I am too inexperienced or too anything to do this work. He has only given me the impression that I can trust my intelligence and instincts to do good work and that I can utilize any situation that might be labeled as a "mistake" to get more information about my own induction. He has given me the incentive to prove him right.

Francis J. Kaklauskas

Soon after my graduation from Naropa, I bumped into Bob in the grocery store aisle. He congratulated me and then said, "Francis, I have one word for you, just one word ... (long dramatic pause) . . . Plastics." For me this reference to the classic scene from the movie, "The Graduate," delivered between granolas and paper towels symbolizes a beneficial memorandum that I often got from Bob: to embrace spontaneity and fun and to not let earnestness get the best of you.

The following is adapted from a talk given at Naropa University at the release party for the book *Brilliant Sanity: Buddhist Approaches to Psychotherapy* (Kaklauskas, Hoffman, Nimmanheminda, & Jack, 2008):

Bob has been the major mentor in my personal and professional life. My guess is that many of us have been deeply impacted by Bob's wit, consistency, discipline, and generous heart. He vividly set an exemplary model of behavior and mentorship that I have thoroughly attempted to emulate.

Given Bob's role as faculty in the Contemplative Psychotherapy Department for many years at Naropa, one might expect I would highlight Bob's ability to integrate western and eastern thought, or to say how he could be likened to an enlightened divinity. For me, Bob has been something much more, and something much more simple than a clever scholar or other worldly guru. He has shown me how to be a good man, husband, father, friend, and person. He has also shown me how to be a thoughtful and dedicated clinician, but one who has life balance, personal idiosyncratic passions (i.e. singing, cycling), clear compassionate boundaries, a sense of humor about himself, the mind, and human folly, and an understanding that life is a blessing to be embraced and enjoyed. Bob has all the skills and knowledge, limitations and annoyances, of any other great clinician, but he is a transcendent angel in at least two areas.

Over his forty years of clinical work and training, he has uncovered every flavor, spice, and potency of human aggression. This is certainly true in my experience of him personally and in his work with clients. What is even more important for me though, is that Bob has helped me recognize, accept, and transmute these feelings inside myself. Suicide, revenge, hatred, murderous feelings are not obstacles, but tools once understood with depth and awareness. This aggressive drive, passionately seductive and destructive, he not only knows, but has mastered. He is an emotional alchemist helping people turn poisonous lead and mercury into life affirming gold.

The other quality I have observed in Bob is a thorough dedication to understand and transcend "narcissism," in western terms, or "ego," in Buddhist language. Bob does not champion himself. He champions everyone. He doesn't take sides. He is on everyone's side. He can take the fall, the blame, the hatred, the wrath, so others can continue to move forward on their path. His behavioral choices are in no manner impulsive or self-motivated. He steps in front of oncoming traffic to protect others, and releases these bruises in little bits of rubber from his bike on the roads and mountains of Colorado.

Twenty years ago, when I was an ambitious psychotherapist still in my twenties, I went to Bob's office and asked what I needed to do to be a good therapist. He appropriately endlessly explored this issue. He asked me why I would want to do this, what were my views about this process, and validated my desire. Finally I wore him down, and he told me what I should do: get into analytic therapy with a well trained therapist, get my doctorate, and have a child. His recommendation of Dr. Dolores Welber for therapy has been profoundly life changing for me. My doctorate has helped me understand I am worthy and have the requisite base knowledge, and starting my family gave me a deeper understanding of human development than I could have ever learned in any textbook, in addition to opening my heart more fully than I could have ever imagined. By many accounts, this type of very specific directive intervention may have been a therapeutic mistake. But I took it and ran with it, and now today, I have accomplished these things. I cannot say if I have become a good therapist, but more importantly, I can say that this advice has led to a rich, engaged, and meaningful life.

Right after my son, Levi, was born, my wife, Elizabeth became very ill, and had to be hospitalized. I sat stunned by her bedside holding my new son as an overwhelmed and petrified new father. Now, I don't know if Bob and his wife Helena had to cancel clients, groups, personal engagement, or whatever, but both came to see us, called everyday, and brought us dinner once we came home. They showed me that psychology is not about theories, ideas, and rigid boundaries, but finding ways to help.

The many years of being a member in groups led by Bob and Helena, not only taught me about myself, human nature, the dharma, and the subtleties and power of clinical work, but more importantly inspired me to forever continue to walk along the long path to emotional maturity.

I know you were doing your job, but I cannot thank you enough.

Jack Kirman

To Bob,

It's been such a long time since you have been in New York, and since then, time and age (I'm 81) have so robbed me of my memory that I can no longer recall specific memories (that would be suitable here). But I still have an emotional memory of you as a sprightly, handsome, very intelligent and very decent young man whom I both admired and felt much affection for. In addition to that, I have heard periodically about your fine and appreciated work in Boulder, which accorded with my feelings and expectations. Bob, take heart, the 70's are a piece of cake! Seriously, they have been one of my best decades. Bonne chance et Vive la Vie!

Fondly,

Jack Kirman

(Gratefully) Tangled up in Bob

Chuck Knapp

Though I'd recognized him from dharma gatherings, the first time Bob and I actually met was in the spring of 1985, now 30 years ago. We were both working at the Alcohol Recovery Center and he was presenting on Modern Psychoanalysis to the staff. We'd also known of each other as our wives, his current, my former, were both pregnant and were heading to Rocky Mountain Dharma Center for the 1985 Vajradhatu Seminary. As they were taking preparatory classes for seminary, they realized that their husbands both worked at the ARC. So he and I were on the lookout for each other.

I was immediately struck by how much energy he (this dark haired young man) had, how quickly and fluidly his mind worked, how thoroughly grounded he appeared to be in the analytic training, and how fearless he was. To the last point, he began the group by asking what people knew about Modern Psychoanalysis and he especially wanted to hear anything negative that we had to say. Unlike so many trainings I'd been a part of, from the outset Bob was not in any way encouraging the group to make nice. That invitation seemed to energize and free the group to play, take risks, speak our minds, and to interact. I was straightaway attracted to his courageous approach, and was very curious about him as a person.

Fortunately and in short order, he and I, our wives, and eventually our children (two boys each), became very close friends. Intensive group retreats, pregnancies, and learning to be the parents of young children were early shared experiences that created conditions for us to really see ourselves and each other: sanity, neurosis, halos and warts. I was so grateful through that period to be sharing the exploration of what it was to be a parent, how to think about it, and to make it into as much of a path of profound, rich uncertainty as any other element of my spiritual training. I learned so much from Bob and Helena through this period, and as our children grew older, a true intermingling of our households created a situation in which a great deal of co-parenting was going on. This was complete with innumerable injuries of various kinds (including stitches, broken bones and teeth), some very serious illnesses, a recreationally flooded basement, heartbreaks, friendship crises all through the ranks, and always supporting each other to find the workability in the situation.

As time went on, middle age dawned, our parents began dying, our boys were moving along in school, and I went through a divorce. Again, Bob and Helena were such stabilizing presences for the boys and me, including when I began a relationship with my life partner, Ellen. Currently, the boys are all in their mid to late 20s and successfully on their own. Middle age has come and gone, and it is much easier to smell the looming of old age and mortality. It's a very tender thing to have closely shared the arc of this span of life, especially as I've watched Bob show unflagging love for my closest loved ones. I know that Bob's presence has had and continues to have an immense positive effect on the health and success of my family and me, and that my gratitude for this is beyond expression.

Interwoven with our personal life paths, Bob and I were always interested in each other's professional work. I saw him expand into the wonderful community environments of Naropa and the AGPA, where his vivid intelligence and compassion were welcomed and transforming. In particular, his presence in Naropa's Contemplative Psychology Masters department influenced decades of therapists who experienced him as an example of how a truly sensitive and open heart can synchronize with a powerful intellect and terrific sense of humor. The Windhorse Project has been just one of the many beneficiaries of his work with these resilient, skillful, and compassionate graduates, many of whom have become Windhorse staff members. Beyond his influence through the Naropa graduates, Bob has always been a strong supporter of the Windhorse work. This was critically important especially when we were in the early stages of trying to establish a stable presence in the community.

Other than frequent conversations and occasionally attending a workshop he was conducting, we didn't work together during the early years of our friendship. Our first actual professional collaboration began in 1997 when Bob became the psychotherapist on a large and complicated Windhorse team. That step was a joyful landmark for me, as I'd wanted to work with him for years. Fortunately since then, we've managed to seduce him into teamwork on a fairly regular basis. With him in the mix, not only do we have a world-class clinician on board, but also one who really can't help but to enhance the IQ, skillfulness, learning environment, and compassion of that fortunate team.

In 1990 while in the midst of some particularly difficult personal tumult, upon request Bob referred me to a colleague of his for therapy. I eventually did a long-term training analysis with her, and she later became my supervisor for many years. And in 2003, another of my most treasured and transformative professional relationships came about due to his invitation. He and I were discussing a particularly difficult clinical situation and his analysis so succinctly combined human warmth, compassion, and clinical soundness, that I found myself wondering aloud if there was any way that I could spend more time with him and around his way of approaching our work. Nothing came immediately to mind for him, but a few days later he said that his best work and his way of understanding was most embodied by his supervisor, Dr. Leslie Rosenthal. Dr. Rosenthal ran an every-other-week supervision group in Manhattan, which Bob, joining by phone, had been a member of for about 20 years. He asked if I would be interested in joining the group, which for me was an absolutely stunning prospect. True to Bob's assessment, in any way I could understand, Dr. Rosenthal was a completely remarkable person and clinician. About 80 years old when we first met, I was fortunate to have known him for nine years as a supervisor. Sharing that space with Bob and six other deeply experienced supervisees, was and continues to be a place where parts of my mind and insights arise that are uncommon and deeply orienting at all levels of my work. A favorite photograph in my home office is of Bob and Dr. Rosenthal, taken about ten years ago, arm in arm, looking like a father and son who really love each other.

In an effort to keep the length of this offering manageable, I'd like to name in a more concise form some of the most enduring lessons I've learned (and am learning) from Bob's example:

There is Tremendous Freedom, Joy, and Power in Simply Being Yourself

If you know Bob, there's no need for elaboration.

Generosity

This includes generosity in the profound sense of letting go of attachment to one's ego; giving up attachment to winning an argument; being endlessly present for family and friends; supporting the professional development of anyone who is genuinely interested; and working hard at being a helpful member of a supervision group. This also includes generosity toward oneself. As therapists we spend a lot of our time and energy working to help others, and Bob's a champion of being sure to take care of ourselves in the process. I believe that he thinks exercise can be helpful in this regard. His generosity has also included lending a friend in need, money for a rental deposit.

Go into the Energy

Avoiding the emotions at hand, thus energizing resistance and defenses in oneself, in a group, or in one's family, only makes a much bigger and more complicated mess of things. In clinical work, it's takes disciplined and sensitive practice to eventually master discriminating between taking matters prematurely to a painful point, as opposed to moving into emotional energy when its overt recognition is timely. On a personal level, one can take more chances with simply moving into the energy, and some of the most intense and illuminating conflicts I've had in my life, have been with Bob.

Likewise, as a parent, Bob's willingness to tolerate intensity allowed him to be wrathfully insistent at times when that was the difficult but only thing to do.

There is Continuity and Connection Between All Aspects of Life

This became immediately apparent when I first heard him describe clinical work. All aspects of the situation were included, especially elements that we may try to ignore, such as aggression in its many forms. Beyond that, our thoughts, communication, actions, relationships, art, music (especially Dylan's), work, politics, great cosmic patterns, schmutz, and the elegance of bicycles, motorcycles, trains, Sandy Koufax, and well-designed highway systems, are all interconnected. I believe that it's Bob's deep realization of all people's interconnectedness that is the fount of his unflagging compassion.

The Health of Being in Community

Bob has a powerful intelligence toward maintaining healthy relationships with individuals and groups, and he appears to draw a lot of strength from community in general. This also extends to his choice of how he is choosing to live at this stage of his life. Community is one of my great learning edges and I watch him more closely than he probably thinks I do.

One of the great truths shared by dharma teachers is that the essence of wisdom is being of benefit to others. By that measure, Bob embodies robust and graceful wisdom, as a father, spouse, friend, psychotherapist, and teacher. I also believe that one of the measures of a teacher is that they beget and inspire teachers and teaching environments. Bob has trained so many group and individual psychotherapists all across the country, who are now in teaching positions themselves. Likewise, magnetizing a festschrift is a powerful teaching environment in and of itself. As we all know, it's easy to take someone for granted when we spend a lot of time around them, and I hope this festschrift helps us all to raise our awareness of what blessings are, and what a blessing we have in our dear friend, colleague, and teacher. I also hope we can appreciate that Bob will no doubt enjoy the fact that a group of us have on some level, been competing to see who can write the best festschrift offering.

Back again to a personal note, for me one of the great treasures of a close friendship is how much I learn in the presence of that person. Trungpa Rinpoche said that one of the basic points of being in relationship is to explore honesty. With Bob, exploring honesty has always been in play. And I always find that when with him, I learn about such a range of things, from Soupy Sales and Mad Magazine, to Edward Snowden and about simply being a person living in the full catastrophe on a spiritual path. Probably most of all, I learn about my heart.

Ellen Knapp

One of my favorite things about Bob is his irresistible grin. This is usually accompanied by a lot of warm wit and close attention paid to what's being told to him. Really engaging and fantastic to be with.

I mostly know Bob as a friend and primarily in the role of him as a dad. I was introduced to being a parent myself kind of abruptly and not via giving birth, the more predictable way. Rather, I began my relationships with my boys and their dad in a kind of combination plate deal with the Ungers. The boys and Chuck were in a transition from their previous version of family, which was such an unsettling process. But, we had the Ungers. Their boys were exactly the same ages as our boys (about three and six years old) and all four boys were already soul mates. You can't imagine the power of the Ungers' friendship at this time. Bob and Helena completely opened their lives to us all, with love, play, collaboration, endless time to listen, cry and just take in the realities of what was present at that time.

Time went on and there were many weeks, months, years of shared life and ups and downs: boy dramas, boys growing, boys leading us all over the place. We had lots of laughs and fun and lots of other stuff too. And Bob was truly unwavering as a friend, partner and parallel parent. So reliable as a vivid, very energetic pillar of our world. There was the day that Bob's son Dylan was over riding BMX bikes with our son Colin, probably around age 14 (they couldn't drive yet). They had built jumps in our back yard and had taken to flying over the jumps on their bikes, practicing for BMX races, but also just having a fantastic time. So Dylan, with a regular (not full-face) helmet on, decided to take a jump on the edge of the yard from the direction of the yard onto the blacktop driveway. His front wheel caught, turned and he flew over the handlebars and landed on his face—and he had braces on his teeth.

Needless to say it was instant bloody emergency, his teeth on the pavement and no grownups around. Our Colin was amazing. He never wasted a moment to wonder what to do. He ran from house to house on our street, found help and Dylan was taken to the ER where Bob met them. Bob was like Colin. He wasted no time in wondering what to do. And it all turned out, 15 years later, to be just another story, no lingering injuries of any kind on any level. All about explosive fun, total commitment and love and trust and just being with each other.

That is how I know Bob. Plus he's been the truest of friends to me. We don't see each other as often now that the boys are grown but my heartfelt appreciation for him and Helena has roots that go so deep with love and are and will always be part of my blessed life forever.

Colin Knapp

If I were to describe Bob to someone who had never met him, three main characteristics would come to mind. First and foremost, Bob is a caring and loving husband, father and friend who would do anything for the people he loves. I have seen this over the years being in close contact with the Unger family and continue to see it to this day. Second would be willpower. I have always looked up to Bob's will and dedication to whatever he puts his mind to. I find this a very admirable trait and something that everyone should aspire to cultivate. Anyone who can ride over 100 miles on a bike in a day has some serious willpower. And third, Bob is a man of many talents. Whether it's fixing bikes, motorcycles, working wood on a lathe or helping people, Bob knows his way around. Last but not least, Bob is just an all round great guy who you would want in your corner any day of the week.

Bob, here's to this one and many more!
Happy birthday!
Colin

I Think It Was The Second Red Minivan, But I'm Not Sure Anymore

Spencer Knapp

Returning from a hot rod weekend/bicycle excursion in Moab, Jooj, Dylan and I were bored out of our minds in the back seat. Until I was around 13, every car ride felt like a frickin' eternity! After staring off in the distance for what certainly must've been years, Bob announced to the car that he had jokes and would we like to hear them. "All right," he said, audibly restraining his laughter, "So . . . a man is eating at this restaurant and the waiter brings him a bowl of soup. He says 'Excuse me, waiter, what is this fly doing in my soup?'"

At this point, Bob is so pleased with his execution of this joke he's almost unable to contain himself. "The waiter looks into the bowl and says 'Well, I believe he's doing the backstroke!" Bob immediately burst into gales of laugher. I looked at Jooj and Dylan, our reactions mirrored in each other's faces, the cringe in that minivan reaching critical mass. In only an instant however, the adolescent parent-shame evaporated and we all laughed to tears at what had to be the most endearingly amateur delivery of what is certain to be one of the world's most pathetic jokes.

It may be embarrassing but I think about that joke frequently. I think about what made that joke so funny, and (shocker) it wasn't the punch line. The thought of this hyper-intelligent, remarkably accomplished man laughing the most enthusiastic, side splitting laugh at a ludicrous joke in the middle of nowhere on a long drive with three sullen teenagers is something that makes me chuckle every time it comes to me. This perfectly exemplifies Bob's ability to find/create humor in bleak situations, and it's helped me get through some dreary times on the road, or otherwise. I will cherish that memory as long as I'm lucky enough to remember it. I hope to share moments like it with my own children, and I hope someday my kids are lucky enough to share moments like this with Bob himself.

Happy Birthday, Dr. Robert!

Love,

Spencer

Uğur Kocataşkin

I first met Bob Unger in 2004 at his house at one of the legendary Unger parties that used to kick off the academic year for the Contemplative Psychotherapy community at Naropa University. I was a first year student at the time, and the well-attended event held in the beautifully bloomed garden was my first introduction to the community. At some point in the afternoon, when our paths crossed in the bustling gathering, Bob welcomed me and introduced his wife Helena. When he heard that I was from Turkey, he immediately said that Helena is of Greek origin and told the story how Turks hanged her grandfather in Izmir during the First World War after he managed to get his family out of the defeated city. An awkward welcome, I thought, not knowing what to say. I felt defensive and at the same time some level of responsibility for what had happened to Helena's grandfather. Bob seemed to enjoy the awkwardness and kept looking at me as if to say, "What are you going to do now?" Seeing my discomfort, Helena immediately came to rescue and jokingly reprimanded him for having told the story. Needless to say, I avoided Bob for the rest of the party.

I could not avoid him forever though as he taught one of the courses in the first year of the program, the Evolution of Central Concepts in Western Psychology. He came in on the first day of the class and announced that there would be no note taking. The group exploded with resistance and he held his boundary with grace and with some level of amusement, which he did not bother to hide. He knew how to teach in the moment, in relationship, with fearlessness.

Since these first encounters, Bob continues to be a teacher, mentor, supervisor, and a friend. His ability to bring everyone around him out of their comfort zone and into the present moment is uncanny. The magic however is in his ability to do this always with kindness, gentleness, and heart, which seem to transform the moment into an invitation and sometimes a thrust to get in touch with one's brilliant sanity.

I did call Bob a friend above, perhaps a presumptuous gesture. Yet this speaks to his immense generosity of heart and to his ability to let his students become his colleagues and peers.

Thank you, Bob, for all that you continue to give.

I love you.

Uğur

Bennett Leslie

I first got to know Bob after moving to Boulder in the early 1990s. The connection was through bicycles, and to a lesser extent, our shared occupations as mental health professionals. On the bike, as well as in life, Bob is indefatigable. He's always up for going harder, longer, faster, but is able to put his drive secondary to his consideration for his riding buddies. He can't resist the temptation to push towards the top of the hill, almost always leaving everybody else in the dust, but there's no gloating. In this way, he serves as a true inspiration, balancing his personal dedication with his sensitivity to the qualities that make relationships rich and rewarding.

I was surprised the first time I heard Bob swear. I didn't think this was part of his vernacular until I saw him crash on a sandy stretch during one of our annual trips to Moab. This also let me see another side of Bob's personality which he mostly keeps in check. It's nice to know his feet are made of clay, if not his skin, when he suffers rock rash. But one usually sees his optimism, appreciation, interest in other people, and a continuing commitment to be the best person that he can be.

Bob is also an instigator and a bit of a provocateur. This has been especially apparent as I go through the process of researching and buying my first motorcycle. All along the way, Bob has expressed great interest, one suspects partly because of the vicarious satisfaction that he gets from being involved in this process, but it also feels like I am being welcomed into a new fraternity. He has a knack for understanding while at the same time instigating me to "go for it". Along the way, he has shown great interest in the details and the possible considerations. He understands that I'm inherently cautious in an undertaking such as this, and it's been very helpful to have him encourage me to consider bigger, faster, sexier motorcycles than I might initially think of. I suspect that many others have felt this blend of understanding and fortification from Bob. I look forward to many more rides and conversations.

Jeannie Little

In 1997 I was encouraged by two people to meet Bob Unger at AGPA. Paul Geltner and Richard Wein, both old colleagues of his, insisted that I would like him very much. I introduced myself that year, then again in 1998, and again in 1999. Not knowing at the time about his face blindness, I assumed I just was not very memorable. Nevertheless I persisted. I wanted a supervision group and there was none in Northern California, so I asked Bob if I could join one of his. That was the spring of '99, and he finally began to remember me, even though I came to the group by phone.

Bob has put his stamp on me in many ways in my roles as a therapist, a supervisor, and a boss. Often I felt like an adopted child who sounds and behaves like her revered Daddy. It's taken many years for Bob's teaching to become sufficiently internalized that I *think* I no longer sound like his mimic.

Over the years Bob has said or done things that enter my mind like a dart and stick forever. His clarity of thought and simplicity of speech certainly help to lodge his ideas in my consciousness, but I think they are also ideas that have been honed over decades of conscientious work on his part so they go straight from his mouth to my mind. First and foremost stands out the radical neutrality that he conveys with a warmth that allows him to say the most provocative things with the greatest of innocence: "How do you know I'm a man?" "I might be angry, I might not," or, "I might have an opinion, I might not," followed by a graceful redirect such as, "But if I did, what do you think I would be thinking?" or "What would I be angry about?" or "Why in the world would I be angry at *you*?" to the person or group who is trying their mightiest to find out what he *really* thinks and feels.

I got into trouble with my first group when I tried a Bob intervention. I asked two group members whom I overheard orchestrating a trade of pet products for wine if they "would like to drop out of the group while they conducted this other business and then rejoin the group when they were ready to meet each other only in group." Not being skilled in the art of working in the hypothetical, this intervention blew up, both members quit, and the rest of the group was thoroughly confused and angry. Fortunately, one rejoined the group and the incident became part of group lore regarding my belief in the primacy of group relationships until I ended the group 15 years later.

I like Bob's devotion to group and his persistence in referring to "the group" as a living breathing entity in and of itself. This has stood me in good stead for many years and helps enormously with the severely mentally ill homeless drinkers and drug users that are the clients of my agency. They are able to feel a part of something without the individualized attention that can evoke discomfort and paranoia in some and rejection and isolation in others.

In 1978, coincidentally the same year that I started my career as a social worker, Bob published an article called, "Sustaining Transference in the Treatment of Alcoholism" (Unger, 1978). In it he proposed several notions that would have, had he gone further with his ideas, made him the first harm reduction therapist in the world. The two most important points to me, ones that I pass on regularly to others in the harm reduction field, are that the entire field of addiction treatment has been based on a countertransference reaction to the (perceived) loss of control of the user. More specifically, he draws a parallel between the "alcoholic's" impulse to act by drinking rather than to experience uncomfortable feelings and the therapist's induced impulse to *do* something : "the client's impulse to act gives the therapist the impulse to act." Just last month at AGPA, one of my staff and supervisees, a second generation harm reductionist and supervisee of Bob, said those very words in a workshop. The group lit up and spontaneously moved in their seats. You could see the idea land with them and reorganize the many impressions and discomforts that they had not before had words for.

As a role model, Bob has influenced my practice in three vital ways: to be clean, in the ethical sense of the word; to be focused on the work, not on my own ego; and to use a beaming smile in my work.

Bob has given me personal gifts too. A few years ago, during one of my many visits to Boulder, he took me downhill mountain biking at Winter Park. Mind you, I had never been on a mountain bike. But I was hooked, and I now own a very nice one. And yes, I now also own a road bike that is much nicer than the old hybrid I commuted on. So, like many others who are no doubt contributing to this Festschrift, I drank the Kool-Aid, spent a certain undisclosed sum that makes me a special customer at my favorite bike store, and believe that the bicycle is the most amazing machine ever invented.

Bob also gave me Helena. I can't explain it, but from the moment we met (and she was quite ill with flu on that occasion and only able to say a groggy hello), we clicked like two BFF's in junior high. I have that same feeling each time we get together – that we could talk and gossip and cook and walk and shop and talk some more for days and never sleep. She's so much fun!

Finally, Bob has given me love. He seems to find in himself love for everyone and everything. While that can't possibly be entirely true—he certainly is no Pollyanna—he manages to gather the people around him into his embrace and make us all his tribe. I think that's the reason that I feel more a part of the Boulder group than my own in California. We are Bob's tribe.

What do I want in my future with Bob? To co-write that article on countertransference in the substance abuse field (really, Bob, I mean it!) and for Bob to live a good while longer, though no longer than he wants, and to keep bestowing on me his beaming smile and belly chuckle, his bouncing enthusiasm, and his unmoving dedication to clean practice.

References

Unger, R. (1978). Sustaining transference in the treatment of alcoholism. *Modern Psychoanalysis*, *3*, 155-171.

Kathleen Lowe & Vic Harris

We first met Bob in 1983, all of us colleagues earning our stripes as Boulder therapists working with court mandated drinking drivers. We survived the experience together with humor and camaraderie and an enduring friendship developed. We all married the same summer and Kathleen had the honor of being present at Dylan's birth as Bob's support person. Eventually she and Bob both decided to go into private practice and shared office space.

Having known Bob for 32 years as therapist, bicyclist, family man and friend, two qualities stand out most for us. First, Bob's discipline and willingness to completely throw himself into whatever he has chosen to take on (his success as a therapist, teacher, athlete, and artist illustrate this point). The second quality is his open heart. Bob is willing to be completely moved and touched. We remember sitting next to him at a Claudia Schmidt concert with tears rolling down, heart wide open and a big grin on his face. Bob isn't afraid to fall in love. He loves deeply and openly. It's a privilege to know him.

Isha Lucas

When contemplating Bob Unger's contribution to my life as a student, potential therapist, and person, I am not sure where to begin. I have an overwhelming feeling of joy whenever I hear his name mentioned. This is not because Bob is squishy or tender but because he is so real, honest and open. My experience of Bob, for the duration of my time at Naropa, was that he manifests integrity at his core. Because of his ability to show-up as he is, he offers others an opportunity to join him with authentic presence.

One of my favorite memories of Bob is when he called me a curmudgeon. It was during a class at Naropa. We were discussing a suicidal patient and I was questioning the idea of suicide and our societal judgment of the act, when Bob called me out. He said it in such a matter-of-fact manner that it forced me to contemplate my state of mind, the way in which I interact with others, and my reasons for challenging such social norms. Rather than pushing me to a place of defensiveness, Bob opened a space for reflection. This way of engaging, rather than alienating, is at the center of every interaction I have had with Bob. He is a truly amazing and insightful teacher and I feel honored to have been his student.

Charlotte Malkmus

I was a student of Bob's at Naropa in 2001. At the time, I asked him to be my thesis advisor. I wrote about shame and competition for women, a theme that, unsurprisingly, turned out to be of great importance to me personally. Bob was generous with his time and his knowledge, but also I remember having lots of fun talking to him on the phone during our appointments. What a revelation—that writing a thesis could be fun!

Then a great thing began to happen: my Naropa-assigned second advisor, a recent graduate with an administrative position, began to enact with me the very phenomenon I was trying to elucidate for myself in the paper. At each of our meetings, she began subtly shaming me, letting me know, for example, that she "never" felt competitive with any of her patients and repeatedly disavowing all competitive strivings with me. As I returned from these meetings, discouraged and confused, Bob helped me to see what was going on, and to understand it.

In a final, public enactment, I presented the paper in a large group, Bob-style, with everyone sitting in a circle that filled up the room. During the discussion that followed the presentation, the advisor launched one of her attacks in the form of follow-up questions. It was only a matter of seconds before Bob intervened, in his quick way, managing to stop the attack without shaming the attacker. I don't remember all these years later exactly what it was that she said, or what he did. What I do remember is how protected I felt.

Later, when discussing the incident, I remember Bob saying the advisor "threw a knife in my back." At that point in my own development, I couldn't appreciate that I was experiencing a sense of validation. I just knew that being with Bob felt good. Looking back I recognize that this was a first, powerful lesson for me in the forces of the unconscious.

Over subsequent years of study with Bob I discovered that being able to detect these forces at play is unendingly compelling, akin to being able to see the wind. I've also learned that engaging these forces is my life's work. Bob has continued to be generous with his time, his knowledge and his spirit, again and again inviting me and others to compete with him, grinning all the while. He has shown me and my fellow group members to be irreverent and kind, to play, to enjoy ourselves in the effort. To my mind, he is the consummate teacher, someone so many of us want to be just like when we grow up.

Eric Maxfield

I write to honor my teacher, mentor, group leader, and friend, Bob Unger. Bob runs a group for homeless shelter staff, and I was a participant in that group from 1996-1999. During that period, Bob provided our group with an outlet for stress, a forum to foster shared identity, and a place to explore and test out our individuality. We were engaged in emotionally exhausting work with a much larger group, averaging 1,200 homeless individuals a year, who were often in some type of crisis. Bob's group was a special place where we, the caregivers and limit setters, were cared for. This was the first place I encountered Bob and his unique dual abilities to set a tone of propriety and expectation while at the same time accepting each member of the group. I was intrigued by the quiet authority and guiding hand that Bob used to tug, tweak, and push us and so I joined some of his group classes.

Bob's group classes defied my expectations completely. I thought that, unlike his group at the shelter, he would hold classes and simply explain what it was he was doing. I would then have the keys, the method to use this powerful tool. The tool (group) that could help people explore their feelings and find support. Instead, he asked us, all 20 or so of us, mostly therapists (though I am a lawyer), to go ahead. And it was even less direct than that. It was implied by his presence that yes, here we were, and here he was, together. We were a group, we behaved like a group, and we exhibited the dynamics of a group. Bob was the leader and teacher, though I found that the learning didn't happen right away, but took time, from that time until today, in fact, to start to take hold. I started to reflect on how the group, in all its various manifestations, is the place where we learn how to get our needs met, and to perhaps grow to meet the needs of others, to be present with others and feel the bump and abrasion and resonance of one's self in the group.

In my work at the shelter I decided to see what would happen if people were not controlled with rules of "should" and "must" but rather were asked to come together as a group. So I started a group. I would say, "Meeting at 7 pm." People would come to the group and sit down and start to talk and express themselves. In a simple and beautiful way they increased the dignity of the environment simply through their participation. I observed the profound effect of dignity in a crowded shelter of people who were experiencing stress and crisis. I imagined Bob's guiding principles, encouraged group members to explore and take risks, and worked to protect the outliers from becoming scapegoated.

Years later as an attorney manager I joined a group run by Bob for professionals who met together to discuss work and leadership dynamics, ways of progressing in work systems, and ways of helping and encouraging others. Over the next few years I encountered what I came to think of as Bob's avuncular encouragement toward personal growth through grouping. The group provided the opportunity for continued reflection on the utility of the group and the responsibility of a group leader. The group also offered a sense of increased identification, a drawing in of the outlier, and a pushing away of the inlier, toward a balanced place of individuation and connection. And the opportunity to try and fail, to test, to push boundaries, to apologize, to take risks, and to succeed.

Bob's many years as my teacher, mentor, group leader, and friend have helped me develop my self and a vision of a possible ideal self—unrealized in many ways—but with the ability to be supportive, compassionate and encouraging, to find a harmonious and dignified place in the larger group.

Thank you, Bob Unger.

Sara Mayer

Dear Bob,

I can hardly believe that you are 70! Happy Birthday! I hope you have several more decades of living, loving, riding, laughing, and teaching. Your spirit is a gift to all of us whose lives you have touched.

First, I want to thank you for telling us about da Vinci tandems. We would never have known about them otherwise, and our tandem has given us so many hours of wonderful riding . . . relatively conflict free . . . thanks to the da Vinci transmission system. I doubt we would have lasted three months on a standard tandem!

Then, Tom is so appreciative of your help buying his road and mountain bikes at the Veloswap. Again, he never would have been able to do it without your knowledge and confidence. We found the Veloswap totally overwhelming and did not buy a thing the one other time we went.

And even more important, I want to thank you for our Tuesday group. I don't think we would have made it this long nor would we have grown so much without your faith in and knowledge of group process. I have learned an enormous amount from you in the group and have deep respect and affection for you. I think the group has taught us how to be our "best selves" more of the time both in group and in our lives. Your positive energy and willingness to take risks with us has ended up being quite contagious!

Your life is a gift to your family, your clients, your friends, your students, your colleagues, and the larger Boulder community. Congratulations and happy, happy birthday!

Catie McDowell

When I went in for my brief one-on-one consultation with Bob, before joining one of his groups, we had an uneventful, comfortable chat. As I left his office he off-handedly remarked, "You seem like you'd be fun to have around." That comment stopped me in my tracks. Me? Fun to have around? I am a serious and brooding introvert, a reserved and contained WASP. Never in my life had anyone ever said, nor have I ever thought, that I'd be "fun" to have around.

That was several years ago. I truly don't remember how many. But since that time I have had the pleasure and honor of sitting with Bob every other week. He is a fount of wisdom, knowledge, and instructive stories, usually shared with a wry smile and not a bit of ego. He is also deeply kind and generous of spirit, like when my son became ill and I needed a safe place to share my unbearable worry and sorrow. He gently challenges my habits as a clinician, and inevitably asks a question that I would never think to ask. Being with Bob is like watching a really good magician perform sleight of hand tricks—he is doing so much in every moment, but he makes it look so easy.

Finally, it is remarkable to me that in all my years in Bob's group, with various members coming and going, I have always felt that I belonged—from day one. Bob has a way of making each of us feel uniquely welcomed and valued. And while I've learned so much about the work of psychotherapy, I've also had *fun*. It's as if that "off-handed" comment in our first meeting wasn't off-handed at all. Instead it was a purposeful invitation for me to become a better version of myself. And I'd like to think that I have. And for that, and so much more, I am forever grateful to Dr. Bob Unger.

Barbara Mitchell

In the summer of 1976 a friend of Bob's let him know she wouldn't be using her country house in Columbia County, in upstate New York, for a few weeks. Within minutes he collected a group of friends, mostly motorcycle buddies, to rent the house and its already-planted gorgeous vegetable garden. Most of us didn't know everyone else, we just knew Bob. There was an atmosphere of relaxed hilarity that carried us all through those few weeks. When the zucchini ripened and we'd made bread, pancakes and stir-fry and still couldn't use them up, we played softball, using the huge ones as bats. I remember waking at dawn one morning, lying in bed and watching the curtains move in the breeze. I thought about my new friends, scattered in beds around the house. I was infused with a sense of joy and peacefulness that I had never before experienced. Bob, a natural group leader, had created a family.

Mary Sue Moore

In conversations over several years, Bob has helped many of us overcome obstacles again and again, often by reminding us of some great song lyrics from the 60's that apply perfectly to whatever situation we are discussing. While Bob Dylan has figured prominently (of course), the lyrics that will always be linked in my mind to Bob's generous support and my deep gratitude were written by Leonard Cohen, in his song *Anthem* released in 1992:

> The birds they sang at the break of day.
> Start again, I heard them say.
> Don't dwell on what has passed away
> Or what is yet to be.
> Ah, the wars they will be fought again.
> The holy dove, she will be caught again.
> Bought and sold and bought again.
> The dove is never free.
> Ring the bells that still can ring.
> Forget your perfect offering.
> There is a crack, a crack in everything.
> That's how the light gets in.

Thank you, Bob, for your brilliant musical reminders of life's ironies and joys!!

References

Cohen, L. (1992). Anthem. On *The Future* [CD]. New York, NY: Columbia.

In Tribute of Bob Unger

Melissa Moore

Graying and shrinking . . . yet ever expanding that mischievous open heart
How else could you abide? Impossible!
Endlessly enmeshed . . . ceaselessly trolling the nether oceanic layers of consciousness
Always the Cheshire cat smile
Dylan lofts gently in the eros-sphere around you . . .
Go 'way from my window
Leave at your own chosen speed
I'm not the one you want, babe
I'm not the one you need . . .
"Good, good," the doctor snorts. "It's all good."
Let me express my heartfelt thank you . . . by the way
For your kind yet direct intervention on bad decisions I once made.
My darkest hour, well one of them, many moons ago,
You said, "Helena and I love one another and thus we can endure all the crap . . . but you, you're confusing love with loneliness, now let go and move on!"
I did let go, thanks to you . . . a real game changer in hindsight.
A heartfelt loss for sure, beyond a wakeup call—more like "Phew . . . close call!!"
Thank you, dear brother friend for your love, intensity and heart.
When a thought of you flies by, I sigh . . . I feel your strength and courage.
Married for life we are once removed . . . and may there be many more lives to share.
On your seventieth solar return I wish you a safe and joyous ride to the end.
For the loser now
Will be later to win
For the times they, they are a-changin'

All my love,

Melissa

Ode to Bob

Edward Rockendorf Morey

Round and round the track of life—
He goes
Forever chasing Dylan

Only oats and grains
Fuel his legs and brains

Bob should eat a stack of steaks
And take a break
Maybe with some wine
Before and mid sleeping time

The track at the Home will be short and steep
His bed in the middle with a bag of eats
The speakers will blast Dylan

Into the sunset he will ride, again and again
In perpetual motion—whether alive or dead

Grateful

Rivvy Neshama

Bob sees what is special in *everyone* and makes everyone feel special. And that's just one thing that makes him so special too!

I am grateful for Bob's presence in my life.
I am grateful for Bob's presence in the world.
I am grateful for Bob's presence.
I am grateful for Bob!

Happy Birthday, Doc Bob!

With love from Rivvy

Sabrina Neu

In an article on supervision, Spotnitz wrote, "One aspect of training the student analyst . . . is to create for the student . . . the atmosphere of total acceptance that the student must create for the patient" (Spotnitz, 1977, p. 202). I think that was the biggest gift that Bob ever gave to me. In over nine years of participating in Bob's supervision group, and in all other interactions with him, I have always felt Bob's unwavering acceptance. There were many times when I wondered if the profession of psychotherapy was for me, but Bob helped me tolerate these feelings so that I could keep going back to helping people understand themselves. Whenever I'm sitting with a supervisee or a group, Bob is always in the room, too, and I still find myself quoting his pearls of wisdom. Of all the supervisory experiences I've had in a 17 year career, it's Bob that I carry within me. Bob's passion and zest for life are inspiring: teaching, Bob Dylan, cycling, dancing at AGPA, singing lessons. I only hope that I can live with half as much of his curiosity, energy and openness to new experiences.

Thanks for always walking your talk, Bob, and heartfelt wishes for a happy 70th!

References

Spotnitz, H. (1977). Trends in modern psychoanalytic supervision. *Modern Psychoanalysis, 1,* 201-217.

Susan Nimmanheminda

Bob! Hmm . . . I'll start at the beginning.

I was looking for a supervision group and someone recommended Bob Unger, albeit with reservations. From what I was told, he had a mixed reputation. Some loved him. Some found him provocative and manipulative, others genuine and tender. He was a psychoanalyst, and in my book (though I'd never met a psychoanalyst) that wasn't a particularly positive credential. My stereotypical image of a psychoanalyst prepared me to meet someone who rubbed me the wrong way— someone who was distant and hierarchical. So I was more than a little surprised that at our initial interview I experienced Bob as warm, interested and interesting, engaged and engaging, *and* even funny.

That was the beginning of, what adds up to now as a 20-year-long relationship with Bob. When I contemplate all this relationship has been to me it ranks as one of the most enriching and influential of my life. His impact on me ranges from the bike I ride, to my analytic training, to my affiliation with Naropa, and beyond.

I'm ever aware of Bob's impact on my work. The supervision and mentoring I got from Bob, including not only his various professional attributes but also who he was as a human being, showed me that I, too, could bring all of the various parts of myself into the therapeutic relationship. Though he no longer considers himself a Modern Analyst, I saw Bob model the Modern Psychoanalytic ideal of being able—and enabling one's clients—to have the full range of feelings, from love to hate and everything in between. There is sometimes a tacit taboo in the profession of psychotherapy that the therapist shouldn't have certain feelings. But I never heard Bob even hint that someone's feelings were "wrong." Instead, he encouraged a wide-open affective field, one that embraces emotions as the seeds and fuel for a skillful, therapeutic relationship.

I learned from Bob the difficult skill of working with the negative transference. I knew, of course, that people often reach out to a therapist for help healing their interpersonal wounds. What I didn't know, and also learned from Bob, was that the therapeutic dynamic at its best is often one where these wounds become enacted within the relationship. Bob is a master at holding and transforming this dynamic.

Bob has a strong reputation as an endurance cyclist, a reputation that stands as well for him as a psychotherapist. On more than one occasion, I've heard him say, "Psychotherapy is an endurance sport." Though this festschrift marks Bob's 70th birthday, I trust he'll be out on the roads—and in the office—for many years to come.

Jenna Noah

I remember sitting in that group at Naropa. My heart simultaneously melted and trembled looking out at that mass of 30 people.

"Who killed Jack?" Bob's voice bellowed.

This was shocking for two reasons. Firstly, Bob Unger rarely remembered anyone's name. And then secondly, Jack wasn't dead. He left our program and was no longer in large group.

And then, the fireworks began. Cries, moans, protests, anger, guilt all billowed out.

That's how it was with Bob. One poignant sentence and then the emotions burst forth.

He was one of the few who could hold the entire storm of us, and of me.

Elizabeth Olson

My father died when I was quite young, leaving me missing a father-like figure in my life. Bob has held this father transference for me, as well as been supervisor, and mentor through out my professional and much of my personal life. Bob has given me countless interventions which, while perfect for clients, were sometimes uncomfortable and dreadful for me to say, but always propelled the talking forward in sessions. I know that an intervention is just right for a client when I shrink and squirm, feeling like I could never say that. Yet I find the courage (hearing Bob's voice) to associate to the suggestions most of the time, surprised at how helpful and life changing they are for my clients. Over time, these interventions have become much more enjoyable. Something new will be said with the potential for real change.

Bob's courage and selflessness as a clinician have taught me that even though you are scared, you say the unsayable. Feelings, impulses, thoughts of all kind are welcomed, tolerated, studied and metabolized. These inductions inform the emotional understanding and mental conceptualization of what a person is experiencing, especially the ways that they repeat their early experiences in the transferential relationship. Responses to clients are delivered with genuine feeling and a range of different vocal tones that communicate with the unconscious subtly, yet potently.

I had a client once who tortured me with horrific, sickening stories about genocides, sexual torture, and world atrocities. After a couple of years of torture, Bob encouraged me to come up with even more horrific stories and to share them with the client in a matter-of-fact tone, thus surprising and neutralizing the client's sadistic streak; no one had ever responded to her in that way. I started talking with the client about some of the most disturbing historical events that I had ever heard in a flat, conversational tone as though I was just really interested in that kind of information. It felt outrageous, but took the torture out of our sessions. Matching a neutral tone with disturbing words and images was the key to the emotional communication. Those kinds of interchanges altered the client's emotional experience in that it was no longer gratifying for her to be sadistic with me and she could feel it; she knew it on a deep unconscious level. Rather quickly following these interventions, she became much less interested in sadism, and much more interested in living her life with enjoyment, meaning, and empathic, reciprocal relationships.

About seventeen years ago my husband, Francis, decided that he wanted to become the best therapist he could and he wanted Bob's advice. When he met with Bob, he asked him, "What do I need to do to become a really good therapist?" Typically, before Bob gives advice, he asks, "Will you promise to do what I recommend?" In this way, any unconscious resistances will be teased out, and any reluctance to follow the advice can be put into words. Francis agreed to follow his advice wholeheartedly, so Bob said: 1) Get your doctorate, 2) Have children, 3) Get into analysis with the best analyst you can find. Francis and I followed through on all of these recommendations. This advice has guided my life. For all of this and so much more, I am grateful to Bob.

Joan Ormont

Lou and I always had the greatest respect for Dr. Unger. Whenever Lou was invited to speak at Naropa, Dr. Unger was always present to welcome us with his warmth and hospitality. Over the past many years we had the pleasure of meeting some of his students who always spoke very highly of his teaching and analytic skills.

Best wishes to Dr. Unger on his 70th birthday!

All the best,

Joan Ormont

Jeffrey M. Price

I first met Bob around 1995 when I was in my first year as a graduate student at The Naropa Institute. I fell in love when he told us to put away our pens and papers and pay attention. There would be no note taking. Wow. You mean a teacher could trust me to pay attention . . . and that would be enough?? Revolutionary! I was giddy. Then, later in the semester, when he was teaching us about "resistance" and the resistance on the part of one of my classmates grew too unyielding, he said, "This class is over," and left us sitting there with no teacher and no teacher's assistants in the room. Wild! Cool! This guy rocks!! He certainly got my attention.

When I took his class on group theory a few semesters later, I was hooked. At the end of that class I wanted more. There had to be more and I let him know it. Two things happened: he suggested I look further into the American Group Psychotherapy Association (which I did and have been involved with ever since; this was a great referral!), and he invited me to join one of his therapy groups (which I have also been involved with ever since; another great referral). In this group I not only get to explore all those wonderful nooks and crannies of my unconscious, but just as valuably, maybe more so, I get to watch Bob work every week, up close. I consider him a master and I happily continue to be the willing and eager student. Every week he models another aspect of being a group leader. Whether it is laughter, self-deprecation, tender tears, or somehow being able to care about so many people at the same time, he is still showing me how to do it.

There was one more thing about referrals I wanted to mention and this was most significant to me personally and professionally, and for which I will be forever grateful. He sent me to the well-known and highly esteemed Dr. Leslie Rosenthal for clinical supervision. Dr. Rosenthal was there at the beginning of group psychotherapy in this country. He practiced in New York City so our supervision sessions had to be over the phone. Over several years this proved to be no obstacle and, in fact, was as rich and rewarding as supervision could be. It was a unique opportunity and I was tremendously honored. What a gift this was from Bob. I could not possibly thank him enough.

In all of the incarnations of our relationship over the last almost twenty years, I guess the one I cherish most is the way he has served as an inspiration to me to be a better therapist and a better person.

Thanks, Bob.

With much love,

Jeff Price

Chris Randol

Bob Unger saved my life. I had graduated from Naropa in 1989, a couple years after my teacher Trungpa Rinpoche had died, and close to the time my second teacher, the Regent, passed away. The Regent had been a translator for me. With incredible humor and insight, he made some pretty dense teachings accessible. The Buddhist community was shaken, and no one yet filled the void.

Then along came Bob, importing the Modern Psychoanalytic teachings from 10th St. on the lower East Side to Boulder, Colorado. A modern Marpa the Translator, full of Hyman Spotnitz, Louis Ormont and Leslie Rosenthal.

Bob introduced me to Modern Psychoanalysis, which made room for primitive feelings that didn't feel acceptable anywhere else. And he did it with humor and lust for life, which was always mother's milk for me. Having grown up with a mother who was a bit of a raconteur, who behaved as if personality was a fiction and being yourself was always a bit of play acting, I longed for the crazy wisdom teachers, resisted those who played it safe and small. Spotnitz did not play it small, and neither did Bob.

The group that we put together as the original Colorado Group Psychotherapy Society (COGPS) created a community of siblings for me, older siblings. They had mostly intact marriages, and I began to see this as a new normal. Still married to my beautiful wife after 30 years, I feel my kids and my family have benefitted tremendously from what I observed, assimilated and integrated. For my work at the Boulder County Jail and beyond, my group training has been the gift that keeps on giving. I am ever so grateful to Bob for working with me and the larger Front Range community. "Jolly good show," as Trungpa Rinpoche would say.

Jeremy Rhoades

It has been wonderful learning from Bob about working with groups, as a member of his supervision group. Many of his teachings are applicable on multiple levels, and yet somehow he seems to be able to cut through jargon and concepts, and address what is actually happening from a perspective that keeps the well-being of the group in mind. Thank you so much for your shared experience, Bob!

Mary Riendeau

As a graduate student in the contemplative psychotherapy program at Naropa I first met Bob at his house, for the department's annual fall garden party/cake cutting shenanigans. I remember very little about Bob on that occasion as an overwhelmed, overheated new student, except that he resembled my father quite a bit, which made me a little suspicious of him.

I next encountered him as a group facilitator at the Boulder Shelter for the Homeless, where I worked part time. He joined our weekly staff meeting once a month, in order to presumably support some sort of group process. Alas, in pure Bob Unger style, he would come into the staff meeting and sit, mostly silent, while the rest of us wondered what was happening. We program staff would talk about him in the weeks leading up to the meeting, wondering what he was up to, and what sort of mystery lay in store for us next. Eventually as the shelter season progressed we began to talk more as a group during those staff meetings, and he would make completely non-sequitur process comments, often sparking ire in many staff, myself included, especially because his remarks seemed elusively effective.

Outside of our Shelter interactions, what really confused me and annoyed me is that Bob Unger never seemed to remember who I was, ever. Whether it be in the group psychotherapy class I took with him, in the halls of Paramita (the north campus of Naropa University) or at the Boulder Shelter, he never used my name or did anything to suggest a spark of recognition.

Finally, Bob was one of the staff who led the final retreat for our program, up at Shambhala Mountain Center (SMC). I didn't think much of spending that week with him, since I had accumulated some mild annoyance and irritation toward him over the years. However, in that final retreat it seemed somehow that I was finally seeing Bob unfiltered, instead of through the lens of my many unwanted and uncomfortable projections. I'm not quite sure what the process was that released me from that suffering, but suddenly Bob was there, in generous and humorous relationship with me. He was warm, funny, engaging, conversational, wise, and completely available, and I grew to deeply enjoy his laugh and antics at the dinner table.

Thank you Bob, for being a teacher to me in the most profound experiential way, by offering yourself so generously as a blank canvass on which I could project everything, only to be disarmed by you in the end, especially by your beautiful and horrendous rendition of Bob Dylan :).

Reuben Robbins

I first met Bob as a student at Naropa about 18 years ago. Soon he was a supervisor on a Windhorse team I was working with. After Naropa, I asked if he would be a supervisor for the clients I was working with. I remember vividly leaving that first private supervision, thinking, "That was the best $65 I ever spent" (which was a lot of money for me then). Bob advised me on the first journal article I wrote and published, which was about a "joining" intervention he helped me craft for male spousal abusers in court mandated group treatment. When I moved to back to New York to get my doctorate in Clinical Psychology, I didn't have much contact with him. Several years went by, and then during internship, I had a challenging case. I was frustrated with my internship supervisor, and immediately thought that Bob would be "the" person to talk to. And he was. Talking with him helped me talk much more effectively with the young man I was working with. When I moved back to New York again and began my practice, the one person I thought of that I wanted to work with to help me with my clients was Bob. Not only has he been very helpful and supportive in my development as a psychotherapist, he has been very helpful in my development as a psychologist (with a research career) and a husband.

It wasn't until I began working with Bob more regularly, while developing my practice that I quickly learned about his other "inspirations" besides Hyman Spotnitz, especially Bob Dylan and Alan Watts. Among these three, I can't think of one meeting that went by with out Bob referencing one, two or all three. "Well, you know, Spotnitz would say it's all 'hot air'," and, "It's like Bob Dylan said, 'To live outside the law, you must be honest,'" and, "Well, you know what Alan Watts would say about that..."

I wish more people, particularly psychologists and psychotherapists, would have the opportunity to work with Bob. In this field of ever increasing specialization, acronyms (e.g., CBT, DBT, ACT), and empirically rigid approaches to working with people, it's been inspiring and exhilarating to know there is a well-seasoned, successful therapist who can engage in meaningful life conversations that help and who agrees (at least seemingly) that all therapies are really the same.

Neil J. Rosen

Writing about Bob is almost too easy. He's there for people. That's it. It's simple except that he's there for so many people in a way that draws them to him that he practically has a line out the door like a deli counter. Take a number. "Pastrami, please. Two pounds, end cut." Lots of tender, spicy and rich Bob love for everyone. He listens and wants to know more, ever more with the idea that more is usually better because talking itself is a curative activity that leads often to a desire for still more talking and listening. He's well suited to his daily gig and is often called into action to instruct others in the art, humbly and generously, I would add.

It's not always about life's travails. Bob is also happy to talk and listen on a broad array of topics with an angle of perception that is uniquely his own. Politics, culture, engineering, sport, medicine, mental life, history, philosophy, and ethics, yet this is still a partial list which, itself, misses an essential point. It's his sense of curiosity and frequently wonder that makes exchanges with him delightful and instructive. The topic is, in a sense, merely a frame for his "Bobosity." He is always who he is. There's a frequent kind of courage about being open, passionate and taking risks. I don't always agree with him about everything. I often do, but I always know that his faith in dialectical, synthesizing or Socratic exchanges, a libidinously alive way of talking will get us to an interesting place that is hard to bring to a close even when the coffee's all gone or the ride is over.

Now, seventy is no mean age. It's a substantial one, but it's a very good one for listening and talking. At an age of, say, fifty, one has learned a whole lot of words and a few facts, but making them all sing gets better and better over time if one is the right sort of student. Bob, it seems, might be just getting started.

Robin Rosendale

I certainly count myself among those who consider Bob Unger a teacher, mentor, and genuine source of inspiration. My first relationship with Bob began as one of his students. Although more then a decade ago, I can still remember the details of the first class we had with him. Within a few short minutes Bob managed to weave his genius into an emotional web that constellated intense feelings and opinions within our entire class. Some of us were enamored, others outraged, and one particularly astute individual noted, "I'm not sure if I love him, hate him, or want to sleep with him." That is what it feels like to encounter Bob. He is an original and irreplaceable character. Such an individual can't help but evoke strong reactions in the people he encounters because his presence reminds us of that inner mandate of the soul, that each of us carries a similar potential to become our own unique and irreplaceable selves.

Despite moving to New York City after leaving Boulder, I've been lucky enough to maintain an ongoing relationship with Bob as a member in one of his consultation groups. I cherish these encounters, not simply because I'm in the presence of Bob's undeniable genius, but because the group itself has become something sacred to me. I've come to believe a genuine education has its roots in the sacred, as it requires the indwelling spirit of the student to participate with the awakened spirit in the teacher. As a result, both teacher and student leave the encounter affected by the other. Over the years I have witnessed something transform within each of our group members. Sure, we're still subject to our own projections on Bob, and we certainly still compete for his affection, but more then that, each of us has gotten closer and closer to occupying a therapeutic style and a way of knowing that is uniquely ours. I often learn just as much from my fellow group members as I do from Bob, and this is what I've come to experience as one of Bob's greatest gifts. Yes, it goes without saying that he is a master of playing with the field phenomena of transference and countertransference, of how to recognize and normalize aggressive feelings, as well as to playfully trust in the unconscious's endless capacity to surface up images for association, but ultimately, Bob's most lasting gift to me is his role as teacher and true educator. Beyond his valued instructions, Bob's irreplaceable character has been integral in helping me discover my own.

Joseph Schultz

I met Bob over twenty years ago when I was in my first year of graduate school at the then Naropa Institute. I was immediately struck by his outspoken honesty and spontaneous response to the present in a seemingly fearless way. He always seemed to be able to direct his focus on whomever he was speaking to and to truly have that person's interest at heart. What impresses me the most when I think of Bob is that whenever I feel like life has become too overwhelming— especially in clinical work—he comes to mind as someone I can reach out to with the knowledge that I can say whatever I need to without fear. A few times I have actually met with him in those moments, but more often the mere thought that he is out there and that he will be there for me is enough in itself to get me through. I know that he has made such a difference to so many people over the years.

Why My Computer's Name is Shapunger (and Why I Fly Yearly to Florida to Visit Bob's Uncle)

Jed Shapiro

The paths are intertwined. In about the summer of 1981 I was sitting around a campfire at a place I had never been to before named Rocky Mountain Shambhala Center with 3 people I had never met before: Bob Unger, Diane Rudine, and James Evans. The three males all inquired whether Diane might like to hang around with them that night, but that's another story. 34 years, five marriages, and four children later we are seriously Bouldery, Buddhistly, and relationally intertwined.

Bob and I have backpacked in the Rahwah Wilderness, babysat each other's kids, gone to graduations and weddings, biked to Ward, 4th of July campground and Elephant Rock. He has inspired my life in countless ways from "As The Wood Turns," to living in a co-housing setting, to helping me get famous analytic therapists to give in-services at the Boulder Mental Health Center. But his biggest influence on my life (Helena helped) has been to bring a cousin-in-law named Helaine to Boulder from 2000 miles away just so I could meet her and entice her to move here and live with me for the past 10 years.

Yeah, Bob!! We're family!! And that is how my household (and computer) came to be Shapunger!

Lodi Siefer

I was feeling angry. I'd come to class and Bob hadn't set up the room. Again. There weren't enough chairs out for everyone, and I just had the sense that Bob didn't care. He didn't even know our names! He always wasted the first ten minutes taking the attendance, fiddling with his glasses to read the name and then looking up to find the person who was raising a hand or saying, "Here." So frustrating! I wanted something to happen. I wanted to be *learning*. Do you know how much I was paying for this class? And why were we supposed to sit in chairs anyway? This was Naropa, after all, the land of meditation cushions. So I sat on the floor. And so did several of my classmates. It was our little silent protest against Bob, against chairs, against doing what we were told. I'd checked the syllabus, the "contract" as Bob referred to it, and he didn't have anything written about sitting in chairs. Yes, he'd written that we weren't allowed to take notes (how was I supposed to learn anything?!?), but nothing prohibiting meditation cushions.

When Bob got to class, he told us to sit in chairs. I said I'd rather sit on a cushion. He said we had to sit in chairs. A couple students moved to chairs. Other students shifted in their seats, uncomfortable at the scene we rebels were making. Bob said that if we didn't sit in chairs, he would mark us absent. Two more students moved to chairs. My blood boiled. Here was another person in authority (read: white, straight male) abusing his power. I said, "Do what you want to do. For the record, I am present today no matter what you write down." Class continued, with me on the floor, and as my anger ebbed, I started to feel shaky and shutdown. My face felt mask-like, and I could only look at the floor.

After the lecture, we counted off for discussion groups. And I got Bob. Of course. We circled our chairs (I sat in one for this part), and I felt frozen. Then, right at the start, Bob spoke of how the conscientious objectors of Vietnam stood their ground in the face of all the negative consequences that the authorities gave them. Bob sounded admiring, "They went to jail for their beliefs." I looked up. Something shifted inside. I could look others in the eye. I felt proud, too, in whatever way my protest hadn't yielded to authority. But mostly I felt intrigued by Bob. He didn't shame me or abdicate his power and give me what I wanted. I didn't know what had just happened, but it was a new experience for me.

If I had to describe now what Bob did that day, I'd say that he metabolized my aggression. He didn't take it personally, but held his role, willingly stepping into my attack, unthreatened (seemingly anyway) by my anger toward him. He chewed up the neurotic elements and handed me back the seed of wisdom within. And he has done this again and again with me and with others I've witnessed.

I still don't know how he does it. And I'm so grateful.

Deborah Silver

I recently came across my final project for analytic certification from the Center for Modern Psychoanalytic Studies (1993). The second paragraph of the "Acknowledgements" page reads as follows, "I am indebted to Robert Unger for providing my first exposure to the innovative workings of Modern Psychoanalysis. It is because of his fine example and encouragement that I found my way to the Center."

It all began in 1980. I was a fairly new Social Worker at the Bellevue Hospital Alcoholism Treatment Program in New York City. A new clinician/administrator came on board named Bob Unger. The way he worked was different and compelling. He treated some of his patients on the couch, including Mr. F, a tall, homeless, schizophrenic man who had once been a professor. The clinic staff was perplexed, but fascinated nonetheless. Bob soon had us looking at how we were all "induced" by the patients' impulsiveness. We stopped smoking and eating while working. We started hearing about countertransference and resistance, defenses, joining, mirroring, etc. We were captivated. I was hooked. I wanted what he had, and began my psychoanalytic training at the Center for Modern Psychoanalytic Studies, graduating in 1993.

When Bob moved on from Bellevue to a new opportunity, he encouraged me to apply for his position. I did, and was given the new role. I may have taken his place, but I'm not so sure I filled his shoes. His warmth and charm, his humor, his ability to pull people together, his way with the patients, were skills I only aspired to.

Now, all these years later, I echo those words I wrote in 1993. Thank you Bob, for the wonderful path you pointed me toward and helped me follow. I wish you the happiest of birthdays and many more to come.

Bob and Me: The Odd Couple

Mark I. Singer

Bob Unger and I met approximately 48 years ago through a mutual friend, John M. Paige. We were in our very early twenties, each looking for a roommate. And so we roomed together in a one bedroom apartment in Brooklyn on Butler Place. Bob had the bedroom and I was in the living room. Yes, the odd couple of Brooklyn, with Bob as his namesake, Felix Ungar, and Mark as Oscar Madison.

Mark, true to his character, Oscar, was a pig: slovenly, crude and aesthetically ignorant. Bob, true to his character, was always requesting Mark to clean up his act, with his requests becoming more animated and desperate as time went on. Both Bob/Felix and Mark/Oscar were neurotic as hell, each in his own way. Each was trying to find his place within himself and within the world, and not doing a very good job of it. Both were aware of the struggles of the other, and under the often edgy surface interactions, felt the other's pain and anxiety. This was the unlikely beginning of a lasting bond and friendship.

As the years slowly progressed, they kept in touch, by phone and in person. Bob, living in a "commune" in New York, came to visit Mark living in Cleveland in the "dope castle." He brought with him some commune friends and some commune chemicals. Mark had his own commune friends and commune chemicals. Bob and Mark and their friends had a good time as they further scrambled their brains. But, beneath the scrambling, the friendship endured and deepened, as each understood the other's confusion and lack of direction.

Bob and Mark eventually "coupled-up" as each found a mate. Both again learned that living with another wasn't easy, and both revisited earlier struggles. From the beginning, Mark's marriage was not working. His wife repeatedly demanded a divorce, in response to which Mark went uncharacteristically mute. Finally, due to bad behavior, Mark's wife sent him to therapy to get better adjusted to living in the civilized world or to vacate the house. Bob, being smarter than Mark, was in therapy from the beginning. Mark's marriage eventually worked; Bob's didn't. And the friendship endured as each understood that their "coupling" had deep emotional consequences.

Bob left New York for Colorado and visited Mark on his westward quest. He was convinced that New York had been poisonous and his marriage had been anything but an antidote. Mark was very worried about Bob, as he seemed truly disheartened and lost. A few years earlier, a close friend of Mark's had committed suicide. How would Bob handle this crisis?

Colorado was a much better setting for Bob. He found a place that nurtured him: intellectually, emotionally and physically. He also found a mate that was able to understand and admire his complexities, and help limit some of his eccentricities. Bob has done very well for himself and for those around him.

So, aside from the brief history of our friendship, what do I think of Bob? Of all the people I have met in my lifetime, Bob is without question the most talented, emotionally intelligent, and insightful. I think of him as a Renaissance man. No one I know has a greater depth of skills: motorcycle mechanic, bicycle mechanic, motorcycle racer, bicycle downhill and road racer, dancer, marathon runner, wood artist, craftsman, builder, city planner, psychotherapist, group therapist, academic, etc., etc. He comes by these talents honestly—he works hard and long. He also comes by his insightfulness honestly. He has thought and reflected endlessly over the years, experienced and re-experienced, examined and re-examined.

We have shared important parts of each other's life history, thoughts and emotions for over 48 years. I love Bob and value his friendship and counsel.

So, Bob continues to traverse through life. From the son of humble beginnings to a well-educated, well-integrated and well-intentioned man. And how do we make sense of this? What is the meaning and description of life? As agreed upon by

Bob and his friends almost half a century ago while eating together at a dining room table, "Life is a burnt hamburger." It's not perfect, but you still gotta eat it!

The Anger Whisperer

Suzanne Smith

He can hold it
If you can throw it
From your chair
In the air
Then on the ground
It bounces around
Where will it land?
In the palm of his hand
There's nothing to fear
He holds it so dear
Sit still and be strong
It was you all along

A View From the Back Room

Joel Solomon

What's all this fuss about Bob Unger? I'll speculate that he still deserves all this admiration, adulation even in his 70th year. Would he tell us to burn it? Really? Is he that evolved?

New York

Thirty years ago I was partnered with the most narcissistic psychiatrist in America on a project that was going to revolutionize mental health care and also make us rich. We were looking for a clinician/administrator to run "the business." I think it was an ad in the New York Times that brought Bob to our Center which was really a back room in my home office. His clinical and administrative skills were apparent, but at that point in time inadequate to harness the combined unfocused, unavailable, disorganized, old-fashioned neurotic confusion that my partner and I demonstrated. Of course that business never got off the ground and my business partner and I went our separate ways. Bob and I, however, stuck. At that point in his career, I think Bob was astute enough to recognize there were forces in the universe that were beyond his control.

Perhaps it was the chaotic "New York State of Mind" or Bob's internal state, but as much as we all are taught to disdain geographic change, there are some situations which call for nothing less. Bob felt his combined emotional, professional and financial situations outweighed any reasons to remain in New York. He hopped on his bike and away he rode to the new land.

Boulder

Out of the ashes rose the Phoenix and our deep, loving friendship which has endured the test of geography and time. Enter Helena, the wise, the beautiful, the catalyst.

To me, Bob's essence (aside from Helena) is profound humor, unremitting optimism, ironic insight and an unfailing commitment to his moral compass. Bob knows the right thing to do in his therapeutic work and in life. He knows what to do when boundaries have been so thinly stretched they are about to burst. He knows when a situation is so secure that boundaries need not be defined.

Husband, father, humanist, vegetarian, teacher, guide, experimenter, adventurer, explorer of internal and external worlds.

Therapeutic poet. Poetic therapist.

Doctor who doctors. Doctor's Doctor.

Bicyclist, motorcyclist, wood-turner but not of wooden phrases. Trances, transference and counter.

Romantic.

Instead of thirty or forty more essences to define Bob I would simply say: Helena. Dylan. Julian.

Happy Birthday, Bob!

Anna Soref

Dear Bob,

Working as Dylan and Julian's babysitter when they were both very young gave me an intimate view of you and your family. In those early years my impressionable 18 year old self saw a man deeply dedicated to his work and his family. You balanced them both beautifully and managed to get in some time for bike rides. Your tenderness to your children—sitting with each every night for their special time, for example—has modeled my own parenting. I remember the time the first Gulf war happened and you helped draft and sign an opposition letter in the Daily Camera. Then there was the time that you opened your home to me and my husband and let us live with you for six weeks. Granted, we had to share a room with Iggy (the iguana).

For my young self, seeing such actions taught me more than I'm sure you realize. The bottom line is that when you live your life from a place of goodness it affects others. Your goodness has affected me in more ways than I can list here. Thank you for giving me that.

Love you Bob,

Anna

Gil Spielberg

Bob and I have worked together as co-therapists for over 20 years. Once each year, we have co-led a training group at the annual conference of the American Group Psychotherapy Association. These 2-day training institutes have been oriented around particular themes or even "continuous" groups composed of the same members for more than a single year. Working with Bob in this way has been my most enduring professional association. I have watched Bob struggle, succeed, fail brilliantly and fail not so brilliantly. As unique as it is to have a colleague relationship lasting over such a significant period of time, that is not the most astonishing aspect of our relationship.

What is truly astonishing is that in our two decades of work together I can safely say that I have not learned a single thing about group therapy technique or theory. Not a single thing. And this has been Bob's greatest gift. Let me explain.

During our time together I have and continue to be inspired, amazed, stimulated and comforted by Bob. For me this experience always occurs in the same way. For example, we are about to begin a training group. I usually lay out some of the ground rules and timelines. Then I try to emotionally locate myself within the group. This tends to take a bit of time. Then Bob does it. His first intervention is never what I expect. It is never anything I have heard him say before or would have expected anyone to say. He is engaged. Now I am awakened and begin to engage as well. Bob's absence of predictable technique and fresh engagement has brought me back to the present. I treasure those moments.

I also treasure our "thread dialogues" about group. These "thread dialogues" are a series of five or six parallel conversations about group, relationships, therapy and whatever else. They never end and actually it is unclear how they ever begin. We always learn something completely unexpected. It is our own method of integrating the personal and the professional learnings of the conference.

And there is more I treasure about Bob. Bob has a rare commitment to learning how to be a good group member as well as a group leader. As far as I have seen, Bob is the only person to consider that being a good group member is an art or craft that is essential to being an excellent group leader. Bob is the master of being a conscious group member and a conscious group leader. Yet, the deepest basis of my friendship with Bob, and what I treasure above all is that Bob has been a conscious colleague and conscious life long friend who never tries to teach me anything.

Elizabeth Stahl

It's hard to take your problems and worries seriously for any length of time while talking to a smiling elder bouncing up and down on a large exercise ball. Talking to Bob is like getting an adjustment. I go in all tied up in knots, with all sorts of tensions and resistances to what is going on in my mind and life. By the time our session is over, I feel lighter, though nothing has changed, and no problem has been solved. Maybe just a shift in perspective was all that was achieved. My mood shifts to feeling lighter, unburdened. I enter into the world with a feeling of delight at how complicated it all is: a sense of "This is life!"

The mood Bob induces in me, or I transfer onto him, is in sharp contrast to his essay on disappointment that he offers up readily and often. I have begun to associate disappointment and humility with relief. Bob has encouraged me to view my role as a therapist as a practice in the art of being rejected and as an endurance sport.

In group I often feel neglected by Bob (yet another transference), and there is a way he inquires, accepts, and validates my wounded feelings without enabling the victim within and instead empowers me with the ability to make requests and express my frustration at his inability to meet my needs. Bob supports the warrior within me.

From Bob I have learned that one might not be able to change what there is to work with, but that there are signposts one can count on: the practice of good form and his general rule of thumb to "Be kind."

Liz Stewart

I joined one of Bob's supervision groups about nine years ago looking to gain some insight into the world of transference/countertransference as an educator for Rolf Therapists. Little did I know that joining this group would be such a catalyst for change both professionally and personally.

A few of the many things I've learned:

As a single parent of a teenager, I actually know a lot about induced feelings. I was convinced I had to go back to get a Masters Degree in Psychology. Not so!

That Bob Dylan might have as many great and meaningful lines as the Grateful Dead.

At certain points, knowing a little bit of Yiddish can help when working with tension.

Exercise, exercise, exercise was instilled in me as a way to self-regulate and get things moving through and out of my body. In fact, I have seen Bob bike riding and running in Boulder as well as sightings at different American Group Psychotherapy Association meetings in San Diego, New York City, San Francisco, and New Orleans.

On forming ideas about "doing." He wrote this about his cycling life:

> People frequently marvel at how I can zip up to places like Ward day after day. For me this isn't actually like *doing* anything—there is no psychic effort involved in hopping on my bike and doing such rides. However, ask me to meditate for an hour; this takes a huge effort and represents really *doing* something. Point being that we need to be careful about how we form our own definitions of doing, especially in the culture of psychotherapy, which might be very different from what is uniquely *doing* for each of our client. (Bob Unger, personal communication, February 19, 2014)

Upon a personal hardship, I reached out to Bob and

what he said has stayed with me: "You can always try to look back to figure out what happened, but as you know, if you drive looking through the rear view mirror you'll get in trouble with what's ahead."

Most of all, I continue to experience life unfolding and the importance of putting my thoughts and feelings into words.

What Would Bob Do?

Matthew Tomatz

I wonder how many times these words have been thought. They rang loudly in my mind when I started leading psychotherapy groups, and I imagine they have guided many nascent therapists, myself included, to discover a voice of courage and conviction. And that is how Bob helped us answer this question: by teaching us to be fearless.

I have a vivid memory of sitting nearly frozen and scared during my first experience of flying solo leading a psychotherapy group. This was no joking matter. A small circle of chairs occupied the corner of a large stark room tucked away in the back end of a community corrections center. Inspirational posters falling short of their mission and dull paint attempting to cover the institutional harshness surrounded us. Eight men sat with me, many of whom were disgruntled with their mandatory payment and doubtful they were going to receive any benefit. On top of that, with a fever, aching body, and dull mind, I was struggling to just carry on and start this work of facilitating this group. I sat, imbued with fear, and stared and got stared at. I dug deep, went inside, and tuned toward what my teacher had taught. In some way, in my own way, I answered the question of what Bob would do and said something. I'm not sure what came out. It probably lacked elegance, but it was a start. I spoke with courage and initiated my career as a group psychotherapist.

When I met Bob for the first time, my Naropa University cohort had just returned from a month-long Maitri meditation retreat. Our minds had been twisted and stilled, and it was a challenge to grasp concrete ideas or slip back into the flow of classes, schedules, and academic rigor. I only have one clear memory of that first class, which was hearing a rule loud and clear: No notes!

What? That's absurd! How does he expect me to remember the important parts? What will I do when it comes down to test time? How will it stick if I don't write it down? What I couldn't see was the brilliance in this teaching method. Bob was directing us to allow material to sink in deeper than paper, to use the material to connect with our own personal voice as a therapist, and to foster the courage it takes to trust such a form of learning.

At times, this rule tended to enrage some of my Naropa cohort, and Bob demonstrated an ability to hold frustration and anger with a kind of openness that I had not before witnessed. Not only was he embracing anger, he was purposefully directing it at himself, which struck me as a courageous thing to do. Bob was demonstrating the very fearlessness that he was encouraging by requiring us to forego note taking.

One of the primary teachings of the Contemplative Psychology program at Naropa is fearlessness. Chögyam Trungpa Rinpoche, the founder of Naropa, held fearlessness at the heart of his teachings and as a condition for warriorship (Trungpa, 1984). Here, warriorship conveys a quality of being brave and courageous while remaining willing to be deeply affected by life. Being fearless in the face of suffering, being moved by what is witnessed, and going beyond the terror of one's own vulnerability, the warrior is compelled to action. This teaching reveals the necessity of welcoming fear as a gateway to compassionate action and as a pathway to caring and effective therapy.

Group therapy has been described as complex and at times bewildering. Working with therapy groups requires us to face vast possibility and embrace the ambiguity that is inherent to such an endeavor, which can easily become a path to feeling overwhelmed. What I appreciate most about Bob's teaching is that it emboldened fearlessness. He did not guide us to face such uncertainty with a safe and specific technique that would keep us, and the group, from moving toward the unknown. Instead, he challenged us to rely on something deeper, our wisdom, and to dive, without notes, into the multifaceted depths of the human condition.

So, it happens that when we are faced with uncertainty the question might arise of what would Bob do? Not that we really know, but we can learn that the question itself invites strength and courageousness. The question suggests that it is time to trust your voice and engage with the group and the world. Now, when I ask the question, I know there is a solution in the inquiry itself, that the next step is not hidden, and to trust that the answer lies within myself.

Through his teaching and support, Bob taught me to trust my voice and lead groups with conviction and courage. I also know voice is an important quality to Bob, especially as I understand that he holds a dream of being a singer and musical artist. I have never heard Bob sing, but I have seen him facilitate a group. After years of sitting in music ensembles and witnessing many conductors, I say without a doubt that Bob is a musician. Like a great conductor, he directs groups of people with grace, excitement, and a distinct view, and he teaches his students to do the same. More importantly, he guides people to find their voice, which is truly a great gift. Bob helped me connect with my voice, and for that I will always be grateful.

References

Trungpa, C. (1984). *Shambhala: The sacred path of the warrior*. Boston: Shambhala.

Barbara Ungashick

I first met Bob in October of 1989 at a Colorado Center for Modern Psychoanalytic Studies workshop in Aspen. It was at a time when I was searching for a therapeutic modality that suited my personality and I thought genuinely was helpful. That coincided with the period during which modern psychoanalysis had a number of dedicated therapists who were being taught by analysts who would come out to Colorado from New York City to give weekend workshops on many and varied psychoanalytic topics. During this exciting time Bob gave a very popular workshop on group psychoanalysis. It had the largest attendance of any of the worships I had ever attended.

At one point I wanted to share modern psychoanalysis with my colleagues in my supervision group in Denver and asked him to be the presenter. He accepted and we had a typically lively presentation at which time he offered a new group he was starting to any of us interested. I was completely enthralled with what was possible for me to learn from him and spent about 15 years in individual and group supervision.

Looking back on those years I think I obtusely wanted his complete attention so I would not leave a single stone unturned. Eventually, I had been "fed" enough to join the group I had been avoiding for so long. I loved every minute with him, the group members and the dialogues, and felt that the whole experience completed a therapeutic foundation for me. I retired from the group 10 years ago and have been forever grateful to Bob Unger and what I got from him. Thank you, Bob.

The Art of Asking Questions

Dylan Unger

Like many kids growing up, I was always amazed at how much my dad, Bob Unger, knew about the world. He seemed to have an answer for everything. And that never faded. Even today, at 29 years old, I am still constantly impressed by just how many answers he has.

What impresses me most, however, is how he always knows what to do when he doesn't have the answer. Whether it be changing the question I am asking or picking a better question, my dad always knows what questions to ask me to guide me to the right answer.

Growing up I often found myself questioning my role in life and searching for what would make me happy. Knowing that my father would always be there to help guide me in the right direction was invaluable. Even if he didn't agree with my choices, if he knew it was right for me then he supported me in it. And sometimes I didn't agree with his answers, but looking back I can't think of a single time when he guided me in the wrong direction. My dad always stressed that I should never close a door permanently if I could help it. Back when I was a rebellious teenager and I disagreed with or disregarded most of his advice, that one piece stuck in the back of my mind, and if it hadn't I would not have the amazing life I have today. It was a wonderful feeling growing up knowing that I had the support and wisdom of such an amazing father, not to mention my amazing mother, another example of his great decisions.

Now that I've grown up and can actually appreciate just what an amazing resource I have at my disposal, I hardly ever make an important decision without first consulting him. I am currently in my second year of law school. I didn't enter law school with any clear idea of what I wanted to do, and figuring out which path to follow has led to a lot of major decisions for me. Every time I'm faced with a big decision I call my dad to run it by him. The beauty of his wisdom is that it's not that he has an idea of what I should do and pushes me towards it. He just knows what questions to ask me to get me to properly think about the problem so I can come to the best answer for myself. I now have a real plan for my life and I'm so happy that it feels so right and exciting to me. I know that I would not have found this path without the constant support, guidance, and questioning of my father, Bob Unger.

Helaine Unger

I first met you the day before my wedding in 1991 to your cousin, Richard. You, Helena, Dylan and Julian arrived in Burlington, VT to attend our wedding at Shelburne Farms. I immediately took a liking to your wonderful family from Boulder. Little did I know that you had come with your bike pedals ready to bicycle with Richard from our home in Burlington to the wedding in Shelburne! I was, of course, panicked. Would you arrive on time to get ready? What if you had a flat tire? In the end, it all worked out beautifully. You arrived in plenty of time and the wedding was lovely.

The second time that we met was under much different circumstances. Richard had suddenly passed away and you, Helena and the children returned to Burlington to be with me, Ilana and Richard's parents, Frieda and Lee. You stayed with us for most of the Shiva period and brought much comfort to us all. Your support during this challenging time was very much needed and appreciated. You were able to help me put things into perspective and move on.

The third time, Ilana and I came to Boulder to see you and Helena prior to a rafting trip. You introduced me to Jed and encouraged our relationship and my move to Boulder from the beginning. I feel that you have always been there for me during happy and sad times. You are like the brother I never had and I love you.

Happy, Happy Birthday!

Love,

Helaine

Helena Unger

When we met 34 years ago at SMC, I was working in the kitchen. Bob walked through, lobbing a feisty comment my way. I lobbed a quick retort back and that's when the magic began. It was our first exchange, to be followed by a lifetime of smart remarks.

One year later, we married at the Justice Center in Boulder, going to the ceremony on the back of his motorbike. In those days, Bob was torn between being a psychotherapist or a wood turner. Once our first son was born, he realized we might starve if he were to choose wood turning. So instead he worked full time, earned his PhD, and began to teach at Naropa—all while parenting two sons with me. Today those two children are resourceful, funny, and confident adults who totally trust their father and turn to him for advice—with the exception of fashion, food, or how to barter.

We vowed we would never divorce. Between the former backpacking hippie and the New York Jew, we were two strong, stubborn individuals who earned their lasting relationship the hard way!

We still compete about who is luckier—me to have found Bob or Bob to have found me. I, of course, see the latter as the truth of the matter.

Bob, you continue to show me how to live with integrity, set boundaries, be fearless in the world, and be openly competitive with each other and still share compassion and unconditional love.

When you do something, you do it really well—like riding your bike nearly every day, come rain or shine, with a grin on your face like a young boy on his first bicycle.

You have demonstrated how to be successful in the world, as a person and as a professional. By teaching group psychotherapy at Naropa, you have influenced and mentored countless students who have gone on to share that knowledge and find confidence and joy in their work.

Julian Unger

I have always said that I am extremely lucky to have Bob as my dad, but as I sat down to write this entry in honor of him, I had to really think about why I have always felt that way. Reflecting on this, I realized one of my Dad's most impactful traits is how invaluable his skills as an advisor to me throughout my life have been, and how truly unique my life experience has been as a result of his advice.

When people find out that my parents are *both* therapists they often crack a joke about how I must have had an exhausting childhood. Luckily, when I was quite young I figured out how to call my parents out and not stand for any "therapist talk." While I did learn at a rather young age to, often sarcastically, deflect questions like "How does that make you feel?" and other cliché "therapist" moves, I also constantly took advantage of living with two extremely insightful, selfless advisors. This is not what outside observers meant when they joked about growing up with a 1:1 ratio of therapist to teen, but it was a tremendous leg up that my brother and I received.

Whenever I seek advice, be it over something small, like my latest pickle about apartment hunting, or something more consequential like a career move or picking a major in college, when I go to my dad I am undoubtedly in the hands of an expert. He listens, asks insightful questions, and always helps me understand the problem better then I ever could without him. Most importantly he does this without any objective of his own, patiently giving me the tools to guide myself to the conclusion that is best for me. I have at times taken this for granted, but looking back, I realize how truly lucky I am to have an advisor of this caliber willing to excitedly help me at all hours of the night. People literally pay money for those services! There is no doubt in my mind that without such amazing counsel I would be in a very different place in my life right now. I have been very lucky to have my dad's guidance in my life as a father. It makes me extremely happy to know how many other people have had the great fortune of receiving his advice on a professional level. What makes him so amazing is his ability to guide me in making my own decisions, and I know that these are the same principles that have made him respected and loved in his professional life.

And with that, happy birthday dad! His compassion, wisdom and love for two wheeled vehicles truly makes Robert Unger a fantastic father!

Andrew van Dyke

I am not sure what to say about Bob. He kind of defies words. What I do know is that I have a deep appreciation for what he has done to establish a group community in Colorado and in educating so many fine practitioners who are out there as we speak, sending ripple effects into the community at large. He helped me to learn how to use humor as a tool to regulate the tone of the group and take it into deeper levels of experience. He inspired me to get excited and dive into group facilitation as a professional and the community he helped begin here helps me keep on going.

Kristin Venderbush

(in conversation with Michael M. Dow)

My first memory of Bob—I'm sure I saw him before this—but I think of him in the group class. There were 32 of us, a huge cohort, and Bob is like leaning in, with this total impish smile and he's up in people's faces and he's really challenging the things people are saying and getting people to consider the veracity of their statements. I just think of him as challenging the bullshit we put out there. You know, elbows on knees, and looking at people really hard. It was so scary and weird and we just thought, "What are they going to do with us?" You know, to have faculty relating to us that way. I remember a lot of people thought he was a jerk and didn't know what to make of him. It takes bravery. I think of that as I practice now. I want my clients to like me and win them over, you know. I have a few examples of people like Bob who really put clients first. When I think about those classes, I think of him as being pretty fearless. I mean I know it's the model, to try to draw aggression towards yourself, but to see someone to do it with such skill and with a smile and being willing to push people farther and not be liked in the moment and/or long term was impressive. It was exciting to be around and such great teaching. I think that as a contemplative educator the way Bob contributes is really demonstrating awareness in action.

People could argue and say that he's all about making people uneasy, but it's also a service. It puts people first. You're not concerned about being liked, which is of course my primary objective at all times (wink).

On the other had, as the administrator of the Master's program in Contemplative Psychotherapy at Naropa, I helped with the summer parties. I remember coordinating with Bob and Helena. I think I just remember them being super gracious. I was all nervous going to a faculty member's house, but he's such a sweet guy, generous and welcoming. I think they loved it too, but to me it was such a big part of community and bringing people together. And I remember one of their kids was bleaching their hair and dyeing it purple and I loved the way they loved their children and just let them be and experiment. I mean maybe it's just Boulder, but I thought they were really sweet about letting their children explore.

Laura Volmert

I am currently on what I think of as Bob 2.0 (this, of course, has nothing to do with Bob and everything to do with my own inductions/transferences/counter transferences). As a student of Contemplative Psychotherapy at Naropa in the late 90's and early 00's, I was wowed by Bob's brilliance and clarity. I experienced him as incredibly wise and brimming with insight about human interaction. In addition to having Bob as an instructor, I was also able to experience him in several supervisory capacities where I continued to be awed by his brilliance. I remember working at Friendship House, where Bob would occasionally come in to provide clinical supervision to the staff. What I recall about those groups was that Bob's presence provided us with an opportunity not only to discuss the challenges of working with chronically mentally ill folks, but also to process our relationships with each other, which were just as challenging (if not more so). It was hard to move on from that work environment after experiencing that level of processing among the staff.

Bob 2.0 began for me last year when a former Naropa classmate managed to wrangle me into a supervision group with Bob. As someone not currently working as a therapist but trying to figure out how to move toward private practice, I jumped at the chance. It has been such a delight to once again experience Bob's brilliance, but also to feel his incredibly deep compassion. Of course, that compassion and kindness was always present, but somehow I am able to receive it in a different way 13 years later. I have felt simultaneously supported and gently nudged out of my comfort zone, which has been difficult and rewarding. Most of all, my most profound experience of Bob 2.0 is the experience of feeling really seen in my process toward creating a practice, and has allowed me to become curious about my process rather than feeling simply stuck.

Miscellaneous Thoughts on my Friend Robert

Don Waldman

One of the things I like best about Bob, and there is a lot to like, is that he finds something good about everyone. Numerous times he has described someone he knows or has met as this truly wonderful being. I'm not like that (I mean, I have good friends that I like and everything, but not like Bob).

He takes being kidded so well (and he is such an easy target: think tenting in the desert, food, tastes in music, etc.).
My idea of a father was greatly influenced by Bob as a father. I felt fortunate that his kids are about seven years older than mine, so that I could learn from his experiences.

I wish to thank Bob for facilitating my second mid-life crisis. If it were not for his interest in motorcycling and constant nagging for me to get one, I don't think I would have bought my very large BMW.

And then there is Bob as counterweight:

I'm old, and I hang around with a lot of younger people, so I'm glad there is Bob.

I'm liberal, and I hang around with a lot of liberal people. Sometimes I get accused of being too liberal. So again, I am so glad there is Bob.

My wife, who is somewhat of an introvert, sometimes will roll her eyes at how much of an extrovert I am, so again . . .

A Short Memoir in One Hundred Words (for Bob)

Karen Kissel Wegela

It began with delight: here's a great guy!
Then, a nightmare of a group we co-led.
Leading to the dark ages when we didn't speak for years.
Then, a warming over a breakfast.
Followed by slow, reluctant reconnection.
Then, years of working together, usually disagreeing.
Turning into discovering how much we liked disagreeing.
Understanding that we agreed on disagreeing.
Then, disagreeing for the fun of it even when we agreed.
Years of laughter, sadness, deep joy.
Finally, recognizing that we have been—all along—family.

With great love and respect,

Karen

Dolores Welber

It gives me the greatest pleasure to be a witness to Bob's persistence, personal growth, and generosity with others. His contributions to the world as a husband, father, analyst, teacher, and group leader attest to the personal power of persistence and love of self and others. It is an honor to be among those honoring him.

Never Just Answer

Josh White

(in conversation with Maureen Dummigan)

So, it's 6 am and the extremely busy Josh has not been able to find the time to write anything at all about his mentor, Bob Unger. This is unlike Josh, who usually drops everything to do something like this. However, the two guys with whom he started Red Mountain (a super awesome contemplative-psychotherapy-based program in Sedona, AZ) are no longer in the picture. We are the last ones standing and Josh is creating an amazing program from the ground up—which takes up more time than anyone has. Michael Dow suggested that I, Josh's wife Maureen, just get him talking and write down what he said. Brilliant.

The following "non-versation" took place at 6 am at the kitchen counter as I plied him with gluten-free blueberry muffins.

M: So, if you had the time to say something about Bob what would it be?

J: It would be that I love him but I don't have time to write anything.

(M writes this down)

J: Don't write THAT!!!

(M thinks, "Now I have him.")

J: I remember that he was always cheerful.

M: What else?

J: I remember this one classmate who was really upset that Bob wouldn't answer the question of whether or not he was married. The classmate was getting really upset and Bob wouldn't relent. We were all squirming.

So, finally, Bob said, "What feelings would you have if I told you I was married?"

The classmate answered that it would make her feel that Bob understood the dynamics in that person's marriage and she would feel safe.

Bob then asked, "What feelings would you have if I told you I wasn't married?"

The classmate answered that she wouldn't feel as safe. She then went on to talk about the dynamics in her family of origin and how important it was to feel understood.

Bob said, "So, it's extremely important for you to feel understood by your group leader. If I had just answered your question, we never would have gotten to these feelings. Whenever a client asks you a question it's an opportunity to help them understand themselves."

The classmate cried and the whole class just sat there in awe of what had just happened.

M: Wow. Yes, he is amazing. What else do you want to say?

J: I remember my first American Group Psychotherapy Association (AGPA) conference in New Orleans and I ran into him in the baggage claim. He has this huge metal box. When I asked him what it was he said it was his collapsible bike that he took everywhere so, "He could get away quickly."

Also at that AGPA, everyone wore lanyards with titles or identifiers on there. Bob had like 50 so it was almost as long as his tie. Bob said, "These things are so we can tell how long everyone's penis is." This made me feel a lot better because as a newbie my lanyard wasn't very long.

M (suddenly thinking about penises, trying to focus): What else do you want to say?

J: Well, honestly, I'm really good at group. Most therapists, even really good ones, are not good at group. And I'm very aware that the reason I'm good at group is Bob.

Something About Bob

Maureen Dummigan White

Bob. So much to say about Bob. Bob was the greatest, most terrifying surprise of my first year in MACP back in 1996. There we were, a motely group of people who had some notion about becoming therapists. We imagined our lives in comfy chairs, clothed in velvet and other tactilely pleasing fabrics, tinkling Feng-Shui fountains on our desks in just the correct position to invite tranquility. We imagined gently healing the wounded, listening intently, offering sagacious encouragement or silence. We imagined what it was to be helpful. We imagined.

Then Bob. Bob. Fucking Bob. He burst that reverie and brought us into contact with shadow, with aggression, with the reality of other people. Classmates ran from the room on a regular basis. They declared that his ways were not skillful, that his aggression was dangerous. What in the hell was he doing?

Man, we were so young and naïve.

Now, all these years later, there is not a work day that passes that I don't think about what I learned from Bob. Actually, I think there are very few days in general when I don't apply or ponder what I learned from Bob. When I was a Naropa Baby, I thought individual talk therapy was the kinder, gentler way. I was repulsed by the idea of group. Now I know that even individual sessions are group sessions. We are never alone in the room with a client. Everyone in their personal mandala is there with them.

I absolutely love leading groups whether they are therapeutic, meditative, organizational development or individual (wink). I always wonder how everyone will show up. I wonder who will represent what aspects of the mandala/system and how we will all work together. I am thrilled by a group as a living entity. They fuel my curiosity and expand my heart.

When I think about Bob today it is with so much warmth, appreciation and reverence. What a courageous man to take group after group of Naropeans and hold up the mirror for us. I mean, most of us chose Naropa because we longed for a reprieve from what seemed like the harshness of regular academia. We, or I, thought that Naropa would soften my hardness without me actually having to admit to it, much less work with it. In hindsight, Bob was so playful and gentle. He taught me to notice everything and to play with everything and to always put the group first. He taught me to let go of the need to be liked (although I do prefer it) in the service of actually helping others.

Bob. Fucking Bob. What a sad day for him to leave Naropa. Thank you, Bob. Thank you. You are, and will always be, the quintessential role model for tender-hearted bodhisattva warriors.

Lenore Wian

My dear little brother. Impossible to put into words the lifetime of experiences we've had. You are always there for me —in joyous times and not so joyous times. Your speeches have been a landmark for our family and they always capture the essence of the moment and you make us laugh and cry. You are extraordinarily generous and wonderful and I love you more than words can say.

A Man in Full

John Wilcockson

Tom Wolfe's novel *A Man in Full* is a sprawling 700-page treatise on American mores and minuses of the 1990s whose main character is Charlie Croker, a crooked real estate developer with a crumbling industrial empire. In contrast to Croker—whose life is full of decadence and deceit—our Doctor Bob is truly a "Man in Full." Bob's time on this planet is full of fun, full of fitness, full of family, full of friends—full of life! I don't know any other man who can dance ballet, enthusiastically sing Dylan (even though he can't sing), run half-marathons competitively, nonchalantly do bike races as if they're spins around the block, expertly speed down twisting mountain roads on a sport motorcycle, counsel clients (and his boys!) with in-built wisdom, keep abreast of the latest trends in physiology, technology and politics, treat everyone with loving kindness (especially Helena, Iggy the iguana and their various pets), and all the time lead a life in a calm, Buddha-like manner—with a chuckle and a smile never far from his lips! We love you Doctor Bob, our real-life Man in Full.

References

Wolfe, T. (2010). *A man in full.* New York: Farrar, Straus & Giroux.

Karen Wilding

The Bob Unger that I worked with at Naropa University was a master of understanding knots a la R. D. Laing (1970):

> Jack
>   knows he does not know
> And sees that Jill
>   does not know she knows.
> By telling Jack
>   what Jack knows he does not know
> Jill helps Jack to help Jill
> to know she knows
> what she does not know she knows.

Thank you for your thoughtfulness and endless patience Bob! May your 70's be joyful and full of delight.

References

Laing, R.D. (1970). *Knots* (pp. 5-6). New York: Vintage Books.

Anne Wilzbacher

In spirit of Bob Unger, one of my role models and greatest mentors (not sure he even knows this . . .), I will free associate what comes to mind when I reflect on this genius of a man . . .

I was a student of Bob's at Naropa University (Master's in Contemplative Psychotherapy (MACP) 2010). As a first year MACP student, I remember my sister-in-law, Sarah Kolman (who was a third year MACP student) saying, "Wait until you have Bob. You will love him!" I am not sure what her exact words were, but this was the message I remember. "Bob? Who's Bob?" I asked. He runs the group class. Group class was the class I was most looking forward to. This was my jam.

This class changed me. I was inspired. I was intrigued. I was engaged. I was home. I felt empowered. I knew I loved groups, but this class facilitated a congruence within me I did not even know I was waiting for.

I attribute to Bob my ability to see my path more clearly and continue to decide to lean toward the wild, chaotic wisdom that is the territory of group dynamics. Bob believed in me and challenged me. Looking back on my 33 years, there are just a handful of people in my life where I had the pleasure of experiencing *being believed in.* What a gift. So I thank you, Bob Unger, because you are one of them.

Along with Jeff Price, Bob introduced me to the American Group Psychotherapy Association—a conference I look forward to attending every year. I have attended for 6 or 7 years and it is really something special. The first time I attended this conference, I could feel it. This was also my jam! This is what I am interested in and intrigued by. This is what I want to become a part of. This is the territory that I want to explore. Being encouraged and empowered to participate and become a member of this association has contributed greatly to who I am and what continues to drive me. It has been invaluable to simply have an individual gently steer me toward something that has been profound in my life.

I had the privilege to work with Bob as his Clinical Support Professional (CSP) (the new word at Naropa for Teaching Assistant) for a few years in the MACP program. Bob is so sweet, skilled, hilarious, smart, caring. I admire his ability to enter a group, let go of his agenda, and work with whatever it is that arises. True meditation practice in action. I wanted to do that! How does he do that so gracefully?!

It was a true honor to get to sit next to Bob as his CSP and be the recipient of his infamous "head turns" to his co-facilitators. I am not sure he even knows this is a *thing*, but it was definitely *a thing* that I noticed from the first day in his class. He turned to his CSPs in that class and talked to them about us . . . or asked them questions about something that might be happening in the group. While there were all sorts of reactions, feelings, and thoughts about this sort of "intervention," I thought it was brilliant. I liked it. I am aware that Bob was also the recipient of many levels of aggression at times due to something as simple as the "head turn." Well many things actually: uproar, silent stewing, frustration, rage, love, pain, sadness, and so on . . . But how incredible, to get this all seen or recognized more clearly in the group. We know it's all there already. This "head turn" illuminated feelings that perhaps would not have surfaced otherwise. Illuminating human experience is how I saw it. So to say the least, to be on the receiving end of that "head turn" when he asked me a question about the group and that moment of answering out loud what I thought, was an honor. I was participating in a very crucial moment in time where perhaps we were creating a "gap," a pause, a doubt, confusion, a closer connection . . . whatever it was, I believe it contributed to a sense of "waking up to the moment." This might seem simple, but to me, it was profound.

My relationship with and experience of Dr. Bob Unger has been profound and moving. I revere him deeply. He was a pillar in my graduate training experience. He remains as someone I bow to with respect and continue to learn from. It is no small thing to get the beautiful opportunity to feel empowered and seen. So Bob, I thank you for giving me that experience. I do not take it lightly. And now, on to the next moment. That's my jam!

Brooks Witter

One of my proudest moments was to keep up with Bob—a man 30 years my senior—on a bicycle over 100 miles of mountain roads. Bob rides as he lives: with full commitment, lots of energy, and talking away to anyone who will listen, demonstrating a relentless desire to connect with those around him.

Another bicycle themed moment of Bob-ness is reflected in my attempt to gain advantage in a triathlon. Bob generously let me borrow his ultra-light mountain bike, as I could use every ounce of economy I could buy or borrow. In my anxious and early morning haste of getting out the door and to the starting line, I must have cranked the headset of the bike a bit too far, for when I pulled the bike from my car I discovered the rear brake line had lost its seal, rendering me with only a front brake for my first competitive race of my life. Well, it's Bob's bike, and it figures this is how I would do it: headlong and with full commitment. If I am to use brakes, I do so sparingly, as too much will throw me over the handlebars, and not enough I spill off the trail. Riding a dynamic balance of chaos and control, I ended up racing for an hour as I imagine Bob lives: with full commitment, wide awake, and ready for whatever comes his way on this great adventure.

Thanks, Bob, for being such an example of the breadth of capacity of the human heart.

On Ecstasy, Banality, Disappointment and Deep Sorrow: Group Therapy and the Perpetual Struggle against Narcissistic and Antisocial Ideological Hegemony

Jean-Marc C. Wong

(in conversation with Michael M. Dow)

I have no idea why I joined Bob's group, and I'll probably never know exactly what in Hell I've gotten out of it. Wasn't it you Michael that came to me singing Bob's praises? Urging me to join one of his supervision groups? Well, I tried. It's your fault. He didn't offer me a supervision group. He stuck me in a patient group. Every Wednesday morning. A full hour and a half, starting promptly at 7 AM and ending exactly at 8:28 AM or 8:29 AM . . . minus the minutes I miss for showing up late every week. That was fifteen years ago. And I'm still going.

You ask me why. I don't know why. Now I've said before that only one thing is clear about fifteen years of group with Bob: it's been a corrective financial experience. That's what I got out of it. Financial ruin. That's my running one line joke about long term analysis for all these years. But whose fault is that? I make my choices. And it was only in the past few weeks that I realized that it's possible that this alone—throwing money into a bottomless dark hole—is what has saved my life. With the cash in pocket, what other shiny trinkets might I have hoarded to fill the space? How many more hours would I've been forced to endure in the aisles of T. J. Maxx? A life filled with empty schlock! It's terrible to imagine! As it stands, despite years of therapy, I have rooms of crap to get rid of!

What is group analysis anyway? What's group? I haven't the slightest idea. I should've done the readings. Bob probably knows, but he cleverly never really lets on. Maddening! Keeping all the secrets to himself! Oh, a comment here and there over the decade and a half. "Just say what comes to your mind spontaneously. We'll deal with the fallout later," he might suggest. Or, "Some would say that the group's purpose is to serve as . . . " My urge is to pull out my iPhone and jot notes on these rare occasions, but I find myself immediately tuning out. So what does Bob do? Do I really want to know? He sits there on that ugly silvery blue ball and let's us do the talking. It seems good enough. Seven or eight of us. Some have been there well over 20 years, some brand new babies. All in various embryonic stages of malformation. These Others. A shared experience? Yeah. But also . . . like parts of me. Bob stuck me in a group with all the other parts of me that I find pathological, frustrating, endearing, feel compassionate towards. Parts of me that I haven't had the courage to acknowledge. Easier to identify these parts when they're one step removed, my God. He's created a space in my life, a place to come quietly and solemnly. Open the door. Walk up the stairs. Turn the knob on an interior door and peek inside. Yes, we're all here. I recognize myself. Deformed! I think he wants us to revel in it.

Is Bob analyzing me? Doubt it. He's riding his fucking bicycle. As the clock ticks! Who cares? Who needs interpretation when we got meds? Prozac! Viagra! Do I really need to find the key which accesses my most primal urges? That vault might lie in a well-hidden mud pit deep in the forest, but there's holes blown in it and the contents are seeping out! I don't see Bob as attempting to understand the unconscious underpinnings of my behavior. Sure he likes a good dream, and I suspect he's much more comfortable with homicidal impulses than he is with sexual urges! Hard-wired bullshit anyway, that's my opinion. Bob's not so interested in interpreting. My experience is that his goal for me is quite to the contrary: I'm that messy haired muppet wearing shades in the Mah Na Mah Na sketch of the Muppet Show. Bob and the group serve as a reality check for the amazingly unreal, rather fanciful way I've configured my life. (Hey! I'm not alone.) And when I get to improvising or indulging myself too much, the cows shake their heads in disapproval. (Disbelief may be more accurate!) There's something comforting about sticking with the herd.

Bob's kept me out of jail. There are rules in this life: Ties for the men, skirts for the women. And yet Bob allows me a safe place to say, "How useless, this game!"

There're rules in this life, and they're meant to be broken. I quit wearing a tie years ago. I'd like to say it was in protest of the gender discrimination, but it was probably just to fuck with Bob. I can't imagine Bob approving of antisocial behavior, but he's certainly indulged me in my antisocial fantasies. Life can be such a bore! Group becomes a parallel universe, a place separate from real life on this planet. Maybe the long idea is to get these worlds to converge as closely as possible and that's when I'm done. Will I ever be done with treatment? Maybe I'm close (wishful thinking), because the group has become such an integral part of my personal experience that I often wonder if what I'm walking back into as I descend the stairs out the door and off of that green painted porch at 8:30 AM each Wednesday is some fake world—a dream or an imaginary horror. A surreal world, which only exists in the context of the more tangible group. Group is the reality. Ninety minutes becomes a little larger than the entire universe (as Pessoa might say (Pessoa & Zenith, 2006)).

If that's true, than who in Hell is this Bob figure? I saw his name listed in Wikipedia under "Hyman Spotnitz." As furthering the work of this giant. (What a nut job!) Carrying the torch of modern psychoanalysis: Nagelberg, Ormont, Rosenthal, Meadows, Unger. Did you add his name to the Wiki, Michael? It said "[citation needed]." Ha! I don't believe Bob gives a shit about such recognition. Bob's a screw up and he loves it: our flawed hero in ten thousand meandering narratives of perpetual disappointments! The story...it ends tragically for us all. What a bummer! What a ruse! We die! "We're all bozos on this bus," Bob often quips. Ha! I love this quote. I love this about Bob: he recognizes life as great comedy. In the midst of all the grief, humor pervades his groups. Fifteen years of humor and I've had a front row seat. Worth every penny! Bob! He emanates such joy. He is alive as he dies!

Weekly group. Bob's always there. Every time. One day he won't be. We'll see who dies first. For now, he's right there.

He's consistent. His motorcycle is backed into its space. Therefore, unless he's tripped and fallen into a bush or gotten stuck on the crapper, he'll be upstairs sitting on his ugly ball. He joins me in my bewilderment. He has as much hope for me as he has for his own short and miserable life. He expresses an incredible patience. He dabbles in the transcendent. He searches for pearls of wisdom, and he may share one like a cheap prize he just pulled out of a box of Cracker Jacks. He feels pain and suffers with us, his eyes frequently filling with tears upon hearing about loss. It's everywhere. His eyebrows raise and his mouth opens in "ah ha" moments. He understands. He hates the word "authentic." He smiles widely and beams in recognition of the absurdity and futility of it all.

There's more madness than health in this life, and I expect no cure. But Bob's group at least allows me to have the same daydream today as that of my childhood: to one day buy enough bottle rockets to tie onto a large metal trash can that will send me into orbit. Light up that big twisted wick and put the lid over my head! Ah, the solitude of outer space. The impossible escape! And since I'm an adult and got a garage full of tools at my disposal, (no plastic saws!) I know I can cut out a much nicer window to look out of. You see, out there it's the unknown. And maybe that's the best way to describe my group experience, or why I keep seeing Bob despite really not recognizing particularly what I've gotten out of it. Maybe group analysis is more about subtraction than addition. Coming out of it with more questions than answers. A slow but wild journey into the mysterious unknown. Hmmm. Perhaps desire and the illusion of hope are maintained as Bob helps me to "unknow" myself.

So why am I in group? Well, who the fuck wants to be forgotten? And what's my life worth if I didn't at least try to understand my feelings? Sure I may be going in a circle, but I got direction man! Damn it. I guess I believe there's huge value in the simple pleasure of staying curious in the face of being completely perplexed—to know one has played in the game. It's life. It's group. Group. It's my Certificate of Participation. I get one every week by attending group. It's better than any trophy to me. And I'm so grateful to Bob for that.

References

Pessoa, F., & Zenith, R. (Ed.). (2006). *A little larger than the entire universe: Selected poems* (R. Zenith, Trans.). New York: Penguin.

Elliot Zeisel

Bob Unger and I have been friends for over three decades. We are analytic siblings, having been treated and trained by many of the same people. From this vantage point, I've had the opportunity to see Bob grow into the man he is today. For me, Bob is a wonderful amalgam of forces in life. He is by turn, husband, father, therapist, teacher, friend, colleague and athlete. Over the course of our friendship I've learned much from Bob in each of these areas. I am a better father as a result of our annual check in at the American Group Psychotherapy Association (AGPA) meeting, when we'd review the challenges and progress of our growing families. I'm a better therapist for having shared many hours of informal consulting with Bob at the meeting when we'd be working our way through an Institute process or contending with some thorny organizational issue. I am a more conscientious athlete as a result of our association. I will never have his resting heart rate of 42. However, I hold Bob in my mind as a model for self-care, as a model for the integration of mind and body. His early adoption of Buddhist practice has expanded my understanding and practice of mindfulness too. Bob brings a dynamic and mindful approach to whatever activity he's engaged in. He is a much sought after teacher of group therapy in Boulder, at the AGPA Institute and Annual Meeting. His teaching is characterized by a thoughtful blend of theory and group leadership skills that is delivered with clarity and humor. Bob is devoted to refining his craft as a therapist/teacher and will make use of whatever life brings his way in the effort to expand his abilities. He is quick on his feet or in his seat and I'm a lucky man to count him as my friend and colleague.

Dr. Bob engages in a bit of bicycle ballet, avoiding asteroids, as he leads a group of dedicated Phonites[1] into the deepest reaches of outer space.

Jean-Marc C. Wong

---

[1] Group members calling in to group via speaker phone

Articles

Psychoanalysis and Buddhism: Paths of Disappointment[1]

Robert Unger

I'd like to begin with a vignette. A little over 20 years ago, Rangjung Rigpe Dorje, the 16th Galwang Karmapa, head of the Karma Kagyu lineage of Tibetan Buddhism, and thought by many to be next in importance to the Dalai Lama in Buddhist culture, lay dying of cancer in a Chicago hospital. He is said to have refused pain killers, yet he astonished his nurses with his presence, kindness, and compassion (Goldstein, 2003). Just as he died, his attendants reported that his last words were, "Nothing happens." In this chapter, I'd like to discuss the relevance of this simple statement through personal experience.

I entered the field of psychoanalysis with the highest of hopes. It was the end of the exciting 1960s, I was in my early 20s, was new to New York, and was determined to shed a constrained, self-conscious identity. Although at the time I was in another occupation, psychoanalysis seemed like a natural fit for me and, after a couple of years of analysis, I entered social work school, psychoanalytic training, and faced the future with new excitement and optimism.

The years rolled on and, although my schooling seemed to be progressing quite well and my analysis—conducted by a brilliant, exciting, and charismatic analyst—was always interesting, I still found myself uttering a familiar refrain to myself. It took a variety of forms, but its essence was something like this: "Sometime, after some more analysis, I'll be as smart as my analyst," or "a better athlete," or "a more

---

[1] Originally published in Unger, R. (2008). Psychoanalysis and Buddhism: Paths of disappointment. In F. Kaklauskas, L. Hoffman, S. Nimmanheminda, & M. Jack, (Eds.). *Brilliant Sanity: Buddhism and psychotherapy* (pp. 347-353). Colorado Springs, CO: University of the Rockies Press.

desirable lover." What these statements had in common was the notion of my becoming more *something* than I was in the present—internally a combination of more confident, more relaxed, and more accomplished, and externally more revered by others. Given that the content of these fantasies varied, I was not aware that the core thought was being endlessly repeated.

After about ten years, my personal and professional circumstances called into question the validity of this path and I retreated from the psychoanalytic world. It was at roughly this same time that I was introduced to Tibetan Buddhism and meditation practice. That path began to make much more sense to me than psychoanalysis and my allegiance shifted. I left analytic work altogether, moved to a mediation center in Colorado, and became a committed Buddhist practitioner. Eventually, I returned to psychoanalytic work, but I continued my meditation practice and my involvement in the Buddhist community in Boulder.

After several years of meditation practice I began to notice an all too familiar refrain creeping into my meditation. Once again, I found myself thinking that if I continued to meditate, "sometime, after more meditation, I'll become as smart as my meditation instructor," or "a better athlete," or "a more desirable lover," and so on. I eventually realized that I had returned to my former wishful thinking. Although the content of the thoughts and fantasies typically referenced the future, I had learned a fundamental lesson in analysis—as Freud (1923/1989) noted, whatever thoughts and fantasies were occurring in the room were of the present. In Buddhism, I had also learned that whatever arises in the mind has the nature of nowness (Trungpa, 2004).

It was clearly time to explore what information these hopes and fantasies of the future provided about the present. I concluded that fantasizing myself in a different position, state of mind, or circumstance implied that I was less than satisfied with my present state of mind, emotion, and being. And that implied some state of disappointment. Furthermore, I realized that over time, neither psychoanalysis nor Buddhist meditation had offered any particular cure for disappointment. I was spending just as much time fantasizing about the future now as I had when I began following the paths of analysis and meditation. It was hard to acknowledge that it had taken so many years to understand and face this seemingly simple truth.

I decided that it might be useful to view disappointment in context of Freud's pleasure principle (Freud, 1920/1961). We know that it is natural to seek and imagine situations that might result in greater comfort or in reduced internal tension, with the classic example being that of a person stuck on a desert island who fantasizes about a good meal. From the time a baby cries to expresses its response to discomforts such as being hungry, wet, or cold and a parent responds with the appropriate remedy, humans learn to fantasize about the things that will make them comfortable or reduce their internal tension. As we mature, this process increases greatly in complexity and subtleness. Society provides events and circumstances that raise our anxiety and tension while simultaneously promising remedies that can reduce it. In a materially focused culture such as ours, we are bombarded with information about a variety of products and activities that will allegedly make us more comfortable. The increase in ambient stimulation and tension in society over the past 50 to 100 years has been much greater than the human body's ability to acclimate to it, spurring a new urgency for securing relief. As the ambient level of tension rises, that tension becomes manifest in a variety of symptoms and behaviors. People tend to embrace activities or products that promise relief, from buying material goods to turning to alcohol, legal and illegal drugs, exercise, and perhaps even psychotherapy or meditation. In fact, mainstream psychotherapy is moving strongly toward a focus on symptom relief as its primary objective.

The dilemma is that if these panaceas provide any relief at all, it is usually transitory. In a recent article in the *New York Times* entitled "The Futile Pursuit of Happiness," Jon Gertner (2003) describes research conducted by a group of psychologists and economists in the area of affective forecasting—the notion that virtually all of the decisions we make are based on our prediction of the emotional consequences of those events. The research showed that we are not very good emotional forecasters. What we imagine will make us happy probably will not make us as happy as we had imagined and the effects will be short-lived. In an article in *Psychology Today*, titled "Great Expectations," Polly Shulman (2004) emphasized something most of us know from experience—that the "ideal mate" does not exist. This notion is usually some projection of what we *think* will make us content. Writings espousing these notions seem to be appearing more frequently of late, perhaps a natural response to the increasing emphasis on comfort and relief in the culture.

So, if we do not pursue an external solution to our internal state of dissatisfaction or disappointment, what alternatives do we have? What happens if, as in psychoanalysis or Buddhist meditation, we are directed to study our own internal states, moment by moment? What seems to come into focus is a state of disappointment that may initially be experienced as hunger, fear, anxiety, tension, loss, sadness, or some other distressing feeling. In a culture largely driven by promises of solutions to uncomfortable states, it is deeply frustrating to spend years in analysis or a meditation practice only to discover, in the words of the 16th Karmapa, that "nothing happens."

Why engage in such often expensive and time-consuming yet disappointing activities? Here we might turn to the notion of addiction as it becomes more widespread in the culture. Although it is common to think of addiction in material terms, the list of other kinds of addictive behaviors, such as sexual addiction, exercise addiction, relationship addiction, and so on is growing. To break free of any form of addiction, one must go through a withdrawal process that can be both painful and lengthy. Recent neuropsychological research has supported the enduring Freudian concept of repetition compulsion, as it has become apparent that addictive processes are woven into our brains from our experiences (Siegel, 2007).

In fact, the cinematic experience in our present culture clearly reflects the overwhelming availability of diverse, intense simulative forces. Which of you readers has been to a movie lately and not felt bombarded by the emotionally explosive excess of the trailers for coming attractions, never mind the movie you came to see? Few among us can imagine life without cell phones, computers, television, and other modern electronic stimulants that did not exist a short time ago. No sooner do we purchase one of these technological wonders than it becomes obsolete, with the next generation of gadgets providing even more complex stimulation. In a very interesting and entertaining book titled *Faster: The Acceleration of Just About Everything,* James Gleick (2000) describes more than thirty areas of stimulation that have seen exponential acceleration in recent years.

When considering life without the everyday stimulants we have come to take for granted, it is instructive to monitor our emotions when one of these agents of stimulation is suddenly unavailable to us. Think about how you feel when the phone does not work, the TV breaks, the power goes out, a friend cancels an appointment, or another source of stimulation is withdrawn. We might say that we are disappointed, but physiologically or emotionally what we experience might actually be akin to withdrawal. Rather than accept the unexpectedly empty space or time in our lives, our need for constant stimulation often leads us to quickly find an alternative source. We might decide to head out for a neighborhood bar, call someone else, or maybe go to a movie. The experience of disappointment or withdrawal is very hard to tolerate. Today, in too many cases, our culture defines the uncomfortable experience of disappointment or withdrawal with a diagnostic label such as depression or anxiety—diseases that need to be cured. Large corporations make a great deal of money creating medicines to *cure* these uniquely modern ailments.

It can be helpful to take a step back and study the internal state created by a culture that provides and supports a rapidly increasing level of stimulation. In those moments when we are not engaged in stimulating activities—which are frequently moments of disappointment or withdrawal—what is actually occurring internally? That is, when we are not focused on participating in environments of stimulation or reducing the discomfort caused by lost stimulation, what happens when we find ourselves doing nothing? We must face the possibly extreme discomfort of merely experiencing our internal state with no explanation or solution to it.

This introspective activity is not well-supported in our society. Addiction loves company. I think of a patient of mine who in his 30s had been a heavy social drinker since his teens. After receiving his third DUI three years ago, he came to me with a resolve to stop drinking. He has been sober since, but he is astonished at the persistent efforts of his friends to get him to return to drinking. The media continually promises health, wealth, relief, and happiness to those who adopt stimulating/addictive activities. People who choose to abstain are often thought of as square, not cool, old-fashioned, boring, or timid.

Given this environment of stimulation, what occurs when we chose to engage in psychoanalysis or Buddhist meditation? In the mainstream culture of psychotherapy today, now that the practice of advertising therapeutic services has become accepted, promises of comfort abound—make an appointment and get relief from depression, fix your marriage, or improve your sexual functioning. It is hardly surprising that someone would enter psychotherapy with the expectation that this activity is going to make him or her feel better. The increasing popularity of so-called "evidenced-based approaches" pressures therapists to relieve a patient's symptoms right away. Similarly, the popularization of Eastern religions in our culture has also come with promises of peace and happiness, relief from whatever state of dissatisfaction or disappointment you may be struggling with.

But what really happens in psychoanalysis? Once the initial stimulation of entering analysis and gaining the exclusive attention of the analyst recedes, we know that what we term the *transference neurosis* develops—that is, the patient's fundamental intrapsychic and interpersonal repetitions emerge and he or she is likely to experience frustration because nothing is happening. The patient's impulse to leave or to find some way to stimulate the analyst increases. During this period, the patient might be said to be experiencing withdrawal or disappointment as his or her fantasies of relief or fulfillment go unanswered, particularly if the analyst remains an essentially neutral, investigative object. If the analyst is successful in helping the patient put hopes, wishes, and fantasies into words and then to describe their underlying emotional experience in the present, the patient might be able to learn how to tolerate the momentary, ongoing experience of disappointment or "nothing happening."

Likewise, in Buddhist-oriented awareness mediation, fascination with one's thoughts begins to recede once the endless patterns of hope, fear, and expectation are recognized. Frustration, boredom, anxiety, and physical discomfort emerge in the moment, while meditating, as one realizes that nothing is, in fact, happening and nothing will. How disappointing!

In analysis and meditation, once outside stimulation has been minimized, one's own internal state of stimulation moves to the foreground of awareness. Accustomed to denying this reality through fantasy or action, we find this to be a most uncomfortable state. With little identifiable context, it might be experienced as disappointment, withdrawal, anxiety, or depression. I recall a conversation I had with my wizened meditation instructor shortly after beginning to meditate. I was telling him how terrific I thought meditation was. He commented ruefully, "Wait until you discover that it's not so terrific."

When considering the ramifications of disappointment in psychoanalysis, perhaps the most important variable to consider is countertransference. All analysts are acquainted with the subtleties and vicissitudes of countertransference, as a response to induction from the patient as well as to forces emanating from our own unresolved conflicts. The induction of disappointment from the patient is perhaps one of the most difficult manifestations of countertransference to tolerate.

Most of us want to feel helpful to our patients, to witness progress, to alleviate suffering. A disappointed patient induces equally uncomfortable feelings of disappointment in the analyst. In addition, because today's culture of psychotherapy places so much emphasis on measurable, definable progress and symptom relief, an analyst's professional sense of self is challenged by patients who induce disappointment. Given these circumstances, it is inevitable that an analyst will feel the impulse to act in ways that will relieve disappointment in the patient, and by extension, in his- or herself. Even our most genuine attempts at understanding, our most brilliant, insightful, and accurate interpretations can be unconscious attempts to alleviate our own feelings of disappointment and anxiety by injecting *progress* into the treatment.

If it is true that psychoanalysis and Buddhism are, in fact, *paths of disappointment*, why walk those paths at all? One alleged reason for Freud's unpopularity was his so-called pessimism, his notion that in the best of worlds, psychoanalysis could only help people come to terms with the arduousness of daily living (Freud, 1905/2000). The fundamental tenet of Buddhism is impermanence (Trungpa, 1976), the obvious implication being that at best, we might prepare for our own impermanence or death. So if psychoanalysis and Buddhism might merely help people live an ordinary life and prepare for the inevitability of death, why bother?

In context of everyday life, the less able we are to tolerate disappointment—or withdrawal from constant stimulation, as I have focused on in this paper—the more dependent we are on external sources of stimulation and fantasies of accomplishments, rewards, or relief to distract us from immediate internal and perceptual experiences. Because external sources of stimulation are forever transitory and impossible to control, anxiety is inevitable. Therefore, we waste considerable energy trying to solve the inevitable and ever-present experience of disappointment.

If instead, through psychoanalysis or Buddhist meditation, we become more acclimated to and familiar with our own immediate state of disappointment, several things may become possible. As dependence on hope, solutions, and external sources of stimulation or distraction recedes, we may be able to experience a sense of freedom and true independence.

We can learn to live with, and fully experience, the negative emotions of fear, sadness, frustration, loss, yearning, and so on. In familiar psychological terminology, this might mean that we could learn to accept and appreciate ourselves for who we are; neurosis, defenses, and all. We might be able to tolerate anxiety and intense emotional states, become familiar with our own minds, and become less reactive to the ups and downs of others.

Disappointment would become just one part of the total experience of being alive. This might be akin to what we think of as true individuation or a healthy ego. We would begin to see that this state of being is actually universal, and that could foster genuine connectedness to and compassion for others.

References

Freud, S. (2000). *Three essays on the theory of sexuality.* (J. Strachey, Trans.). New York: Basic Books. (Original work published 1905)

Freud, S. (1989). *The ego and the id.* (J. Strachey, Trans.). New York: Norton. (Original work published 1923)

Freud, S. (1961). *Beyond the pleasure principle.* (J. Strachey, Trans.). New York: Norton. (Original work published 1920)

Freud, S. (1957). Instincts and their vicissitudes. In (J. Strachey, Trans.), *The standard edition of the complete psychological works of Sigmund Freud* (Vol. 14, pp. 109-140). London: Hogarth Press. (Original work published 1915)

Gertner, J. (2003, September 7). The futile pursuit of happiness. *The New York Times*, pp. 45.

Gleick, J. (2000). *Faster: The acceleration of just about everything.* London: Vintage.

Goldstein, J. (2003). *One Dharma: An emerging western Buddhism.* New York: Harper Collins.

Siegel, D. J. (2007). *The mindful brain: Reflection and attunement in the cultivation of well-being.* New York: W. W. Norton.

Shulman, P. (2004). Great expectations. *Psychology Today*, *2*, 32-42.

Trungpa, C. (1976). *The myth of freedom and the way of meditation.* Berkeley, CA: Shambhala.

Trungpa, C. (2004). *The collected works of Chögyam Trungpa* (Vol. 4: Crazy Wisdom; (Ed. C. Gimian), Boston: Shambhala.

Sustaining Transference in the Treatment of Alcoholism[1]

Robert Unger

Psychoanalysis is not usually considered to be an effective tool in dealing with alcoholism. It is a therapy mode that is rarely sought by the alcoholic, and is looked on with disfavor by the alcoholism treatment community. The image is often of the cold, intellectual and emotionless analyst, who is primarily interested in the past. Some of these preconceptions are true: the analyst is there to analyze rather than to gratify. People with impulse disorders, such as alcoholism, are likely to attribute coldness and lack of concern to anyone who is not gratifying.

Most treatment of alcoholics deals with trying to improve the alcoholic's life, and solving the problems created by the drinking. While this process may be gratifying enough to the patient to keep him in treatment for a while, the underlying impulse disorder is not addressed. I have found in my work that the alcoholic does need gratification from the analyst. If the analytic situation is experienced as too frustrating, the patient will either leave treatment prematurely, interminably continue the drinking pattern, or discover some new way of destructively acting out his impulses. Traditional analytic approaches need to be modified, then, so that sufficient gratification can be provided to prevent a more serious regression or termination of the treatment. The amount of gratification provided needs to be delicately balanced, however, between too little and too much. If too many needs of the patient are met, the transference will not form, and the analyst will have lost the usefulness of that most important treatment tool.

---

[1] Originally published in Unger, R. (1978). Sustaining transference in the treatment of alcoholism. *Modern Psychoanalysis*, *3*, 155-171.

The issue of gratification is closely tied in with the notion that alcoholism reflects an underlying impulse disorder. The alcoholic is compelled to drink in order to assuage his feelings rather than go through the uncomfortable process of experiencing unpleasant or negative feelings. The impulse to act, then, becomes the overwhelming feeling, and the alcoholic gets addicted to an impulsive manner of discharging feelings, as well as to the bottle itself. The addicted person feels unable to control himself, generating terrible feelings of shame and helplessness. Fenichel (1945) elaborates on the narcissistic needs of the addictive personality:

> Addicts . . . are persons who never estimated object relationships very highly. They are fixated to a passive narcissistic aim and are interested solely in getting gratification, never in satisfying their partners, or for that matter, in the specific personalities of their partners. (pp. 377-379)

In the psychoanalytic process, the analyst is not actively taking away the addiction, but is asking the person to experience the feelings underlying the addiction.

The alcoholic addictive process is described by Gitlow (1968). He states that alcohol is a sedative, a depressant of the central nervous system. It diminishes psychomotor activity, which in observable terms, reduces tension and anxiety. This effect usually lasts for about two hours, the time it takes for the blood alcohol level to begin to fall. The problem is that there is also a longer term effect, lasting about 12 hours, which increases psychomotor activity, thus producing more anxiety and tension. This is characteristic of all sedatives. Thus, a person who uses alcohol as a sedative, will need more alcohol to counteract the longer term effect after the short term effect has worn off. Very simply, this cyclical process leads to alcohol addiction.

The debate over whether alcoholism is a physiological disease or psychological problem arises out of the difficulty of dealing with the addictive process. The disease concept is the popular one among people working in the field and with recovering alcoholics. The point of view of Alcoholics Anonymous (AA) is that alcohol is basically a physiological problem created by some systemic, hormonal, or genetic problem. This view has advantages. The alcoholic has been stigmatized as morally bankrupt, out of control and inferior. The disease concept helps him to feel less persecuted morally and psychologically. If alcoholics have no control over their drinking and can think that it results from physiological problems, they may be less prone to feelings of self-attack and worthlessness. In my experience, however, alcoholic patients do criticize themselves severely for their drinking, problem, so I must conclude that there are few alcoholics who actually believe in the disease concept, although it is frequently invoked.

If the alcoholic believes that alcoholism is a physiological problem, why does he go to a psychotherapist? Most who go voluntarily seem to want to learn to adjust to their alcoholism. Psychotherapy is expected to serve a supportive function rather than to deal with the addiction. For modern analysts it is not important whether alcoholism is a disease or a psychological problem. As Spotnitz has often noted, many diseases are psychologically reversible. The important thing is learning how to treat the addiction psychologically.

This brings up a difficult question. Perhaps the reason for the popularity of the disease concept of alcoholism is that no one, neither patient nor therapist, really wants to deal with impulsive behavior because of the discomfort it gives rise to in the therapeutic relationship. Most alcoholics do not want to be analyzed—it is too painful to give up impulsive behavior. Should an analyst therefore attempt to analyze the patient if all he wants is supportive help? Should the analyst set up a situation in which the impulse disorder gets worked on, or should he ask the patient what kind of treatment he wants, whether he would like his impulsivity worked with? I experience the desire to be supportive, but the challenge is to be an analyst and work with the transference. Thus, just as the alcoholic drinks to become emotionally and physiologically comfortable, the therapist will often find some way to be supportive, giving, or gratifying to make himself more comfortable in the treatment situation. Using a psychoanalytic approach, where thoughts, feelings, and wishes are basically explored rather than gratified might give rise to the uncomfortable feelings which both patient and therapist would like to avoid.

Forming a Relationship: Initial Phases

The problem with how to conduct the treatment begins with the way in which patients enter treatment. Since most alcoholics do not enter treatment to deal with their alcoholism and may have been referred by somebody who has been affected by the drinking—family, the courts, an employer, or a doctor—they enter without internal motivation to change, or even to come. If the alcoholic agrees to come to treatment, it may be because of the threat of a major loss such as job or family. In my clinic, the largest referral source by far is the Department of Social Services, which requires people claiming to be alcoholic to be in treatment if they are to receive public assistance.

In many, if not most cases, the person does not feel he has a drinking problem, and if he does, he would prefer to resolve it without giving up drinking. The analyst must remember that alcohol provides the kind of gratification which is virtually impossible for a human relationship, particularly the kind which most alcoholics have previously experienced, to match. Alcohol ingestion usually provides an immediate feeling of security, well being, and tension relief. The patient has entered treatment because some aspect of his drinking behavior has become dystonic; the desire for the patient to isolate himself with the bottle has not necessarily diminished. If drinking is an important source of gratification or serves as a protection from experiencing undesirable feelings there is no reason to want to give it up unless the consequences of continued drinking become more dystonic than the thought of a sober life.

This situation makes it difficult to know how to proceed. I have a case now that is a good example. I work in the alcoholism clinic of a large hospital. D works in another department and is being considered for an important promotion. His department, aware of his history of alcoholism, referred him to the clinic for a "checkup." D presented himself in a casual manner, assured me that his drinking problem was solved, that his wife was the main cause of his problem, and that he has had no desire to drink since leaving her. I am always suspicious when told that someone no longer has the desire to drink, since nothing has usually happened to make the desire (impulse) leave. The only thing I felt I could do was to be nonjudgmental about his feeling that his drinking problem had been solved, and we arranged to see each other for a few sessions. As we talked, always in a relaxed casual tone, D mentioned that he had been drinking more than he first led me to believe. It has become more and more apparent to me that his drinking problem is not yet solved.

The question now is, do I confront D with my feeling about his drinking problem? He obviously does not want treatment for it, so I can't see doing anything other than joining this resistance. My present plan is to try to have pleasant, enjoyable conversations with him, so that he will want to continue coming in to talk even after he has been cleared by his department. Resistance to dependency feelings will interfere with the patient remaining even when the sessions are comfortable and gratifying, so the psychoanalyst works to provide ego syntonic narcissistic gratification. Although there are no present crises in D's life, his promotion is coming up soon. It is apparent that he is going to want to leave treatment then. Eventually I will be contacted by his department for a progress report. I could at that time recommend that he continue in treatment, but since he does not feel that he needs treatment, this would not be respecting his resistance.

Generally, I find that a person who drinks does not want to deal with the drinking when coming for treatment, but would like specific problems to be solved by the therapist.

Because of the dependent nature of most alcoholics, they often appear to be immediately and intensely involved with therapy. They offer what sound like transference communications, and the analyst prides himself on getting a transference established quickly. Then, suddenly, the patient decides to leave treatment. It is important for the analyst to realize that, as with any narcissistic disorder, object transference takes time to develop. Narcissistic attachment must be used to help the person stay in treatment. The analyst should be on guard for signs of resistance that threaten to destroy the treatment. The goal in the initial phases of treatment is merely to make the sessions comfortable enough to keep the patient returning.

The question that always comes up in my mind is to what degree you act in a supportive manner to solve or help solve the patient's immediate problems, and to what degree you concentrate on the long-range goal of forming and working with the transference. One of my first clinic patients was a woman who had several crises in her life which seemed to result in her drinking. Her son occasionally beat her up, relatives were trying to take her house away, and her boyfriend was also an alcoholic who needed a great deal of support. All of these problems led to drinking episodes. She was always overwhelmed by these situations and wanted me to help her solve them, assuring me that this would help her stop drinking. It took me quite some time to realize that these urgent situations were life-sustaining and my attempts to help her solve them were bound to fail because they threatened to remove her justification to drink. She solved this dilemma by leaving treatment.

If the therapist does concentrate on the long-range goal of forming a transference relationship, there is a chance that the patient may continue drinking longer, or may have more slips than when a directive approach is used. This makes for difficulties, particularly in an agency, where successful treatment is usually judged primarily on the basis of the patient attaining and maintaining sobriety. The therapist risks being seen as a failure by the agency, the patients, and himself, if sobriety is not achieved.

This always leads me to ask myself how directly I should deal with the sobriety issue. I think the feeling of being a failure is an induced feeling originating from the alcoholic and affecting most people in a treatment agency. The feeling is that the patients always seem to be challenging me to get them to stop drinking. The drinking has a rebellious tone. The patients can't function in certain ways so they drink—they're out of control and they want the therapist to give them enough so that they don't have to go out and drink. I find it draining to always be trying to give the patient enough so that he doesn't have to go out and drink. The induced feeling is that you should do something—the patient's impulse to act gives the therapist the impulse to act. My question is, should the therapist work specifically to get the patient not to drink, which might be acting on the induced impulses, or is it more important to demonstrate that the therapist can act non-impulsively, even if it means that the patient will drink for some period of time after treatment begins?

I feel the therapist should only act directly when the patient's drinking becomes directly treatment destructive. If the patient is so ill that drinking could result in death or hospitalization, or if drinking could result in jail, loss of job, loss of family, or anything else which might interrupt treatment, then the drinking should be dealt with as a treatment destructive resistance. In one sense, drinking can be thought of as always being treatment destructive, but this is not always so clear. I have one patient who suddenly stopped drinking and taking pills, and became so disoriented from withdrawal that he missed several sessions. In this case, stopping drinking was treatment destructive.

Transference and Countertransference

I have reviewed my work with alcoholics to try to pinpoint some patterns that have emerged, particularly the kind of transference-countertransference relationship to be expected in alcoholism treatment. The most consistent feeling I experience is that I can never do enough for the patient, that I'm failing and there's really not much hope in working with the person so I may as well lend a supportive ear and help organize his life and not bother analyzing him. To understand this situation it helps to consider the transference-countertransference that occurs when an alcoholic is in treatment. The alcoholic may be regarded as suicidal. Excessive intake of alcohol over an extended period of time systematically destroys the central and peripheral nervous system, liver, heart, muscles, and the gastro-intestinal tract (United States Department of Health Education and Welfare, 1971). The alcoholic is choosing to destroy himself rather than tolerate the emotional-physiological sensations which would arise without drinking. The drinking behavior serves to protect those around the alcoholic from his murderous impulses. This helps to explain the difficulty in using the transference to treat alcoholics. Spotnitz (1976) notes that people in a relationship induce feelings in each other. If the alcoholic is experiencing intense suicidal, angry, or helpless feelings, these feelings may be induced in the therapist through the transference relationship. So the only thing for me to do is to continue feeling uncomfortable, frustrated, and like a failure, and not try to get the patient to induce different feelings in me. I find this problem with many alcoholic patients; I have an impulse to get the patient to give me different feelings, and have to be careful not to act on the impulse.

I have one patient who demonstrates this problem, particularly around the issue of initial engagement. The patient, B, an 18 year old boy, was referred by the courts for a drinking-related arrest. Working with drinking adolescents is more difficult than working with drinking adults because of the greater strength of the denial system. Most adolescents experience a great deal of peer pressure to engage in impulsive behavior, yet are scornful of those who admit losing control while engaged in these activities. In addition, adolescents receive mixed messages from adults who superficially disapprove of drinking but present it as "adult" behavior. Much liquor industry advertising is directed towards young people.

I have been seeing B for about a year, and we almost never discuss drinking. At first, he was so uncomfortable that he could only stay for about 15 minutes of the session. I then discovered that he liked sports, so we talked about basketball. Gradually, he became more comfortable, and after about 4 months was able to stay for the whole session. Since I felt that I was supposed to deal with his drinking if I was doing my job, I decided to try an experiment. I told him that I was working with another youngster who was only interested in talking about mathematics, and asked him if I should broach the topic of drinking. B told me that if the kid was talking only about mathematics he probably was not ready to talk about drinking and I shouldn't bring it up. Since this incident, B occasionally asks me how this kid is doing.

B has gradually revealed more of his feelings about himself and his family, and particularly about his father, who raped one of B's sisters before leaving the home. He is finding it helpful to talk about his home life, which troubles him greatly. Recently I changed agencies, and B decided to come along. As part of the intake procedure, we had to fill out some forms which included questions about drinking. B was still reluctant to talk about drinking, and I felt it necessary to deemphasize this area.

After a year, B comes to appointments regularly, and a transference does seem to be slowly forming. I still find myself experiencing feelings of futility, particularly surrounding the drinking problem, as the treatment inches along. B, in the meantime, has become involved in a job training program, and his life does seem to be stabilizing.

Special Parameters: Are Active Techniques Necessary?

Since beginning work with alcoholics, I have been asking myself how to modify my techniques to treat drinking problems. It has become clear that alcoholics need much more active participation by the analyst than is usually provided because drinking is so immediately gratifying that the alcoholic learns to drink at any point of discomfort. This creates a cycle; the more he drinks, the more the ability to withstand frustration decreases, resulting in increased drinking. Assuming that in some way this discomfort emanates from or results in problems in interpersonal relationships, the analytic relationship is potentially the source of great discomfort.

I have found that it is particularly important in the beginning of treatment for the analyst to be aware of the patient's need for gratification and stimulation. In most cases, to provide the correct amount of stimulation, the analyst bases the frequency of his communications on the direct contacts made by the patient; that is, he essentially talks to the patient only when the patient asks him to. This principle might have to be modified with alcoholic patients, however. Many alcoholics have not yet learned to use words to get what they want for themselves. That is, they cannot necessarily ask the psychoanalyst for what they want and may become extremely uncomfortable with a silent analyst while not being able to ask him to change. If the analyst senses that this is happening, he should provide enough verbal gratification to help the patient be more comfortable in the session.

The patient usually has strong preconceived feelings about the analyst as another in a long line of people who want to change his behavior and do not understand that his drinking is necessary. If the patient enters treatment voluntarily there are usually mixed feelings. He would like to learn to drink socially, or clear up the life problems surrounding the drinking, but would still prefer to drink.

The alcoholic's preconception about the therapist's wanting to control his behavior would probably not be considered actual transference because it is not yet personalized. It is a characterological transference-like feeling and elicits a strong set of reciprocal feelings: most therapists get the feeling that they should be controlling the alcoholic's drinking; the alcoholic probably wants the therapist to try to control his behavior. The fact that it is usually impossible to control the alcoholic's behavior suggests that the alcoholic wants the therapist not only to try, but to fail. This would reenact the early parent-child relationship, where the parents were probably failures in providing the right model for impulse control. It thus seems helpful to demonstrate an understanding of the patient's desire without acting on the impulse to control; that is, it is okay for the patient to want the analyst to control his behavior, but the analyst doesn't necessarily have to do it unless it is mutually agreed. To test this out, I have sometimes asked patients if they would like me to order them to stop drinking. This is an attempt on my part to get the patient's conscious participation in any control I might assert over him. I have never had a patient give me permission to order him to stop drinking. Patients usually change the subject or say they are not interested at this time. They are not interested in cooperating consciously in my ordering them to do something, even though I get the induced feeling that I should attempt to control their behavior. If I get their permission to order them to stop drinking, and exploration reveals they need a command, the order is part of a cooperative venture.

Another issue is gratification. Nothing is quite as gratifying as a drink, but if the therapist can provide some interpersonal gratification, the patient may begin to want to come in on his own initiative. If the analyst is too frustrating, the patient may have to leave to protect himself; and if he cannot leave, the excessive frustration may lead to increased drinking. Most alcoholics are very uncomfortable when sober, particularly in the presence of other people. They are particularly uncomfortable in the presence of an authority figure like a therapist.

What seems to work is providing words. I know therapists who talk a lot to alcoholic patients, but in a way that is supportive—they answer questions, provide a lot of personal information, and help patients with problems. This appears to make patients momentarily comfortable, but I think it makes long-range progress impossible, and also offers a degree of intimacy that can be anxiety-producing for the patient. Many alcoholics report a pattern of becoming intensely involved with people, only to break off relationships when things get too close or gratification isn't readily available. The analyst can provide a quantity of words, but must carefully choose what he says so that the patient's ego boundaries are not impinged upon, remembering that the long-range goal is the formation of the transference.

I am still somewhat uncomfortable doing much talking to alcoholic patients. The basic analytic model is to be quiet, to listen and to reflect questions. Sometimes this is obviously intolerable to the patient, and more talking is clearly called for. How much more is a subtle matter—it's not always clear whether my desire to talk is my subjective discomfort, or an induced feeling from the patient. What I try to do is to provide the quantity of words needed to maintain an acceptable level of gratification, without providing the quality of words that inhibits transference. I feel that attachment to the treatment is achieved when the patient begins to participate more in directing the conversation. A patient, for example, who had difficulty saying anything, picked up on a discussion we were having about her son's school, and began talking, without questions from me. I felt her anxiety decrease as she became comfortable talking.

I try to keep discussions as object oriented as possible, and to balance my talking with the amount of patient talking that will decrease tension. Many therapists feel that it is important to get the alcoholic to talk about his feelings about himself and drinking, but I have found that that often results in excessive stimulation and narcissistic concern. It is generally more useful not to encourage the alcoholic to become involved in his feelings, but to engage in comfortable casual communication.

Stimulation and Depression

Another concept I have employed in trying to understand how to treat alcoholics is that of stimulation. In a recent workshop led by E. G. Clevans (personal communication, 1978) on the subject of depression in children, it was noted that many children grow up with and seem to become addicted to a great deal of stimulation—television, violence, and sexual stimulation. Most alcoholics I treat report stimulating lives; drinking itself is stimulating. Most of these patients report crises and urgent situations they must constantly contend with. No matter what the social class, drinking usually provokes family, medical, economic, and legal problems. There always seem to be emergencies which have to be resolved immediately. There is too much to handle so the person must drink.

There seems to be a vested interest in maintaining this level of overstimulation. Many patients report overstimulating lives as youngsters; they were either too gratified or too deprived, or exposed to drinking, fighting, and sexual activity by their parents. If stimulation is removed, depression often surfaces. It is common knowledge that people who stop drinking usually go through a period of depression; suicide may be attempted or another drug substituted for alcohol. In treatment, if a basically nonstimulating environment is provided, the patient may become very depressed and continue drinking or leave treatment to deal with the depression. The rationale for the analyst talking is to provide enough stimulation so that the patient does not become too depressed too early in treatment.

If the analyst has to keep providing stimulation, how does he work with the impulse problem? I think that a goal of treatment is to gradually reduce stimulation so that the patient can begin to feel measured doses of depression. One problem is that the alcoholic is used to drinking anytime he has a feeling he doesn't like and the analyst will have little effect outside the sessions. The analyst, then, should help the patient find an activity that provides enough stimulation so the analyst can work towards reducing stimulation in the sessions. As treatment continues and the transference forms, the patient incorporates more of the analyst into his psychic structure, and the effects of the sessions will be more ongoing.

The best example of an environment which provides enough stimulation to deter drinking is Alcoholics Anonymous. AA does not claim to be a therapeutic organization—its goal is to help people stop drinking. AA provides gratification through sympathizing, identifying, socializing, and other activities which provide a stimulation substitute for the alcoholic. Meetings take place around the clock; the alcoholic has a sponsor who can be called anytime there is danger of drinking. If the analyst is successful in getting the patient involved in AA and other activities which provide substitute gratification for drinking, he can gradually reduce the stimulation in the sessions and allow the feelings underlying the impulsive behavior to surface.

Many patients resist becoming involved in AA. Some are afraid of the interpersonal contact or do not like to identify with other alcoholics. Many realize that involvement with AA spells the end of their drinking. I find the best way to deal with this is to treat it like any other resistance, since AA involvement is almost always a positive indication for successful treatment. If the patient refuses to become involved in AA, other activities which are gratifying and stimulating can be substituted.

I have found group therapy valuable too. Many alcoholics prefer group treatment because they get to identify with others like themselves—it is much like AA in this sense. Also, the intimacy of the one-on-one relationship can be threatening, particularly with a non-alcoholic therapist. Most alcoholics prefer to be in groups composed of alcoholics because they feel threatened by non-alcoholics.

Fostering Object Relations

Group therapy affords, as well, a good opportunity to work on object relations. Many therapists use groups to focus on an individual alcoholic's problems, and encourage the others to identify. This, however, encourages the person to think about himself and ignores the group. In groups I try to emphasize the idea of people merely talking to each other—about anything, not necessarily their problems. Most group members are surprised when I tell them they do not have to talk about their problems; they think that is all they are supposed to do. I try to focus on group resistances, such as silent or monopolizing members, or treatment- or group-destructive resistances such as absence or lateness.

Two experiences with alcoholic groups come to mind. One group was depressed and could not sustain any interaction. Every two or three weeks, however, the members would realize what an inadequate therapist I was and berate me. During these attacks they came alive, interacted and were satisfied with the group. Even though there was an element of sadism, by projecting inadequacy feelings, the group functioned much better during these periods. In another group, members were friendly on the outside, mostly in AA, and consequently talked easily with each other and ignored me. I found that whenever I said anything it didn't seem to contribute much. I discovered that my' feelings of being left out caused the to want to talk. Even though the content of the discussions remained superficial and the group did not seem to be moving forward very quickly, the members were, in fact, talking to each other with increasing ease and comfort. I decided to resist the impulse to talk, and instead remained silent. Helping group members to feel comfortable talking to each other sometimes takes precedence over giving them understanding about their problems.

Resolving Countertransference Resistance

The treatment of alcoholics lends support to the concept that the transference-countertransference relationship can be used to cure a disorder with physiological components. Much revolves around the feelings generated between the patient and analyst. The alcoholic's impulse to drink induces such strong impulses in the analyst to act that the feeling of needing to do something is quite uncomfortable. I have one patient who constantly tells me that he can't sleep and has nightmares; he suffers so much that I have a tremendous urge to provide relief for him. The solution is to provide something verbally. Because of the feeling of not being able to do anything, I want to do more. If I don't do the right thing he is going to drink, and I'm not sure what the right thing is, or even if there is a right thing because nothing is quite as fulfilling as a drink. I always have the impulse to try to be as soothing as the drink. If I don't, something terrible will happen—he will fail and I will fail. He called the other day to tell me he had his first slip after three months of sobriety and I felt relieved.

I find, in fact, that one of the hardest things in working with alcoholics is getting used to feeling like a failure. I think that this is a necessary feeling, however, because in one sense you are failing—failing to provide the gratification patients feel they need, and certainly failing to provide as much gratification as alcohol provides.

Many therapists avoid the feeling of failure by placing responsibility for the success of the treatment on the patient. While this may be acceptable for a more advanced patient, in the beginning and intermediate stages of treating an alcoholic, it is advisable for the analyst to take full responsibility for any failure in the therapy. Just as an infant is not responsible for his own upbringing, the severely regressed alcoholic should not be responsible for his therapy. This will ultimately help the patient to stop attacking himself and focus on the object (analyst). Treatment progresses when the patient can complain in words rather than action.

I have also learned from working analytically with alcoholics that impulsive behavior takes many forms besides obvious ones like drinking. The analyst is capable of acting impulsively in subtle ways, and it has been challenging to attempt to weed impulsiveness out of my communications with patients. I have also begun to learn that an addiction is really a horrible thing. The addicted person feels unable to control himself, generating terrible feelings of shame and helplessness.

In the analytic process, the analyst is not actually taking away the addiction, but asking the person to experience the feelings underlying the addiction by relinquishing the drinking behavior. The transference has to be firmly established to work this through. Almost every alcoholic patient I have treated has told me that he wanted the desire to drink to go away. I don't know if the impulse goes away when the addiction is finally resolved or whether the person just learns to control the impulsive behavior.

I think that working with alcoholics provides a great opportunity to learn about the relationship between psychological and physiological disorders. We already know that diseases such as ulcers and other stomach disorders are, in part, psychologically induced; alcoholism too may be classified as one of the diseases with psychosomatic components. The challenge for the analyst is to focus on how talking helps the alcoholic to control his impulsive behavior, and to use the transference in this endeavor. We can see now the possibility of altering bodily functioning with emotional, verbal communication. The understanding of this will have brought us a long way towards scientifically using emotional communication to affect the body.

References

Fenichel, O. (1945). *The Psychoanalytic theory of neurosis*. New York: W.W. Norton and Company.

Gitlow, S. (1968, October). A pharmacological approach to alcoholism. *The AA Grapevine*.

Spotnitz, H. (1976). *Psychotherapy of preoedipal conditions*. New York: Jason Aronson.

United States Department of Health Education and Welfare. (1971). *First special report to the U.S. congress on alcohol and health*. Office of the Assistant Secretary for Health and Scientific Affairs, Alcohol, Drug Abuse and Mental Health Administration. National Institute on Alcohol Abuse and Alcoholism.

Contributor Biographies

Robert Backerman, LCSW has been a Clinical Social Worker in private practice in Boulder since 1982. He received his undergraduate degree from Tufts University and his Master's in Social Work from Smith College. In addition to a general therapy practice, he specializes in providing psychotherapy for children and families impacted by divorce, as well as parenting time and decision-making evaluations, mediation services, and consultation. (303) 449-8098.

Blake Baily, MA, LPC is a graduate of the MA in Contemplative Psychotherapy program at Naropa and an intensive psychotherapist with Windhorse Community Services where he helps create "individually tailored, therapeutic living environments for people with a variety of mental health challenges." He lives in Boulder with his exceedingly talented wife and two beautiful daughters. (303) 818-8046

Helen Balis, LCSW is a psychotherapist who specializes in working with Older Adults. She worked in Community Mental Health for 31 years and is recently retired.

Sue Bell is a Naropa Graduate turned designer/artist.

Paul Bialek MA, LPC is Core Assistant Professor in the MA Contemplative Counseling Psychology Department at Naropa University where he has served on the Leadership team for the past five years. He has a private practice in Boulder. (303) 941-9577 / bialekpaul@gmail.com

Marsha S. Block, CAE, CFRE is Chief Executive Officer of the American Group Psychotherapy Association. (212) 477-2677 / mblock@agpa.org / www.agpa.org

Mike Block is program director at the Boulder Shelter for the Homeless in Boulder, CO.

Justin Bogardus, MA, LPC has a part-time psychotherapy practice and runs Dream Tree Film, a film production company, most recently responsible for *NatureRx* (Mountainfilm 2015), an award-winning satire that explores the cure to society's ills: more time outside in nature. Prior to completing an MA in Contemplative Psychotherapy at Naropa University, Justin was a successful film/TV producer based in New York City, where he made everything from films and animations to reality television shows and hard-hitting documentaries that exonerated wrongfully convicted prisoners. justin@dreamtreefilm.com / (347) 342-8922 www.nature-rx.org

Deb Bopsie, MA is neighbor, friend, mentee and sister. She runs True Nature Contemplative Psychotherapy dbopsie@gmail.com / (207) 284-5509

Stacy Boston, MA, LPC is in private practice as a licensed professional counselor. She works with individuals, tweens and teens, young adults, and families in both Longmont and Boulder. (303) 956-9147 / stacy.boston@gmail.com

Annie Brier is a wandering writer and artist. She can be reached at anniebrier@gmail.com.

Brooke is a preschool teacher at Alaya Preschool in Boulder, lives with her wife in the co-housing community with Bob and Helena, loves to hike and dance and especially loves her 3 grown children.

Wendy Buhner, MA lives in Vermont with her family on a small working farm raising herbal medicinals and Nigerian Dwarf Goats for milk. She is the mother of 3 children and devotes most of her time to home schooling, farming and figuring out what "wife" means in it all. For fun she sees clients at the Clara Martin Center on the Adult Outpatient Team as a FFS Clinician. prasadana@Ymail.com

Casey Burnett, MA, LPC is a lunatic with a license. He was a student of Bob Unger's at Naropa University. Casey lives and works in Boulder, CO. For the past three years he has been the president of the Colorado Group Psychotherapy Society. casey@caseyburnett.com / (720) 722-4070

Hilary Callan, LMHC is a licensed mental health counselor in Northampton, Massachusetts. She co-leads Modern Psychoanalytic Group training workshops as well as maintaining a private practice with individuals, couples, and groups. hilary.callan@gmail.com / (413) 923-1556

Jason Carpenter, PsyD works as a licensed clinical psychologist in the San Francisco Bay Area. He completed a doctorate at the Wright Institute and is also a graduate of Naropa University's Master's in Contemplative Psychotherapy program in 2003. (415) 820-1484

Lauren Casalino, MA, LPC is a Licensed Professional Counselor and Associate Professor in the Master's Program in Contemplative Counseling Psychology at Naropa University. She works therapeutically with individuals, couples, and groups in her private practice and she facilitates groups of many kinds locally. casalino@naropa.edu / (303) 898-2943

The Center for Harm Reduction Therapy is a certified drug and alcohol treatment program that combines substance abuse treatment with psychotherapy. They work with substance users with co-occurring disorders in a wide array of settings. From private practice to AIDS service organizations to homeless drop-in centers to Golden Gate Park, they engage the hardest-to-reach people. They facilitate a dozen groups a week and are highly skilled at running drop-in groups. They have been working in group supervision with Bob Unger since 2003.

David Chrislip, MS, MPA, is Principal of Skillful Means in Boulder, CO where he teaches leadership for the common good.

He loves his family and friends along with books, bikes, good wine and Italy. (720) 841-0864

Angelo Ciliberti, MA, LPC is the Clinical Director of AIM House where he has been working with young adults for the past 10 years. In addition to this, Angelo maintains a small private practice in Boulder, CO and enjoys teaching at Naropa University. When not working, he enjoys practicing Ashtanga Yoga, cycling, playing tennis, and spending time with his wife and daughter. Aciliberti2782@gmail.com (303) 949-5577

Michael Cohn-Geltner is a graduate student at N.Y.U studying public administration. In the past he has been a bike mechanic, City Year corps member, and U.S. Census Bureau enumerator. (718) 753-0951 / mcohngeltner@gmail.com

Susan M. Cooper, PhD has a doctorate in counseling psychology from the University of Denver. She is a licensed psychologist in the State of Colorado as well as a Certified Group Psychotherapist and has a private practice in Colorado Springs where she specializes in group therapy and eating disorders. She was one of the original founders of the Colorado School of Professional Psychology in Colorado Springs and has made numerous presentations in the areas of group therapy and eating disorder treatment. (719) 635-7242

Michelle DeCola, LPC, CGP is in private practice in Louisville and Denver and she does therapy with individuals, couples and groups.

Abigail Dembo graduated from UC Berkeley with a Master's in Social Welfare and works for the Center for Harm Reduction Therapy. Abigail's work takes place in the community programs of San Francisco, offering both individual and group harm reduction therapy on a drop-in basis, and at no cost to the client. She can be reached at abigaildembo@harmreductiontherapy.org / (303) 903-4135

Teri Dillion, MA, LAC, CGP is a licensed professional counselor who specializes in integrative mind/body treatment for addiction and trauma both in private practice and through the Boulder Alcohol Education Center. (303) 551-3923 / www.WakingHeartTherapy.com

Michael M. Dow, PsyD, CAC III is a Licensed Psychologist. He is the Program Manager of Integrated Services (Primary Care Behavioral Health Integration) at Mental Health Partners and maintains a private practice with individuals and couples in Boulder, CO. (303) 229-5937 / Michaelmdow@gmail.com

Karen Drucker, PsyD, TEP is a Licensed Psychologist and a Trainer, Educator, Practitioner of Psychodrama, Sociometry and Group Psychotherapy. She has a private practice in Boulder, CO and works with individuals, couples and groups. She is adjunct faculty at the Graduate School of Psychology at Naropa University. Karen has a monthly psychodrama training group which has been on-going for eight years teaching therapists how to work with action methods, and works with attorneys using psychodrama to support their clients. (303) 442-2561

Andrea Dugan, MA, LPC has a private therapy practice in Boulder, CO. Using a present moment holistic approach, she works with children, adolescents, families and individuals. (720) 530-4095 / andreajdugan@msn.com

Raymon Elozua is a visual artist living and working in New York City and Mountaindale, NY. His work has been featured in many solo and group shows and appears in numerous public and private collections. (212) 260-1239 / raymon@elozua.com His websites include: elozua.com /www.popsongpoems.us / eggbaskey-scny.us / www.vanishingcatskills.us / www.homescrap.us / www.rustybucket.us / www.lostlabor.com / www.stoveburner.com

Sara Emerson LCSW, CGP, FAPGA is a Licensed Clinical Social Worker, Certified Group Psychotherapist and a Fellow of the American Group Psychotherapy Association. She has held multiple leadership roles in AGPA as well as the Northeastern Society for Group Psychotherapy. She has taught at Boston College and Massachusetts Institute for Psychoanalysis, and has a private psychotherapy practice located in Cambridge, Massachusetts.

Ashley Eyre is completing her Master's in Transpersonal Counseling at Naropa University with an emphasis in Art Therapy. She is an avid mountain biker and looks forward to working with children with art and movement as vehicles for transformation. aebracelets@gmail.com (303) 842-7181

Michelle L. Fields, MA, LPC is a psychotherapist in Boulder, CO. Trained in Contemplative Psychotherapy, she joins experiential and mindfulness techniques with traditional talk therapy, seeing individuals, couples, families and running groups at La Luna Center.
(720) 470-0010/redpomegranateseeds@gmail.com

Gabriel Fortuna has just returned from New Orleans where he received his Bachelors degree in English Literature. He thoroughly enjoys riding his bike. This passion was inspired by his friend and the Man of a Thousand Pedals, Bob Unger. Gabriel is seeking out new energy in far away lands where he hopes to engage the youth of coming generations to find passions in the art of language.

Dan Fox, MA, BCN is keeping busy with four children and his therapy practice, specializing in the letter A: adoption, adolescence, ADHD, Autism Spectrum Disorders. Last year he finished his work to get board certified in neurotherapy. He's been running long distances very slowly to stay sane.

Valerie Frankfeldt, LCSW, PhD is the Director of Training, training analyst, supervisor, and instructor at the

Psychoanalytic Psychotherapy Study Center in NYC. She is a graduate of the Center for Modern Psychoanalysis and specializes in addiction, couple treatment and clinical supervision. She maintains a private practice in Greenwich Village, NYC. (212) 253-2625 / www.valeriefrankfeldtphd.com

Perri Franskoviak, PhD is an assistant professor at Holy Names University who maintains a small private practice in San Francisco and Oakland. He tries his best to stay out of trouble. Sometimes he succeeds.
(415) 789-8309 / www.drperrif.com

Paul Geltner, DSW is a psychoanalyst who lives in Brooklyn and practices in New York City. Dr.paulgeltner@gmail.com

Jack Gipple, MSW, CAC III is a psychotherapist both in private practice and with Windhorse Community Services, where he is also Clinical Supervisor of community based treatment teams. He has had a long association with the Boulder Shelter for the Homeless: board member since 2008, program consultant since 2000. He frequently hums to himself while caring for his family, garden, trees, and bees.
(303) 359-2166

Paul Gitterman, LICSW, MSc, CGP is a licensed clinical social worker who provides psychotherapy, supervision, and outreach services for Williams College, is an adjunct professor for the Smith College School for Social Work, and has a private practice in Williamstown, MA.
(413) 441-8093 / paul@paulgitterman.com
www.paulgitterman.com

David Gross is a 72-year-old retiree, with a "colorful" (OK, checkered) past. Among his careers have been the practice of law, ice cream making, catering, male stripping, and selling wine. The latter occupation took up 25 years of his career. This makes him older than Bob and with more careers. He can also state with a 100% certainty that Bob has never been a male stripper. Currently he spends a lot of time gardening. This involves growing vegetables, not flowers, with the exception of nasturtiums, which are a food. He lives with his wife of almost 25 years, his 21-year-old son and three heads of cat in Woodstock, NY.

Stephen Hansen lives in NYC, loves life and treasures his friendships. If you are a friend of Bob and Helena's, you are a potential friend of his. He wishes everyone true happiness and the best of everything. eflnoseeum@me.com

Theresa Harding is the mother of three caring, effective adults, and the manager of a federal program funding projects that support homeless persons and organizations working to end homelessness. The 34 years since meeting Bob were rich with ups and downs that have evolved to the rich okayness with whatever is today. Bob and Helena have uniquely nourished her journey like an oasis sometimes, a spring rain other times, and mostly a lake of compassion, touched by the blue sky of their prajna.

Greg Harms has been the Executive director of the Boulder Shelter for the Homeless since 2002. He has an undergraduate degree in engineering and a Masters degree in Business Administration. greg@bouldershelter.org

Mike Harris, LPC, LAC graduated from the Master's program in Contemplative Psychotherapy from Naropa University in 2006 and is CEO of Crest Counseling Services in Salida, CO.

Vic Harris, PhD is a retired university professor and public health administrator in Boulder, CO. kloandv@gmail.com

Steve Henne, MA, RCC is the Team Leader, Clinical Lead and primary developer of Stepping Stones Concurrent Disorders Service and a registered clinical counselor in private practice. Stepping Stones is a public health service providing free group and individual therapy to a catchment of over 200,000 people in North and West Vancouver, British Columbia, Canada. It is an award winning program that has initiated a group clinic philosophy for people struggling with substance misuse problems and/or mental health issues. He can be reached at stevenhenne@hotmail.com / (604) 765-2563

Adrianne Holloran, LPC is a bilingual psychotherapist in private practice and specializes in trauma, grief and loss, anxiety disorders and postpartum issues and works with individuals and groups.
(303) 641-5281/ ah@adriannehollorantherapy.com

Matthew C. Holloran, JD, LPC, CAC II is a Licensed Professional Counselor. He gave up a successful white collar criminal law practice to move to Boulder and pursue an education in Contemplative Psychotherapy. He currently maintains a private practice in Boulder, Colorado working with individuals and groups to explore issues of addiction, interpersonal challenges and midlife transitions.
insightcc.net / (720) 837-0236.

Phillip Horner, LCSW is a licensed clinical social worker. He maintains a private therapy practice with individuals, couples, and groups and also is a contract therapist for The Collective of Psychological Wholeness in Boulder, CO. / (720) 316-7774 / pcphorner@gmail.com / www.phillip-horner.com

MacAndrew S. Jack, PhD is a psychologist in Boulder, Colorado. He has been the Dean of the Graduate School of Psychology at Naropa University, Ambassador of the Royal University of Bhutan, and holds a private practice. A student of Lama Tsultrim Allione in the Vajrayana lineage, he enjoys integrating his contemplative practice with modern relational psychoanalytic psychotherapy, and with the vicissitudes of daily life as a father, husband, and amateur mechanic.

Marc Jalbert is a mortgage banker in Boulder, CO. Prior to that he was in the software industry for too long. He was born in

Alaska, raised in New Mexico, moved to Aspen, CO after college to be a ski bum in 1980. He succeeded. He moved to Boulder in 1985 for "higher" education, met Bob Unger soon after and they've been riding various bikes together ever since. He's managed to finance dozens of Bob and Helena's properties over the years. Bob still talks to him.

Francis J. Kaklauskas, PsyD is a Certified Group Psychotherapist and a Fellow of the American Group Psychotherapy Association. He is core faculty at Naropa University's Graduate School of Counseling and Psychology and facilitates the Group Psychotherapy Training Program at the University of Colorado, Boulder through Wardenburg Psychological Health and Psychiatry.

Gretchen Kahre, MA, LPC has been practicing Contemplative Psychotherapy in Boulder since 1990. She is from Denver and received her BA from the University of Colorado and her Masters degree in Contemplative Psychotherapy from Naropa University. She has also been a student of Tibetan Buddhism for over 25 years.

Jack Kirman, PhD is a psychoanalyst in private practice in New York City, having retired from Queens College of CUNY where he was professor of psychology. He has taught at Center for Modern Psychoanalytic Studies and at the Center for Group Studies, and at other psychoanalytic institutes.

Chuck Knapp MA, LPC is a long-time friend and colleague of Bob and also a Co-Director at Windhorse Community Services in Boulder, CO.

Colin Knapp works as a carpenter in the front range area and lives in Longmont, CO. He was born and raised in Boulder, and grew up with the Unger boys so Bob and Helena are like parents to him. He's 29 years old. (720) 939-7701

Ellen Knapp, MA, LPC, CSA, GSM works with older people and their families in later life transitions and complicated times as a consultant as well as companion. www.ellenknapp.com / ellen@ellenknapp.com / (720) 217-9614

Spencer Knapp is a professional drummer. He lives in New Orleans with his wife and his best friend Norma, the dog, and enjoys his time off at the golf course and beating the heat in the local watering holes.

Uğur Kocataşkin, LPC, CAC I is a licensed professional counselor who is in private practice working with individuals, couples and groups. He currently serves as chair of the Master's in Contemplative Counseling and Psychology program at Naropa University in Boulder.
uktaskin@gmail.com / (303) 520-7233

Bennett Leslie, PsyD is a Licensed Psychologist and a Partner at the Boulder Center for Cognitive and Behavioral Therapies where he sees individuals and couples.
(303) 579-6029 / www.bouldercbt.com

Jeannie Little, LCSW, CGP is a founder and the executive director of the Center for Harm Reduction Therapy in San Francisco, CA. Beginning with her work with homeless veterans in the 1990s, she specializes in groups for substance users and people with co-occurring disorders. She has been teaching and writing about homelessness, community mental health, substance use, groups and harm reduction for twenty years. She has been a student, colleague and friend of Bob Unger since 1999.

Kathleen Lowe, MA, LMFT is a psychotherapist in private practice in Boulder, CO. kloandv@gmail.com

Isha Lucas, MA is a birth doula, writer, psychotherapist and PhD student in anthropology and social change at the California Institute of Integral Studies in San Francisco, CA. The

broad focus of her dissertation and research is racism. She runs groups on racism in Colorado.
Isha.lucas@cultivatingwildflowers.com
www.cultivatingwildflowers.com / (720) 464-6891

Charlotte Malkmus, MA, LMHC is a psychotherapist in private practice in Tacoma, Washington and a clinical associate with the Seattle Psychoanalytic Society and Institute.
(253) 355-2498 / charlotte.malkmus@gmail.com

Eric Maxfield, JD is a Colorado attorney.

Sara Mayer, LCSW is a retired psychotherapist in Boulder, CO where she has lived for 46 years. She has been in a group of group therapists studying groups and themselves for 25 years! She's married to Tom, and has two children and three grandchildren. She has been retired for nearly three years and enjoys biking, quilting, gardening, and walking with friends.

Catie McDowell, MS, LMFT has been a psychotherapist in private practice in Boulder since 1999. Catie has worked in a broad range of settings over the last 25 years, and currently sees adults and couples in her practice. (303) 494-6877 ext. 2

Barbara Mitchell, LCSW is a licensed clinical social worker and Certified Imago Relationship Therapist. She maintains a private practice in midtown Manhattan and Hastings-on-Hudson in Westchester County, NY. In addition to treating individuals and couples, her work in the addictions field led to the development of a specialty in treating money disorders.
(212) 867-5507 / mitchell.relationships@gmail.com.

Mary Sue Moore, PhD is a licensed clinical psychologist specializing in clinical work and teaching related to healing relationship difficulties resulting from early disturbed attachments and interpersonal trauma. She teaches regularly in Boulder, for the Boulder Institute for Psychotherapy & Research (BIPR), and twice a year, in London, England, as an

Honorary Senior Psychotherapist in the Child & Family Dept. of the Tavistock Clinic. She maintains a small private practice in Boulder, and can be reached via the BIPR website: www.bipr.org.

Melissa Moore, PhD is a Senior Executive of Felton Institute of San Francisco since 2005 and the founding Director of The Felton Research and Training Division dedicated to raising outcomes in community mental health services for marginalized populations suffering from mental illness. She founded the Karuna Training, a 2 year certificate in Contemplative Psychology, that is currently running in 7 Countries. She is also an Acharya in the Shambhala Buddhist tradition and teaches meditation programs around the world. She is an old friend of Bob and Helena's and was with Helena when Helena first noticed Bob's "nice ass" before they had even met, at a Maitri program hosted by the Naropa Institute at Shambhala Mountain Center. She completed the MA Contemplative Psychotherapy program with Bob's wife at Naropa in 1983 and has remained a loyal family friend ever since.

Edward Rockendorf Morey, PhD is the Ned and Nel Nebbiolo Professor of Economics and Classic Skiing at the University of Colorado / Department of Economics / University of Colorado Boulder, CO 80309 / Edward.Morey@colorado.edu

Rivvy Neshama is a freelance editor and proofreader for individuals, book publishers, magazines, and businesses. She is the author of *Recipes for a Sacred Life: True Stories and a Few Miracles*. http://rivvyneshama.com / (303) 444-8201

Sabrina Neu, PsyD is a Licensed Clinical Psychologist at Counseling and Psychiatric Services at Wardenburg Health Center, University of Colorado, Boulder. She is a full-time staff psychologist for campus student health center and the psychology intern training co-coordinator.

Susan Nimmanheminda, PhD, LCSW, CAC III is a Nationally Certified Psychoanalyst and has a private psychotherapy practice in Boulder with individuals, couples and groups. She is on the faculty and Leadership Team of the Masters in Contemplative Counseling Program at Naropa University. Susan's interest in subjects related to psychoanalytic and contemplative thought and practice is broad, and she has a long-standing fascination with material related to Freud's client Anna O's assertion that psychoanalysis (and, probably, in today's world, Anna would have meant by this most psychotherapies) is a "talking cure." How does talking help? When Susan isn't geeking out on things like this she likes to swim, bike and run and uses life-long pedaling as an excuse for traveling adventures.
www.sunpsychotherapy.com / (303) 449-3942.

Jenna Noah, MA, PhD (pending) is a psychotherapist in private practice. She specializes in sex therapy. Jenna is the founder of Conscious Burlesque and leads workshops helping women feel empowered and embodied in their sexual expression.

Elizabeth Olson, PsyD, LCSW, CGP works in private practice in Boulder and Longmont, Colorado. She loves her family and community, modern psychoanalysis, Zen Buddhism, group and family psychotherapy, and yoga.

Joan Ormont, PhD is a psychoanalyst in private practice in New York City, who has been working with individuals, couple's and groups for the past 45 years.

Jeffrey M. Price, MA, LPC, LAC, FAGPA has a private psychotherapy practice in Boulder, CO. He leads many groups including court-ordered, process and supervision groups. (Thanks again, Bob!) www.thecenterforcourageousliving.com / (303) 415-2766, ext. 2 / (303) 817-7565

Chris Randol, MA, LPC has worked for many years as a psychotherapist at the Boulder County Jail where he is currently employed in the Programs office. He serves as the acting team leader on a state grant to reduce recidivism, and runs several therapy groups in addition to seeing individual clients. Prior to that he worked for many years with Emergency Services at Mental Health Partners. He grew up in Baltimore, and first attended Naropa Institute in the summer of 1976. This was not long after being introduced to the "crazy wisdom" lineage through an Outward Bound teacher in Big Bend National Forest in Southwestern Texas. He has been marinating in Shambhala Buddhist and Modern Psychoanalytic teachings for much of his adult life.

Jeremy Rhoades, LMFT is a licensed Marriage and Family Therapist and Professional Clinical Counselor in Arcata, California. He offers mindfulness-oriented therapy by the coast that is compassionate, LGBT-friendly, and respectful of individual choices. He is an advocate of Harm Reduction Therapy and enjoys working with students.
www.curiousjourney.org

Mary Riendeau, LCSW is a therapist working in Denver for the TRIUMPH program, an intensive outpatient treatment program through the Denver Drug Court in collaboration with Arapahoe House for women with co-occurring substance abuse and Post-Traumatic Stress Disorders

Reuben Robbins, PhD is an Assistant Professor of Clinical Psychology (in Psychiatry) at Columbia University and the New York State Psychiatric Institute. He is currently principal investigator of two NIH funded research projects on the development and validation of tablet-based neuropsychological assessment tools in the United States and South Africa. In addition, he conducts HIV and mental health related research, and provides clinical supervision to the psychology interns. He also maintains a private practice of individual, couples and group psychotherapy in New York

City. He is a graduate of the Master's in Contemplative Psychotherapy from Naropa University in 2000. Phone and Fax: (212) 464-7796 / doc@rnrobbins.com

Neil J. Rosen, PsyD has practiced in Boulder as a psychologist and psychoanalyst since 1988.
njrosen@gmail.com / (303) 494-1116.

Robin Rosendale, MA works full time in a private practice as a psychotherapist in the Greenwich Village neighborhood of New York City. She graduated from Naropa's Master's in Contemplative Psychotherapy program in 2006. She's a psychoanalytic candidate at the Jungian Psychoanalytic Association also in NYC.
(646) 588-1387 / rrosendale@gmail.com

Joseph Schultz, MA, LPC is the Director of Outpatient Services for Colorado Recovery. He is originally from New York, and graduated from Naropa University with a Master's Degree in Contemplative Psychotherapy. He has worked in community mental health for 20 years.

Jed Shapiro, MD is a psychiatrist, now 1/2 retired after working at Boulder Mental Health Partners for 38 years. He now works at Imagine! (Boulder County's Developmental Disabilities) and Charg Resource Center on Capitol Hill in Denver as well as various volunteer activities including the Colorado Foundation for Universal Health Care and Interfaith Network for Mental Illness (INMI). jedsshapiro@yahoo.com

Lodi Siefer, MA, LPC is a Licensed Professional Counselor in Boulder, CO. She has a private psychotherapy practice at http://findground.org and teaches in various capacities at Naropa University.
(303) 396-7505 / lodi.siefer@findground.org

Deborah Silver, LCSW is a Licensed Clinical Social Worker (NYS) and a Certified Psychoanalyst. She has been in private practice in Greenwich Village, New York City for over 25 years, seeing individuals and couples for long and short-term treatment. She is a faculty member and supervisor for The Center for Modern Psychoanalysis and the Psychoanalytic Psychotherapy Study Center and enjoys doing private individual and group supervision as well. She started out in the field of Alcoholism and continues to work with people struggling with chemical dependencies and other impulsive and repetitive self-destructive behaviors. She also has a strong interest in working with prospective and new parents, navigating the emotional challenges of this new phase of life. (212) 982-1664 / www.Deborahsilverlcsw.com

Mark I. Singer, PhD is the Leonard W. Mayo Professor of Family & Child Welfare and Deputy Director of the Begun Center at the Mandel School of Applied Social Sciences and, Professor of Psychiatry, School of Medicine, Case Western Reserve University. He has over 45 years experience in the field of youth services, including directing two adolescent psychiatric units. He has served as a consultant or advisor to the U.S. Department of Defense, the American Medical Association, and the National Mental Health Association. He has taught in the Cleveland Police Academy and works with law enforcement to establish linkages between police officers and social services and is currently a member of the Cuyahoga County Metropolitan Housing Authority Police Department. mark.singer@case.edu / (216) 368-6176

Suzanne Smith has worked for 25 years in developing countries. She recently came back to the USA and co-founded CBOs Count which provides a simplified bookkeeping training to NGOs and local community groups. (303) 324 9509 / aplacebytheriver@gmail.com

Joel Solomon, MD is a psychiatrist in New York City in private practice and Medical Advisor to the Major League Baseball Players Association. Friend of Robert Unger for 30+ years.

They talk from time to time and see each other 1-2 times a year when they pick up just where they left off. (917) 470-2862

Gil Spielberg, PhD is a psychologist who has trained in individual and group psychoanalysis. He grew up in Manhattan and still believes he lives there although his corporeal self has resided in Los Angeles for the past 19 years. He has been further trained by his 3 kids and his wife.

Anna Soref writes and edits about everything in the world of natural wellness from her home office in surprisingly lovely Cleveland, Ohio. She has three teenage daughters, a wonderful soul mate of a husband and two black cats.

Elizabeth Stahl, MA has a private practice seeing individuals and groups. She runs DBT groups for a variety of organizations and offers Parenting Coordination for divorced parents who have a difficult time navigating decisions involving their children. She began her professional career as a visual artist, entered into training at the Center for Modern Psychoanalysis in New York and moved to Boulder where she earned a MA in counseling through the Transpersonal Counseling Program at Naropa University.

Liz Stewart is a practitioner of The Rolf Method of Structural Integration in Boulder, CO. www.LizStewartSI.com

Matthew Tomatz, MA, LPC, CAC III, CGP is the Substance Abuse Program Coordinator and Interim Outreach Coordinator for Counseling and Psychological Services at the University of Colorado Boulder. He also maintains a private practice in Boulder, Colorado: (303) 709-5525 / mtomatz@gmail.com.

Barbara Ungaschick, LPC is co-owner of the Denver Counseling Center since 1979. She works with adults and adolescents, short and long term treatments, takes most insurances and accommodates her schedule to suit the needs of clients. She has studied Modern Psychoanalysis at the

Colorado Center for Modern Psychoanalytic Studies in Boulder, CO and Albuquerque, NM since 1989.

Dylan Unger is Bob's eldest son. He is currently starting his final year of law school at the University of Colorado with plans to go into civil litigation.

Helena Unger, MA, LPC is a divorce mediator and psychotherapist in private practice in Boulder, CO. She is English and Greek, graduated from Naropa University in 1983, married Bob Unger that same year, and is the mother of his two children. With her husband's love and encouragement, she recently became an auctioneer for charitable events.
(303) 938-0611 / helenau1@msn.com

Helaine Unger is an early childhood special educator with the Boulder Valley School District and will be retiring at the end of the 2016 school year. She is looking forward to pursuing her interest in music, dance, knitting and spending more time with her grandchildren on the east and west coasts.
ungerh50@gmail.com

Julian Unger works as an Operations Project Manager at Quri in San Francisco. He has a B.A. in Political Science end Economics from the University of British Columbia. He is Bob and Helena's second son. He enjoys travel, food, motorcycles, and mountain biking.

Andrew van Dyke, PsyD, LPC is a Psychologist in Colorado Springs. He is past president of the Colorado Group Psychotherapy Society and maintains a thriving private practice. He runs various therapy groups in the area, and enjoys spending time with his wife and three kids.

Kristin Venderbush, NP is a psychiatric nurse practitioner in Portland, OR. Prior to that she worked in community mental health in Portland for a decade. She also holds an MA in

Contemplative Psychotherapy from Naropa University which she completed in 1998.

Laura Volmert, MA lives in the land of the midnight sun, Fairbanks, Alaska. She currently works with the court system in adult guardianship cases, and is working to build a private therapy practice. (907) 460-4430 / lauravolmert@gmail.com

Don Waldman, PhD is a Professor of Economics at the University of Colorado, and a bicycle/motorcycle rider. He is 67 years old, married with two kids.

Karen Kissel Wegela, PhD is a psychologist in private practice and a professor in the M.A. Contemplative Psychotherapy program at Naropa University. She is also an author who writes about Buddhism and Psychotherapy. Her most recent book, *Contemplative Psychotherapy Essentials: Enriching Your Practice with Buddhist Psychology* (W. W. Norton) came out last fall.

Dolores Welber, PhD is a psychoanalyst in private practice in the New York area. She has been in the field for the past 45 years.

Maureen Dummigan White, MA co-owns and operates a mindfulness-based treatment program for young adults in Sedona, AZ with her partner and husband, Josh White. She was born in Boulder, CO in the sixties. She started graduate school at Naropa in 1996 but left to pursue something else in Central America. She came back eventually and graduated from MACP in 2001.

Josh White, MA, LPC is the founder of Red Mountain Sedona, a mindfulness-based treatment program for young adults in Sedona, AZ. He is also a Zen Sensei in the tradition of Taizan Maezumi, the happy husband of Maureen Dummigan White and proud father of Hunter Taizan Dummigan White.

John Wilcockson is the author of 15 books, including *23 Days in July* (a book about the Tour de France); the former Editor-in-Chief of *VeloNews* magazine; the current Editor-at-Large of *Peloton* magazine; and the copyeditor of high-profile books, including the upcoming *Political Animals* by New York Times bestselling author Rick Shenkman. John likes to run and bike with Doctor Bob.

Lenore Wian is Bob's big sister and she is gloriously retired!!! lwian@yahoo.com / (619) 315-3156

Karen Wilding, LCSW is a Licensed Clinical Social Worker with a private practice in Boulder Colorado. She is a member of Boulder Psychological Services and serves on their leadership team. She was previously the Director of Counseling at September School for 17 years. She has served as chairperson of several non-profit boards including Attention Homes, Boulder County AIDS Project, Tibetan Village Project, and Shambhala Mountain Center.

Anne Wilzbacher, LPC is a Licensed Professional Counselor and currently works as a Clinical and Family Therapist at Open Sky Wilderness in Durango, CO. Previously she worked at AIM House in Boulder, CO. She works with adolescents and young adults and their families as a wilderness therapist and does individual therapy, group therapy, and family therapy and she loves it! (970)426-9207 / annewilzbacher@gmail.com

Brooks Witter, MA, LPC is a psychotherapist in Boulder, CO where he runs a thriving private practice. Previously he served as Clinical Director at Living Well Transitions where he worked for the past decade with young adults and their families. He is a graduate of Naropa's Contemplative Psychotherapy program, and Past President of the Rocky Mountain Chapter of the Association for Contextual Behavioral Science. Brooks' life mission is to integrate ancient wisdom and modern science in service of providing tools for personal liberation. Brooks holds a view that in our confusion lies the opportunity to develop wisdom and confidence, and believes that in every moment—no matter how painful, confusing or blissful—we may awaken to our basic nature that is ultimately free. Brooks practices this credo by mindfully engaging as a father, a husband, a cyclist and mountain biker, an explorer of the natural world, and as a man who works to model the kind of world he'd like to inhabit. www.luminouscounseling.com / brooks.witter@gmail.com

Jean-Marc C. Wong, MD works as a psychiatrist in integrated primary care, student mental health and private practice.

Elliot Zeisel, PhD is a Distinguished Fellow of the American Group Psychotherapy Association. He has served as the Vice Chair of the Group Foundation for Advancing Mental Health and is a founder of the Center for Group Studies. He and his son David were introduced to BMX biking by Dr. Unger.

Publications

Nimmanheminda, S. U., Unger, R., Lindemann, A. M., & Holloran, M. C. (2010). Group therapy training at Naropa University's contemplative counseling psychology program. *Group, 34*, 309-318.

Unger, R. (1978). Sustaining transference in the treatment of alcoholism. *Modern Psychoanalysis, 3*, 155-171.

Unger, R. (1978). Treatment of adolescent alcoholism. *Social Casework, 59*, 27-35.

Unger, R. (1989). Selection and composition criteria in group psychotherapy. *Journal for Specialists in Group Work, 14*, 151-157.

Unger, R. (1990). Conflict management in group psychotherapy. *Small Group Research, 21*, 349-359.

Unger, R. (1991). Cohesion in psychotherapy groups. Unpublished Manuscript.

Unger, R. (1993). Influences affecting therapist attitudes and approaches for managing conflict in psychotherapy groups (Unpublished doctoral dissertation). University of Colorado, Boulder.

Unger, R. (2008). Psychoanalysis and Buddhism: Paths of disappointment. In F. Kaklauskas, L. Hoffman, S. Nimmanheminda, & M. Jack, (Eds.). *Brilliant Sanity: Buddhism and psychotherapy* (pp. 347-353). Colorado Springs, CO: University of the Rockies Press.

Other Books by University Professors Press

	Stanley Krippner: A Life of Dreams, Myths, & Visions – Essays on His Contributions and Influence *Edited by Jeannine A. Davies & Daniel B. Pitchford*
	Bare: Psychotherapy Stripped *By Jacqueline Simon Gunn with Carlo DeCarlo*
	The Polarized Mind: Why It's Killing Us and What We Can Do About It *By Kirk J. Schneider*
	Stay Awhile: Poetic Narratives on Multiculturalism and Diversity *Edited by Louis Hoffman & Nathaniel Granger, Jr.*
	Capturing Shadows: Poetic Encounters Along the Path of Grief and Loss *Edited by Louis Hoffman & Michael Moats*
	An Artist's Thought Book: Intriguing Thoughts about the Artistic Process *By Richard Bargdill*